AF571819

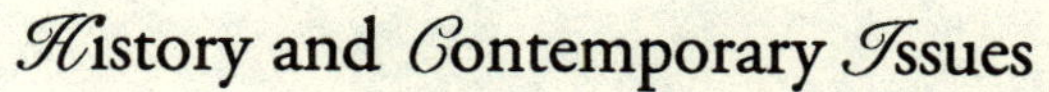
History and Contemporary Issues

CHARLES E. CURRAN

History and Contemporary Issues

~ Studies in Moral Theology ~

CONTINUUM • NEW YORK

1996
The Continuum Publishing Company
370 Lexington Avenue
New York, NY 10017

Printed in the United States of America

Library of Congress Cataloging-in-publication Data

Curran, Charles E.
History and contemporary issues : studies in moral theology / Charles E. Curran.
p. cm.
Includes bibliographical references and index.
ISBN 0-8264-0944-X (alk. paper)
1. Christian ethics—Catholic authors. 2. Church and social problems—Catholic Church. I. Title
BJ1249.C8173 1996
241'.042—dc20 96-26514
CIP

This book is dedicated to those students, colleagues, and friends who ten years ago publicly supported my role as a Catholic moral theologian.

Friends of American Catholic Theology
especially Mary Zelinski Hellwig, Johann Klodzen, and Sally Ann McReynolds

Friends for Charles Curran

Colleagues at Catholic University
especially Gerard Austin, John T. Ford, Elizabeth A. Johnson, Brian V. Johnstone, and David N. Power

Past Presidents and Members of The Catholic Theological Society of America and The College Theology Society
especially Monika K. Hellwig, Richard P. McBrien, Richard A. McCormick, and David W. Tracy

The Law Firm of Cravath, Swaine, and Moore
especially Paul C. Saunders and John F. Hunt

~ Contents ~

Preface

This volume comprises essays and articles written in the last few years in Catholic moral theology. The historical studies in part one trace the development of the discipline of moral theology in general with emphasis on medical ethics and the manual-based approach. The contemporary issues studied in part two indicate the primary crisis in moral theology at the present time. Pope John Paul II has identified that crisis as the dissent between moral theologians and the hierarchical magisterium. No attempt has been made to create an artificial unity, but the context and content of the chapters spell out quite accurately the present state of Catholic moral theology. A concluding epilogue points out the general direction that moral theology should take in the future.

I am grateful to all those who have facilitated my teaching and research here at Southern Methodist University—my students, faculty colleagues, the librarians at the Bridwell Library, and especially Jack and Laura Lee Blanton, who have funded the Elizabeth Scurlock University Professorship in Human Values named in honor of Laura Lee Blanton's mother. I appreciate the support and encouragement of Justus George Lawler of the Continuum Publishing Company. Special thanks go to my associate Jane Cross for her painstaking work in preparing the manuscript for publication, and to Rosemarie Gorman for competently preparing the index.

I gratefully acknowledge the permission of the following publishers and periodicals to republish materials that first appeared in their publications: Presses Universitaires de France, for "Overview and Historical Development of Moral Theology," which originally appeared in *Dictionnaire de philosphie morale*; Simon and Schuster/Macmillan, for "The Historical Development of Catholic Medical Ethics" and "Fertility Control," which originally appeared in *Encyclopedia of Bioethics*, Warren Thomas Reich, editor-in-chief, rev. ed.; Georgetown University Press, for "The Manual and

Casuistry of Aloysius Sabetti," which originally appeared in *The Context of Casuistry*, James F. Keenan and Thomas A. Shannon, eds.; Sheed and Ward for "The Role of the Laity in the Thought of John Courtney Murray," which originally appeared in *John Courtney Murray and the Growth of Tradition*, Leon Hooper and Todd Whitmore, eds., and for "*Veritatis splendor*: A Revisionist Perspective," which originally appeared in *Veritatis splendor: American Responses*, Michael E. Allsopp and John J. O'Keefe, eds.; Westminster/ John Knox Press for "Catholic Moral Theology in the Past Forty Years," which originally appeared in *Contours: An Introduction to North American Religious Thought*, Roger A. Badham, ed.; Center for Homophobia Education for "Is There Any Good News in the Recent Documents from the Vatican about Homosexuality?" which originally appeared in *Voices of Hope,* Jeannine Gramick and Robert Nugent, eds.; *Église et théologie* for "The Theory and Practice of Academic Freedom in Catholic Higher Education"; and *National Catholic Reporter*, for "What Is a Catholic College?" and "*Evangelium vitae* and Its Broader Contexts."

• Part One •

Historical Studies

~ 1 ~
Overview and Historical Development of Moral Theology

The Christian scriptures intimately link faith and morality. The central message of Jesus calls for a change of heart and a new way of life. The synoptic Gospels reduce all the commandments to the twofold love command of Jesus—love of God and love of neighbor. The followers of Jesus are called to discipleship. The famous so-called Last Judgment scene in Matthew 25 maintains that our relationship to God is known and manifested in our relationship with our neighbor, especially those in need. The Christian church as the community of the disciples of Jesus thus sees itself as teaching morality and struggling to know the requirements of Christian discipleship in different times and places.

Moral theology came into existence in this context. Moral theology studies the Christian moral life in a thematic and systematic way in accord with the scientific canons of adequacy, consistency, and coherence. Moral theology is a second-order discourse; morality is the object of its study. Morality refers to the virtues, attitudes, values, norms, and actions of people. Moral theology reflects on Christian morality in a scientific way. Different degrees of systematic reflection on the Christian moral experience exist, with moral theology generally reserved for the highest scientific level of inquiry.

The term "moral theology" is used today primarily in the Roman Catholic tradition. Alan of Lille (d. 1203) first introduced the distinction between dogmatic theology dealing with Christian beliefs and moral theology dealing with actions, but the term only came into popular use at the end of the sixteenth century to designate the particular discipline. Contemporary Protestants often use the term "Christian ethics" which has emerged as a special discipline in Protestantism only in the last hundred years.

Basic Issues in Moral Theology

The primary methodological issue in moral theology concerns the sources of the discipline. Perennial discussion centers on the use of nonrevelational sources usually considered under the heading of human reason. The vast majority of those reflecting on the Christian moral life down through the centuries have accepted some human reason as a source of Christian moral wisdom and knowledge based on the doctrine of creation. Human reason reflecting on the humanity and world created by God can arrive at moral truth. Those who have opposed the use of reason appeal to the sinful character of all human existence or to "scripture alone" or "Christ alone" approaches which allow no nonrevelational source. Many today would accept four sources of moral theology, in accord with what has been called the Wesleyan Quadrilateral—scripture, tradition, reason, and experience.

How to use the scripture in moral theology has been a perennial question. Those who accept critical biblical scholarship recognize the historical and cultural limitations of the biblical witness. Many maintain we cannot and should not follow everything the Bible says about morality in our world today, for some of it is wrong. Scripture affects moral theology differently at the different levels of moral theology. The biblical narrative and story in general very much affect the person and the person's moral imagination, vision, and motivation. The Bible also speaks about important Christian virtues, attitudes, and values, but on specific issues or questions the historical and cultural limitations of the scripture become more apparent.

H. Richard Niebuhr has proposed five logical types for understanding the relationship between Christ and culture. The Christ against culture approach stresses opposition. The Christ of culture approach emphasizes agreement. Between these two extreme positions Niebuhr distinguishes three positions in the broad center—Christ and culture in paradox, Christ above culture, and Christ transforming culture. An anthropology stressing the basic goodness of human beings through creation and redemption and an eschatology emphasizing some continuity between the now and the future are more optimistic about what Christians and human beings can do in this world. Approaches which highlight the presence of sin and the great discontinuity between the now and the future tend to be more pessimistic in outlook.

Most moral theologians and Christian ethicists explicitly or implicitly employ one of three different models of moral theology. The *teleological model* determines the ultimate end, such as happiness, the glory of God, or the kingdom of God, and judges everything else in relationship to that end. Reality, of course, remains much more complex so that proximate ends become means to more ultimate ends. The *deontological model* understands the moral life in terms of duty, law, or obligation, which in moral theology often takes the form of the Ten Commandments, especially in more practical settings. The *relationality model* sees the human person as relating responsibly to God, neighbor, self, world, and the environment. These models are generic, somewhat abstract, and have been developed in many different ways, but they help to orient the basic approach to moral theology.

Moral theology serves three publics—the church, the academy, and the society at large; and these destinations affect the approach taken. In addition, moral theology is done in different settings. The church setting emphasizes the pastoral, the practical, and the role of the church; the academic setting tends to stress the scientific character of the discipline.

Early Historical Development

Systematic moral theology did not develop in the first thousand years of Christianity. The early Christian period, often called the patristic age, lasted until the seventh century or even later in some calculations. The writings of this period, even more so in the beginning, tended to be heavily pastoral, often taking the form of letters from bishops, homilies, commentaries on scripture, various tracts on particular virtues or obligations, and the defense of Christian morality in comparison to the Jewish, pagan, and heretical approaches. The subjects included life in the world, martyrdom, reaction to persecution, relationship with non-Christians, peace and violence, sexual morality, and participating in the institutions of society.

Clement of Alexandria (d. 215?) and his famous pupil Origen (d. 251?) of the Alexandrian school attempted to give a scriptural and a philosophical basis to treating Christian morality, calling for Christians to permeate the life of the city with their charity. But Tertullian (d. 220?) opposed the surrounding culture and adopted a much more rigorous approach to the Christian life.

The fourth century is often called the golden age of the early church. Persecution ceased; Constantine made Christianity the religion of the empire; and monasticism began with St. Anthony (d. 356) in the desert. The Cappadocian Fathers in the East, such as Basil the Great (d. 379); John Chrysostom (d. 407), a proponent of the Antiochean school and patriarch of Constantinople; and in the West St. Ambrose (d. 397), the bishop of Milan, all borrowed from the Greek and Roman culture in their understanding of Christian morality.

St. Augustine of Hippo (d. 430), the most important figure in the patristic period, wrote no systematic moral theology, but he published treatises on particular issues such as free will, Christian discipleship, lying, fasting, patience, marriage, and virginity. Augustine reacted against the dualism and pessimism of the Manicheans on the one hand, and the optimism of the Pelagians on the other hand; but his own thought tended to a more realistic or pessimistic attitude about life in this world. The bishop of Hippo proposed a teleological morality based on God as the end of our longing. Augustine emphasized the grace of God which delivers us from sin and makes Christian living possible. The Christian is called to love God above all things, and the follower of Jesus enjoys God as the end and uses all other things in relationship to God. Sin, like love, resides in the will and consists in our inordinate love of a lesser good (e.g., self) which makes it an end instead of a means. The two different loves give rise to the two cities—the City of God and the City of Man. On particular issues he first enunciated the just war principle, and his pessimistic understanding of human sexuality (conjugal intercourse can be justified only for the purpose of procreation and usually entails venial sin) greatly influenced the Christian tradition.

Later writers in this period include Gregory the Great (d. 604), who in his *Moralia in Job* develops the norms of the moral life, especially patience, and John Damascene (d. 749), whose moral teachings brought Aristotle into dialogue with the patristic tradition. Not much has been written about the morality in the period from the eighth to the eleventh century, but the most significant development came from the change in the sacrament of penance, beginning in Ireland, with its practice of repeated private confession to the priest who assigned appropriate penances. *Libri poenitentiales* arose in response to this new practice giving detailed penances to be assigned for particular sins.

The Roman Catholic Tradition

Roman Catholic moral theology has four distinctive characteristics—an appreciation of mediation, acceptance of natural law, interest in casuistry, and the role of the church. Mediation understands the divine to be mediated in and through the human and is grounded in a theology that recognizes the basic goodness of the human through creation. This emphasis on mediation grounds the Catholic insistence on "and"—faith *and* reason, grace *and* nature, scripture *and* tradition, faith *and* works, Jesus *and* the church. The ultimate end of human existence is both the glory of God *and* human happiness which are one and the same reality.

The acceptance of the natural law illustrates this emphasis on mediation. From a theological perspective natural law recognizes human nature and human reason as sources of ethical wisdom and knowledge for the Christian. To determine what is morally right or wrong one does not go immediately to God but to the nature and reason that God has created. In the human individual the natural law is the participation of the eternal law in the rational creature. From the philosophical perspective, natural law is human reason directing human beings to their end in accord with their nature. The ontological aspect refers to human nature with its innate finalities that are morally normative. From the gnoseological perspective, human reason states the first principle of the natural law, often phrased as "Do good and avoid evil," and deduces from this immediate and then more remote conclusions of the natural law. Before the Second Vatican Council (1962–65) Catholic moral theology developed almost exclusively on the basis of natural law and did not give that much explicit importance to faith, scripture, or theological concerns.

Casuistry has been developed extensively in the Catholic tradition. Catholicism has emphasized the role of works and the need for works in order to obtain eternal life, downplaying at times the role of grace. The Catholic acceptance of the sacrament of penance with its confession of sins according to number and species strongly enhanced the importance of works and the need to determine the number and species of sin. Moral theologians employed casuistry to study the morality of particular actions by comparing these actions with the appropriate norms or principles and with other actions.

The Catholic insistence on mediation highlights the role of the church. God in Jesus and through the Spirit comes to human beings in and through the church as a visible human community with a visible structure. The Roman Catholic Church recognizes the God-given teaching office of the pope and bishops in the church, called the hierarchical magisterium, which has played an increasingly greater role in Catholic morality as time has gone by. After the First Vatican Council, Catholics explicitly recognized an infallible teaching authority and a noninfallible teaching authority belonging to the hierarchical magisterium. The teaching authority must always be seen in its relationship to the whole church, but different opinions exist about the exact nature of the relationship to the whole church, especially in practice. The hierarchical magisterium is exercised generally by the pope, together with the bishops of the church, or alone, or through the offices of the Roman Curia. There has never been an infallible papal statement on a specific moral issue. Many theologians today maintain that there never can be such an infallible teaching because the material is more removed from the core of faith and specific moral teachings cannot claim a certitude that excludes the possibility of error. Others insist that infallibility can and does extend to particular moral considerations such as that of contraception. The hierarchical magisterium itself has never claimed that any specific natural law-based teaching is in fact infallible.

The Catholic moral tradition depends heavily on the developments of the Scholastic period, which began in the twelfth century and coincided with the origin of universities. Systematic and scientific theology in which the various parts are harmoniously related to each other and to the whole began to appear at this time.

Thomas Aquinas (d. 1274), the most significant figure in the Catholic theological tradition, adapted Aristotelian philosophy in a systematic approach to the one Christian theology which he developed in an organic way on the basis of an *exitus–reditus* (coming from and returning to God) approach in his *Summa theologiae*. The moral aspect of the *Secunda pars* of the *Summa* follows a teleological model, constituting an integral part of the one theology. Thomistic morality is grounded in what is for the fulfillment of the human being. Morality is intrinsic; something is commanded because it is good. The approach to what we now call fundamental moral theology (what is common to all moral acts) begins with the tract on the ultimate end of human beings, which is happiness, then discusses the acts by which we come to the ultimate end: the intrinsic principles of our acts, which are powers and faculties modified by habits; the extrinsic principles of human acts, which are the devil and God, who guides us by law and grace. He discusses natural law only in this last section. Thomas develops what we now call special moral theology, or the different actions all human beings do, on the basis of the three theological virtues of faith, hope, and charity and the cardinal moral virtues—prudence, justice, fortitude, and temperance.

The fourteenth and fifteenth centuries saw the criticism of Thomism from the perspective of nominalism under the influence of William of Ockham (d. 1347) of the Franciscan school earlier founded by St. Bonaventure

(d. 1274) and John Duns Scotus (d. 1305). Nominalism emphasized the concrete, the particular, and the individual, and denied the real existence of universals. Starting from the omnipotent and infinite freedom of God, moral good or evil is determined by the will of God not by human nature. From the fourteenth to the sixteenth centuries Thomism came to the fore in the university world of Paris, Cologne, and especially Spain, where some outstanding theologians—e.g., Francis de Vitoria (d. 1546), Dominic Soto (d. 1560), and Francis Suarez (d. 1617)—commenting especially on the *Secunda secundae* of the *Summa,* dealt with many of the developing problems. In response to the Reformation, apologists and polemicists such as Robert Bellarmine, S.J. (d. 1621), discussed issues like free will, sin, merit, and vows. Even during the development of moral theology on the university level more practical handbooks called *Summae confessorum* came into being to help the confessor judge sins and their gravity in the sacrament of penance especially in the light of the Fourth Lateran Council's (1215) imposing annual confession on believers.

Institutiones theologiae moralis, a new genre of moral theology, developed in the seventeenth century (John Azor, S.J., wrote the first of its kind in 1600) and served as the manuals of moral theology until Vatican II. The setting for these manuals was the seminary that just came into existence and not the university; the occasion for their existence was the reform of the Council of Trent calling again for annual confession of sins according to number and species; the format was a very brief exposition of fundamental moral theology dealing especially with human acts and law, followed by the specific acts in the moral life of Christians explained in the light of the Ten Commandments, and finally a third section devoted to how the sacraments were to be celebrated and received; the purpose was to train future confessors as judges in the sacrament of penance to determine which acts are sinful and to what degree. These manuals became cut off from scripture, dogmatic theology, spiritual theology, philosophy, and the developing human sciences, while emphasizing law and church law. Controversies erupted in the seventeenth and eighteenth centuries with the two opposite extremes of Jansenism or rigorism on the one hand and laxism on the other. A major issue of contention centered on how to move from theoretical doubt about whether an obligation or law existed to practical certitude. Probabilists maintained that one could follow an opinion opposed to the existence of a law if it were truly probable—meaning provable. Alphonsus Liguori (d. 1787), later made a saint, a doctor of the church, and the patron of moral theology, brought peace to moral theology by his practical prudence and Christian good sense in adopting a moderate form of probabilism and in his approach to specific issues. However, the manuals as such with their practical orientation, legal bent, and concentration on the minimal aspect of what constituted sin continued in existence until Vatican II and often sought to show that a particular opinion was probable primarily by listing the authorities who held it. Chapter three will discuss the manual of Aloysius Sabetti, the most popular moral theology textbook published in the United States.

In the later nineteenth century, Pope Leo XIII made Thomism the Catholic philosophy and used Thomism in his social encyclicals dealing with the problems of the modern world, condemning much of the Enlightenment approaches and defending the rights of workers. In the nineteenth and twentieth centuries some Thomists criticized the manuals of moral theology, as did the Tübingen school in Germany, using a more biblical and explicitly theological approach. Bernard Häring's *The Law of Christ*, first published in German in 1954, served as a stimulus to the renewal of moral theology that occurred in the light of Vatican II. As a result of the reform of Vatican II, moral theology became nourished by the scriptures and broader theological and liturgical concerns, open to seeking new philosophical partners, in dialogue with the world through reading the Gospel and the signs of the times, focused on all of life and not just the minimum of sin, and concerned about the person as the subject and agent of moral life and not just with acts.

Since Vatican II, popes, bishops, and theologians have been addressing the social problems of the world such as peace and violence, human rights, and economic justice. Liberation theology has come to the fore in South America and in other parts of the world. Many Catholic revisionist moral theologians have challenged the existence of absolute universal moral norms, especially in the area of sexuality (e.g., contraception, divorce), and espoused the legitimacy of dissent in theory and in practice from these disputed non-infallible teachings. In 1968 Pope Paul VI's encyclical, *Humanae vitae*, repeated the condemnation of artificial contraception. In 1993, Pope John Paul II in *Veritatis splendor* strongly reaffirmed the existence of intrinsically evil acts and moral norms that do not admit of exception and called on theologians to give an example of loyal assent. Deep divisions exist within contemporary Catholic moral theologians on these issues. The second part of this book will address some of these controverted questions.

Protestant Christian Ethics

Christian ethics in the Protestant tradition did not really become a separate discipline until the present century, but Protestant theology always included significant ethical concerns. Protestant approaches to Christian ethics by definition have been more diverse and pluralistic than Catholic approaches, but four distinctive characteristics have often been present—the primacy of grace and faith, the importance of freedom, emphasis on scripture, and a negative attitude toward casuistry.

The reformers relying on Augustine stressed the primacy of grace and faith. Such an emphasis strongly opposes works' righteousness, but insists that grace produces its fruits in proper action. The emphasis on grace disagrees with a morality primarily based on human reason and human nature, so that Protestants have generally been quite suspicious of heavy emphasis on the natural law, especially the Catholic emphasis on metaphysics and ontology. The primacy of grace insists on the theological aspects of the discipline such as Christology and eschatology. Protestant ethics, for example, tends to see sin primarily in theological terms as a lack of faith whereas Roman Catholicism sees sin as an act that is morally wrong.

Protestant theology insists on the importance of freedom, both that of God and that of the believer. God is free to act and intervene in human history. Protestant ethics resists any attempt to say that God must always act in a certain way based on some understanding of human nature. History rather than nature becomes primary. The freedom of the believer, a distinctive aspect of Protestant thought, also comes to the fore in moral considerations. Protestantism does not recognize a central hierarchical teaching authority; the ultimate responsibility rests with the freedom and conscience of the individual in the context of the community.

The Protestant Reformation accepted the axiom "the scripture alone," but this axiom has often been understood in terms of primacy and not exclusivity. Protestant churches and ethicists usually look for scriptural justification for ethical concerns. The most significant division in contemporary Protestantism came to the fore in the nineteenth century. Liberal Protestantism and later most mainstream Protestantism accepted a literary and historical criticism of the Bible, whereas fundamentalists insisted on scriptural inerrancy in the light of a literal reading of the scriptures. A fundamentalist approach to Christian ethics finds in the Bible propositional truths and ethical norms that God has revealed for all time's and that Christians are called to obey. Supporters of a critical approach to the scripture cannot accept such a deontological model for the moral life, but in the twentieth century many saw in the scriptures the description of the mighty acts of God to which Christians must respond, thus employing a relationality–responsibility model for the Christian life.

Protestantism in general has not developed a casuistry and has generally understood casuistry in a pejorative way. The primacy of grace and faith, the downplaying of minute philosophical reasoning, and the rejection of the sacrament of penance explain why Protestants did not develop, and even criticized, casuistry. Protestant ethics has been described as an ethic of inspiration precisely because it does not usually engage in a minute analysis of the morality of particular acts.

Martin Luther (d. 1546) did most of his writing in the heat of controversy and therefore did not write as a systematic academic. Justification by faith active in love stands at the heart of his theology and ethics, in opposition to justification by works, merit, and legalism. Luther's profound spiritual quest to find and experience a gracious God is achieved not by works but by faith and experience of faith. Those who are thus justified will then do good works. Dialectic or paradox pervades much of Lutheran thought. The Christian is *simul justus et peccator*, perfectly free and subject to all. Gospel and law are dialectically related. The gospel saves while the law convicts us of our sinfulness. By recognizing our sinfulness we can be saved by faith. Law also works to achieve civil order by curbing human violence and sinful excess in society, but Luther does not acknowledge the so-called third use of the law to indicate the good that should be done.

Lutheran social ethics is based on the two-realm theory referring to the realms of creation (but as a result of sin emphasizing preservation) and the realm of redemption. What we do in our social lives in the temporal order is not determined by Jesus, grace, and redemption, but by the needs of preserving order. God works in both orders, but Jesus works only in the order of redemption. Some later ethicists have accused Lutheran social thought of passivism and accepting the status quo because of this teaching.

John Calvin (d. 1564) shared much of Luther's theology but with a distinctive emphasis on the will, both in God and in human beings. God is sovereign will, electing in love and even predestining human beings. Justification empowers the human will to do the will of God. Calvin, unlike Luther, accepted a third use of the law and even made it primary—law as teaching the will of God. Calvinism, like Roman Catholicism and unlike Lutheranism, has been prone to legalism as in Puritanism. Calvin endorsed the Lutheran notion of vocation in the world but interpreted it in a more transforming and active way. Some later Calvinists believed that earthly success was a sign of God's predestination. Max Weber in the present century proposed the much debated theory that Calvinist ethics provided the spirit of capitalism. The popular notion of the Protestant work ethic is rooted in Calvinist thought.

The left wing of the Protestant Reformation represented by the Anabaptists used many Reformation themes to arrive at a radical ethic characterized by a commitment to following the strenuous gospel teachings of Jesus. These sects, as opposed to churches, are small groups which stand in opposition to the existing culture, cut themselves off from the world which is a source of sin, and bear witness to the gospel demands, especially peace and nonviolence.

No one figure represents Anglican moral theology, but here too Anglicanism has served as a bridge between Roman Catholicism and Protestantism. Caroline moral theology in the seventeenth century often followed Aquinas but rejected "Jesuitry," aimed to make society more just and individuals more holy, and also accepted a type of casuistry. Bishop Joseph Butler (d. 1752) and Kenneth Kirk (d. 1954) developed similar mediating approaches.

In reaction to the period of Protestant orthodoxy or Scholasticism on the continent, Pietism came to the fore in the last quarter of the seventeenth century. Pietism, first proposed in Germany by Phillip Jacob Spener (d. 1705), insists on inner conversion, the personal experience of God, a changed life, and a striving for perfection. In England John Wesley (d. 1791), the founder of Methodism, became the leader, theologian, moral teacher, and organizer of the English evangelical revival with his emphasis on the assurance of the justified sinner and the need to continue in the process of perfection and becoming holy. Jonathan Edwards (d. 1758), the most prominent theologian in the United States at the time, played a central role in the religious revival in the United States which is called the Great Awakening, but he recognized some place in his ethics for human reason.

The eighteenth century witnessed the emergence of the Enlightenment, with its emphasis on the autonomy of human reason, tolerance, and human progress, which greatly influenced Protestant thought while being strongly opposed by Roman Catholicism. The nineteenth century for the first time in Christian history saw philosophy as more important for ethics than theology. Thinkers as diverse as Kant, Hegel, Schopenhauer, Bentham, Mill, Marx, and Nietzsche discussed ethics. In this context Protestant liberalism arose in the nineteenth century insisting on the immanence of God working in human experience and history, the possibility of following the moral teaching of Jesus, and evolutionary human progress while downplaying transcendence and sin. Friedrich Schleiermacher (d. 1834), the most famous theologian of this school, proposed an ethical theory dealing with goods, duties, and virtues, and saw the moral as touching all areas of life—political, intellectual, aesthetic. Albert Ritschl (d. 1889) proposed a Christian ethics free from dogma and metaphysics, centered on the kingdom of God, with the foundational metaphor of "the fatherhood of God and the brotherhood of man."

In the light of liberal Protestantism, in reaction to the conditions of poverty brought about by the Industrial Revolution, and in opposition to the individualistic piety of the past, the Social Gospel came to the fore in the early twentieth century in the United States under the leadership of Walter Raushenbusch (d. 1918). In England and in Germany some proposed a moderate Christian socialism.

The harsh realities of World War I and the Depression occasioned the rise of the neo-orthodoxy of Karl Barth in Europe and the Christian realism of Reinhold Niebuhr in the United States. Their common reaction stressed the transcendence of God, the presence of sin, the dialectical understanding between the reign of God and human existence in this world, and a discontinuity between the present and the future aspects of the reign of God. Barth's famous "no" to Nazism was most influential. Strongly insisting on only one Christian starting point for ethics, Barth rejected natural law, and in contrast to Luther saw the law as a form of the gospel. Barth considered human social reality in the light of his analogy of faith or analogy of relation beginning with the reign of God and applying this analogously to the human situation. Reinhold Niebuhr's Christian realism had a strong social focus, rejected liberalism's optimism, saw love as the impossible possibility, granted some role to reason, and understood justice not primarily in theoretical terms but as a balancing of powers in practice.

Contemporary Scene

Many developments have occurred in moral theology since the World War II period. Chapter five will discuss the specifically Catholic developments in the last fifty years. Perhaps it is too early to judge, but no one school or individual ethicist dominates the scene.

Especially in the last few decades, the ecumenical reality of contemporary moral theology stands out in terms of Roman Catholic–Protestant relations. Catholics and Protestants read one another, belong to the same academic societies, are often trained together in nondenominational institutions, and are facing the same problems. Genuine dialogue has taken place on many issues and approaches.

Churches as a whole continue to address moral issues with a new emphasis on social issues. During the 1950s and later, the World Council of Churches became a strong supporter of revolutionary social change, the rights of the marginalized, and the need for ecological consciousness. Roman Catholic social encyclicals since Vatican II have tended to relate faith more directly to the problems of society and criticized the individualism and materialism of the modern world. Many churches in particular countries have also addressed issues such as the economy, human rights, and peace and justice. On these and other issues such as sexuality, sharp differences exist within most churches.

Moral theology today frequently finds its home in universities so that the academic aspects of the discipline have been developed as illustrated in the growth of professional societies in Europe and the United States and of journals dealing with these issues. The more academic setting and concern have brought moral theology into contact with many other disciplines dealing with human issues such as political science, anthropology, and philosophical ethics. Society at large, the third public served by moral theology, has raised ethical concerns and provided the agenda for the plethora of issues discussed in moral theology.

Pluralism and diversity characterize the question of method in contemporary Christian ethics. No one approach stands out, but there is a discernible move away from the more optimistic approach in the fifties, illustrated by a theology of secularity, to a more pessimistic perspective in the light of what has happened in the twentieth century. As the contemporary period developed, concerns of postmodernism have come to the fore—the questioning of the presuppositions of the Enlightenment and modernity, such as the power of universal reason, the emphasis on the self-directing individual, the myth of progress, and human control over nature. However, within this generally discernible line of change, many other methodological approaches have surfaced.

Many have discussed the existence and grounding of moral norms and their absolute character. Deontological and teleological approaches have emerged with a great deal of variety and nuance. A turn to the subject has occurred with a greater emphasis on the person, character, and virtues. Some have advocated a virtue ethic as opposed to an ethic of obligation. A narrative theology has developed stressing the importance of the Christian story for life within the Christian community. Some of these approaches have been in direct opposition to liberalism and modernism.

Christian ethics in the Protestant tradition has often been associated with the mainline and more liberal churches. Lately, however, the conservative and evangelical churches and theologians have become concerned about public, social, and economic matters and not just personal issues. At the same time a more radical Protestantism has been present, for example, in the work of Jacques Ellul in France and John Howard Yoder in the United States.

Concern for the marginalized and the oppressed has not been just another issue or area of concern. The liberation theologies for the poor in all parts of the world, for blacks, and for women have produced new methodological approaches opposed to the objective, value-free, neutral approach of universal reason. Praxis, involvement, and the epistemological privilege of the oppressed constitute a new methodological approach. Differences exist among liberation theologies, as illustrated by Latin American liberation theology, which finds such great support in the scripture, and feminist liberation theology, which is much more critical of the scriptural witness.

Communitarian approaches have emerged in contrast to the emphasis on individualism within liberalism. In the light of the postmodern perspective, some theologians and philosophers have strongly disagreed with foundationalism—the position that there exists a foundational reality such as a common humanity or human nature from which morality is developed. The discussions about foundationalism touch on the possibility of universal moral concerns, discourse, and agreements. Some opt for a tradition-bound ethics that does not communicate directly beyond one's own tradition, while many hold out the possibility of universal discussion and some agreement despite all the diversity and pluralism.

Bibliography

Angelini, Giuseppe and Ambrogio Valsecchi. *Disegno storico della teologia morale.* Bologna: Dehoniane, 1972.

Beach, Waldo. *Christian Ethics in the Protestant Tradition.* Atlanta, Ga: John Knox Press, 1988.

Forell, George Wolfgang. *History of Christian Ethics: From the New Testament to Augustine.* Minneapolis, Minn: Augsburg, 1979.

Häring, Bernard. *The Law of Christ: Moral Theology for Priests and Laity.* 3 vols. Westminster, Md.: Newman, 1961–1966.

Long, Edward LeRoy. *A Survey of Christian Ethics.* New York: Oxford University Press, 1967.

———. *A Survey of Recent Christian Ethics.* New York: Oxford University Press, 1982.

Mahoney, John. *The Making of Moral Theology: A Study of the Roman Catholic Tradition.* Oxford: Clarendon Press, 1987.

Niebuhr, H. Richard. *Christ and Culture.* New York: Harper and Row, 1951.

Troeltsch, Ernst. *The Social Teaching of the Christian Churches.* 2 vols. New York: Macmillan, 1931.

Vereecke, Louis. *De Guillaume d'Ockham à Saint Alphonse de Liguori: Études d'histoire de la théologie morale moderne 1300–1787.* Rome: Collegium S. Alfonsi de Urbe, 1986.

Weber, Max. *The Protestant Ethic and the Spirit of Capitalism.* New York: Charles Scribner's Sons, 1958.

Wogaman, J. Philip. *Christian Ethics: An Historical Introduction.* Louisville, Ky: Westminster/John Knox Press, 1993.

~ 2 ~

The Historical Development of Catholic Medical Ethics

The Roman Catholic tradition has a long history of concern about the moral aspects of the physical and biological aspects of human life and various ways of dealing with the human body in health and disease. That long history generated many theological and pastoral writings, as well as church teachings and practices. By the 1950s, when the modern interest in biomedical ethics might be said to begin, the Roman Catholic tradition could draw on these sources. Many books on medical ethics were in print in the major European languages (e.g., Alphonsus Bonnar, Edwin F. Healy, Gerald A. Kelly, John P. Kenny, Albert Niedermeyer, Thomas J. O'Donnell, Jules Paquin, Georges Payen, Jaime Pujiula, Luigi Scremin).[1] Periodicals exclusively devoted to medical morality were being published in many of the same countries, among them *Arzt und Christ*, *Cahiers Laënnec*, *Catholic Medical Quarterly*, *Linacre Quarterly*, and *Saint-Luc médicale*. The existence of a well-developed discipline of medical ethics in Roman Catholicism distinguishes this tradition from most others. This chapter will focus on the monolithic discipline of medical ethics that existed in Roman Catholicism before the 1960s. Specifically, the following aspects will be discussed: (1) the general context, (2) the historical development, (3) the specific characteristics, (4) the moral principles, and (5) the particular questions considered. A final section (6) will summarize the very significant developments that have occurred since 1960.

General Context

The Christian tradition, rooted in both the Jewish and Christian scriptures, has always encouraged the care for the sick. Sickness, in the Christian perspective, has a number of dimensions. God as the author and giver of life also heals. Sickness and death relate to the power of sin in the world, but sickness also comes from human weakness and fragility; human beings can and should try to heal and overcome sickness if possible, but ultimately all will die. In the suffering connected with sickness, the Christian tradition sees not only an evil to overcome if possible, but also a mysterious sharing in the suffering, death, and resurrection of Jesus.

The church fostered different aspects of care for the sick corresponding to the multiple understandings of sickness. The spiritual care of the sick ultimately developed into the sacrament of anointing, one of the seven sacraments in the Roman Catholic Church. Recently, the church has recognized a false emphasis in restricting that sacrament to the moment of death (it had been generally known as the sacrament of extreme unction before Vatican II in the early 1960s) and has renewed the emphasis on the sacrament as the anointing of the sick. The sacrament celebrates the presence of Jesus in the community as the healer of sickness but also as the Lord who through death and resurrection has transformed sin, sickness, suffering, and death itself.[2]

Prayers for healing exist both in the sacrament and in the Christian life in general, but the believer knows that healing will not always come. Demonic possession and the rite of exorcism also illustrate the relationship between sickness and sin. However, the church, while acknowledging the possibility both of miraculous cures by God and of possession by the devil, has generally been quite cautious in those two areas because of the dangers of illusion and deception. By the same token, the church has also been wary of the danger of magic and superstition in connection with healing.

The Christian tradition in general and the Catholic tradition in particular have emphasized that God usually works mediately, through secondary causes, and not immediately, without the help of human causes. Acceptance of this principle of mediation characterizes much of Roman Catholic theology and ethical thought.[3] In the area of healing, human means of curing illness have been encouraged, for in that way the doctor is cooperating in God's work, although ultimately sickness and death will triumph. To relieve suffering and strive for healing involve working with God and do not constitute an offense to divine providence, since creaturely existence includes the responsibility to take care of one's life and health. In the light of mediation the Catholic tradition has affirmed that in theory no contradiction exists between faith and reason. While some tensions have erupted between medicine and the Roman Catholic Church, as exemplified in the problem of obtaining cadavers for medical research, on the whole the Roman Catholic tradition has fostered and encouraged the practice of medicine. Thus the Christian tradition encouraged medicine as well as prayer and fought against superstition and magic as opposed to both faith and reason.

The Christian church has fostered and sponsored the establishment of hospitals to care for the sick and the dying.[4] Catholic institutional involvement in hospitals and care for the sick has continued to be a vital aspect of the mission of the Catholic Church. Communities of religious men and women within the church have dedicated themselves to the apostolate of caring for the sick and the dying. Similarly, the church has held in high regard vocations in the health care field for all its members.

Historical Development

Many factors contributed to the growth of what ultimately became the discipline of medical ethics. Catholic theology stressed the importance of works, for faith alone was not enough for salvation. The penitential practices of the Roman Catholic Church emphasized the need to know whether certain actions were sinful or not. Casuistry focused discussion on the morality of particular acts. The discipline of canon law with its complete legislation on marriage, including such questions as sterility and impotence, called for a knowledge of biology and medicine. Great concern for the baptism of the endangered fetus still in the womb occasioned a heightened interest in embryology. The historical development of medical ethics in the Roman Catholic tradition is closely connected with moral theology in general.[5] As mentioned in the last chapter, the definitive history of Catholic moral theology has not been written, but some helpful contributions exist.

Early Development. The first 600 years C.E. are generally referred to as the patristic age, because the principal writers were the fathers of the church. Specific moral teachings were developed and proposed in a pastoral rather than a systematic or academic perspective. Many subjects of interest to the later development of medical ethics were first discussed at that time. Clement of Alexandria (150–220), often called the founder of the first school of

Christian theology, condemned contraception, because marital relations are justified only for the purpose of raising up children.[6] From the earliest times Christian writers condemned abortion, but influential figures like Jerome and Augustine accepted a theory of delayed ensoulment according to which the human soul came into the body some time after conception.[7]

The most creative development in the period from the seventh to the twelfth century concerns the *Libri poenitentiales* (*Penitential Books*) that came into existence with the new format of the sacrament of penance, involving confession of sins to a priest who made a judgment about their seriousness, prescribed a proportionate penance, and gave absolution in God's name. These penitential books consisted of an arrangement of sins by subject matter together with the prescribed penance the priest should give for every wrong act. In the midst of many other wrong acts, such as stealing, lying, cheating, and adultery, one also finds abortion, contraception, and other matters connected with marriage and what was later called medical ethics.[8]

The twelfth century set the stage for the development of modern canon law in the Roman Catholic Church.[9] About 1140, Gratian, traditionally identified as an Italian Camaldolese monk, collected and put in order many of the various laws and norms that had come into existence. His work, known as the *Decretum* or *Decree* of Gratian, was later accepted as the basis for church law. In 1234 Pope Gregory IX published an official collection of laws known as the *Decretals*, which among other things speak about medical examinations to determine sexual impotence as a condition to nullify marriage (*De probationibus*).[10] In 1331 Pope John XXII formed a college of ecclesiastical judges, called the Roman Rota. In his decretal, *Ratio iuris exigit*, he mentioned medical skills and knowledge that help the work of this tribunal.[11] Thus the early stages in the development of canon law emphasize the role and importance of biological and medical science, especially in the area of marriage.

The Thirteenth Century. The thirteenth century witnessed the growth and development of Scholastic theology, which achieved its high point in Thomas Aquinas, whose philosophical and theological approach was later accepted as normative. Thomas Aquinas (d. 1294) proposed a highly systematic theology in his famous *Summa theologiae*.[12] In the second part of this work Thomas treats the questions connected with the moral life of the Christian in the context of a threefold understanding—the human being related to God as ultimate end, the human being as an image of God insofar as he or she is capable of self-determination, and the humanity of Christ as our way to God. The theory of natural law, the moral precepts derived by human reason through analysis of the basic tendencies of human nature, was elaborated by Thomas Aquinas and became the characteristic approach of Roman Catholic moral theology.[13]

The Fourteenth to the Eighteenth Century. In the fourteenth and fifteenth centuries penitential summas assumed the role of the earlier *Libri poenitentiales*. These practical handbooks prepared the priest as confessor for dealing with the sins and problems of penitents. In the third tome of his four-volume *Summa* the archbishop of Florence, St. Antoninus (d. 1459), considers the functions and obligations of different states in life—married people, virgins and widows, temporal rulers, soldiers, lawyers, doctors, merchants, judges, craft workers, and so forth. The discussion of the functions and obligations of doctors extends for five folio pages and mentions medical competence; diligence in care for the patient; the obligation to tell the dying patient about imminent death; the legitimacy of accepting and caring for dying patients and receiving a fee from them; the proper fee or salary for the doctor (the doctor is bound to care for the sick when they cannot pay); the obligation not to prescribe remedies, such as fornication, that are against the moral law; and the question of abortion. Antoninus became a most important source, frequently cited by later theologians.[14]

Beginning in 1621, Paolo Zacchia, a Roman doctor, published a multivolume work entitled *Quaestiones medico-legales*, which makes him the spiritual father of what would become the discipline of medical ethics. Zacchia treats many diverse subjects—age, birth, pregnancy, death, mental illness, poison, impotence, sterility, plagues, contagious diseases, virginity, rape, fasting, mutilation of parts of the body, and conjugal relations. Zacchia's work, which became quite influential, attempts to bridge the gap between theology, medicine, and law, and includes medical knowledge necessary for the pastor as well as the moral and legal issues facing the doctor.[15] Michiel Boudewyns took a slightly narrower perspective in his *Ventilabrum medico-theologicum*. This doctor in philosophy and medicine discussed the questions and cases most often faced by doctors.[16] Catholic medical ethics in the twentieth century adopted the same scope and approach.

Théophile Raynaudus in 1637 in his *De ortu infantium* wrote about the morality of caesarean sections in the various circumstances that might arise in birth.[17] Girolamo Florentinius in 1658 published *Disputatio de ministrando baptismo* in which he talks about the sacrament of baptism and the products of conception that are doubtfully human.[18] Francesco Cangiamila

(d. 1763) in his *Sacra embryologia* discusses questions connected with embryology, such as the animation of the fetus and intrauterine baptism.[19]

However, despite these significant developments in the seventeenth and eighteenth centuries, one still cannot speak of a well-developed and distinct discipline of pastoral medicine or medical ethics in Roman Catholic theology. In the same two centuries, Catholic moral theology in general experienced the growth of the manuals known as the *Institutiones theologiae moralis*, which came into existence in the seventeenth century and continued to be the textbooks of moral theology until Vatican II.[20] These textbooks briefly explain the more theoretical aspects of moral theology but concentrate on preparing the priest as confessor and judge in the sacrament of penance, and they often develop their material using the schema of the Ten Commandments and the sacraments. Questions pertaining to medical ethics are often discussed under the fifth commandment, which explicitly forbids killing and implicitly forbids mutilation, and the sacrament of marriage. Books containing practical cases (*Casus conscientiae*) supplemented the *Institutiones theologiae moralis* and developed ever more the method of casuistry.[21] The manual and writings of Alphonsus Liguori (1789) carried great weight because he subsequently was declared a saint (1839), a doctor of the church (1871), and the patron of moral theology (1950).

The Nineteenth and Twentieth Centuries: Pastoral Medicine and Medical Ethics. Pastoral medicine emerged as a separate discipline in the nineteenth century. In the light of newer developments in biology and medical science, books with pastoral medicine in the title tried to bridge the gap between theology and pastoral practice, on the one hand, and medicine, on the other hand. In 1877 a German physician, Carl Capellmann, wrote probably the most influential of many such works; it was later translated into Latin and many modern languages.[22] In his introduction Capellmann describes his purposes as providing the priest with the medical knowledge needed to carry out his ministry, and communicating to doctors the moral principles necessary to ensure that they act in accord with Christian morals. The chief areas covered by Capellmann are the fifth commandment, including questions of abortion, medical operations, and the use of medicine; the sixth commandment, including masturbation, pollution, marriage; the commandments of the church, such as fasting and abstinence; the sacraments, particularly baptism, holy communion, extreme unction; impotence in marriage; plus other topics of lesser importance. Other significant books of the same type were published by Pierre Debreyne,[23] Alphons Eschbach,[24] and

Guiseppe Antonelli.[25] These and other books published in various modern languages at the end of the nineteenth and the beginning of the twentieth century created the new discipline called pastoral medicine.

The interest in theology and medicine continued and grew in the twentieth century. Ethical problems in medicine were still considered in general treatises on moral theology, but books on pastoral medicine, medical deontology (understood in light of the French word referring to professional obligations), and medical ethics flourished in all modern European languages. In Germany, Albert Niedermeyer published a multivolume work on pastoral medicine, which included a complete and updated treatment of the topics covered in the older works as well as material dealing with psychiatry and psychotherapy.[26] In the twentieth century, especially in the United States, the discipline became known as medical ethics and focused only on the moral issues and problems facing doctors, nurses, and Catholic hospitals. Many of these books served as textbooks for courses in Catholic medical schools and especially in Catholic nursing schools. Father Charles Coppens taught medical ethics at Creighton University in Omaha, Nebraska, at the turn of the century and published his lectures as *Moral Principles and Medical Practice*.[27] The Catholic Hospital Association's "Ethical and Religious Directives for Catholic Hospitals" were first formulated in 1949 and revised in 1955.[28]

As the twentieth century progressed, more and more monographs appeared on subjects in medical ethics. Areas of medical ethics became favorite topics for doctoral dissertations in the area of Roman Catholic moral theology. Also the journals existing in different languages published articles on the subject. Thus by the 1950s there was a large body of literature and a distinct field in Roman Catholic theology generally known as medical ethics, although occasionally the more popular nineteenth-century term "pastoral medicine" was still used.

Specific Characteristics

Roman Catholic medical ethics as it existed in the 1950s (e.g., Healy, Kelly, Kenny, McFadden, O'Donnell), like all Roman Catholic moral theology at that time, exhibited two distinctive characteristics: natural law methodology and the role of authoritative church teaching.

Natural Law Methodology. Natural law is a complex term involving a number of aspects. From the more theological aspect, natural law theory recognizes that reason and human nature constitute a source of ethical wisdom and knowledge for the Christian. Catholic theology historically has recognized both faith and reason, scripture and the natural law. The twentieth-century textbooks in medical ethics based their teaching primarily on natural law rather than on biblical texts.

The philosophical aspect of natural law concerns the precise meanings of human reason, human nature, and natural law itself. Here the Roman Catholic textbooks in medical ethics, like all the Roman Catholic ethical considerations in the first part of the twentieth century, appealed to the teaching of Thomas Aquinas, especially as interpreted by the neoscholastic theologians and textbooks. According to neoscholastic theory, the eternal law is the plan of divine wisdom ordering all reality to its proper end. The eternal law is ultimately grounded in the very being of God.

The natural law is the participation of the eternal law in the rational creature. God directs all creatures to their end in accord with their own natures. There are laws by which the physical universe is governed, such as the law of gravity. However, human beings are governed according to their rational nature. The human being is an image of God precisely insofar as he or she is endowed with reason, free will, and the power of self-determination. Through reason the rational creature directs her own activity toward her proper end and thus is not merely passively directed to the end by God. Right reason is able to recognize the threefold natural inclinations within human nature—the inclinations we share with all living things (i.e., the conservation of one's existence), the inclinations we share with animals (i.e., procreation and education of offspring), and the inclinations we have as rational beings (i.e., living in society). Thus the natural law is understood as human reason directing the individual to her own end in accord with her nature.

The best of the Catholic tradition understood the natural law as an unwritten or unformulated law—the very law of one's being as a rational creature. On the basis of the ontological structures of rational human nature, reason can arrive at universally valid principles or prescriptions of the natural law. The first principles of the natural law are known intuitively by human reason: Good is to be done; evil is to be avoided; act according to right reason. Human reason on the basis of the first principles can then deduce the secondary principles of the natural law, such as "adultery is wrong" and "stealing is forbidden."

The primary principles of the natural law are obligatory universally for all human persons, at all times and places. The secondary principles and the applications to particular cases are less universal, being open to some exceptions and modifications, as Aquinas stated, on rare occasions. However, the Roman Catholic moral theologians of the 1950s tended to take a more strict position, arguing that secondary principles rightly deduced from first principles had the same obligatory force, as did even many applications. Thus such medical ethics questions as euthanasia (involving direct taking of human life), direct attacks on fetal life in abortion, direct contraception, and sterilization were considered as absolutely wrong in all circumstances. Indirect killing or indirect sterilization could be justified according to the principle of double effect, discussed below.

Authoritative Church Teaching. A second distinctive characteristic of Roman Catholic medical ethics involves the authoritative teaching office of the church. Acceptance of the gospel message calls for faith and works. The Roman Catholic Church recognizes a special God-given hierarchical teaching function belonging to the pope and the bishops as well as to councils of the church, called the hierarchical magisterium.

Early councils in the church as well as letters of popes and other bishops spoke about specific moral questions such as abortion and marriage. Mention has already been made of authoritative collections of canon law beginning in the twelfth century. The papal teaching office—especially the Congregation of the Holy Office (now known as the Congregation for the Doctrine of the Faith), which deals with faith and morals—made significant interventions in moral matters in the seventeenth and eighteenth centuries. Papal encyclicals addressed to all the bishops and faithful of the world and speaking on specific areas of faith or morals became prominent only in the nineteenth and twentieth centuries. Encyclicals on marriage by Pope Pius XI, *Casti connubii* in 1930,[29] and by Pope Paul VI, *Humanae vitae* in 1968,[30] strongly reiterated the condemnation of artificial contraception.

The growth and development of medical ethics in the nineteenth and twentieth centuries corresponded with the greater emphasis on the papal teaching office in the Roman Catholic Church. Between 1884 and 1902, for example, the Holy Office responded to a number of inquiries from bishops and theologians about abortion and eliminated some of the exceptions that had not been previously condemned. The Holy Office declared that one could not perform a craniotomy or directly kill the fetus to save the life of the mother, nor could one extract an ectopic pregnancy. The next chapter will discuss these nineteenth century controversies about abortion in greater detail.

Perhaps the most significant development in the matter of authoritative church teachings was the number of allocutions and addresses given by Pope Pius XII (1939-1958), very often dealing with questions of medical ethics. This corpus of papal teaching shows a wide-ranging interest in the problems of medical ethics as well as a penetrating knowledge of medicine and its problems. Pope Pius XII spoke to various medical groups on such subjects as the duties of the medical profession, blood donors, artificial insemination, contraception, sterilization, abortion, the moral limits of medical research in experimentation, genetics, painless childbirth, transplants, death, and the various means necessary to preserve life. Obviously, the interest and concern of Pope Pius XII also sparked the growth and development of the discipline of medical ethics.[31]

It is important to recognize the various grades or degrees of the hierarchical magisterium or teaching authority in the Roman Catholic Church. In the nineteenth century the distinction became formalized between infallible church teaching to which one owed the assent of faith, and the authoritative noninfallible teaching to which the faithful owed the religious assent of intellect and will. Catholic ethicists acknowledged in the 1950s that teaching in the area of medical ethics ordinarily does not fall under the category of infallible teaching, which in reality is very limited. Gradations also exist in the various forms of the ordinary noninfallible papal teaching office. However, Pius XII, in the encyclical *Humani generis*, 1950, declared that whenever the pope goes out of his way to speak on a controverted subject, that subject is no longer open to free debate among theologians.[32] In the light of such an understanding, any Roman pronouncement or decree both theoretically and practically ended debate about a specific question, but the papal teaching office recognized the need for theological input and advice.[33]

Moral Principles

Since the method of natural law proceeded by first establishing the principles of natural law and then applying these principles to particular cases, Roman Catholic medical ethics developed a number of important principles. In fact, the textbooks of the 1950s often began their discussion with a brief summary of the more important principles governing medical ethics. These principles were generally accepted by all Catholic medical ethicists; only in the 1960s did the monolithic look of Catholic medical ethics begin to change.

The Right to Life. Both the gift of God and the natural law itself ground the right of the individual to life. Neither the state nor any human person can deny this right to life. This natural right which belongs to all human beings is inalienable: it cannot be renounced by a person (such as someone who attempts suicide). However, the Roman Catholic ethical tradition recognized conflict situations and cases where the life of another may be taken; for example, killing another as a necessary way of defending one's life, or just war, capital punishment, and accidental killing. The most precise formulation of the principle maintains that the direct killing of an innocent person on one's own authority is always wrong.[34]

Right of Use or Stewardship. Much in the area of medical ethics follows from the moral principle that the individual as a rational creature possesses the right of use of the faculties and powers of one's human nature in accord with their God-given and natural purpose. Since the individual is a user and not a proprietor, she does not have unlimited power to destroy or mutilate her body or its functions. The principle of stewardship serves as the basis for the care one should take of her own body as well as the justification in general for surgery and other procedures.[35]

Principle of Totality. Thomas Aquinas pointed out that a member or part of the body exists for the good of the whole body so that one may remove a diseased member if this is for the good of the whole. This principle was reaffirmed by Pope Pius XII as the principle of totality, which maintains that the good of the whole is the determining factor in regard to the part, and one can dispose of the part in the interest of the whole.

The pope and Roman Catholic moralists were very aware of the abuses of totalitarian governments in sacrificing individuals for the good of the state, so they carefully spelled out the meaning and limits of the principle of totality. Since the individual person does not exist totally for the good of the state, the individual cannot be totally subordinated to the state. The obvious example where the principle of totality applies concerns the individual organs and functions of the total bodily organism.[36]

Principles Regarding Sexuality and Procreation. In traditional Roman Catholic thought, the faculties and powers of human beings must be used according to the purpose for which God made them and nature intended them; for example, one perverts the finality of speech by using it to communicate to another what is directly contrary to one's thought. The sexual function and organs have a twofold purpose—procreation and the love union of husband and wife. Any use of sexual powers is immoral when it impedes the very purpose for which God created these powers. As a result contraception and contraceptive sterilization are wrong. The individual person may not positively interfere to thwart the sexual act or faculty of its God-given finality. According to this reasoning, the sexual organs and functions differ from other organs. The sexual organs exist not only for the good of the individual but for the good of the species. Hence, one cannot invoke the principle of totality to sacrifice the species aspect of the sexual organs and functions for the good of the individual as in the case of direct sterilization.[37]

The Principle of Double Effect. Catholic moral theology has recognized the existence of conflict situations. What is the morality of actions that have two or more effects including a bad effect? Catholic medical ethics employed the principle of double effect to solve these dilemmas. It is morally permissible to perform an act with two effects, one good and one bad, if the following conditions are present: (1) The act must be good in itself or at least morally indifferent. (2) The good effect must follow as immediately from the cause as the evil effect. This condition recognizes that the end does not justify the means. (3) The intention of the individual must be good. (4) There must be a proportionately grave cause for doing the action. This principle was used at times to justify the possibility of indirect abortion (e.g., removing a cancerous uterus during pregnancy), as well as indirect killing, indirect sterilization, and indirect cooperation.[38]

Cooperation and Scandal. Especially in the work of doctors and nurses, questions arose about cooperation and scandal. "Cooperation" was generally defined as participation in the wrong or sinful act of another. Formal cooperation, described as intending the evil act, is always wrong. Immediate material cooperation, defined as participation in actually performing the wrong act, is likewise always wrong. Mediate material cooperation, which presupposes there is no intention to do evil and involves doing an act that is good or indifferent, may be permitted if there is a sufficient reason for so doing. In such a case the individual person neither intends nor does an immoral act. The morality of mediate material cooperation depends on the principle of the double effect, with special attention to the proportion between the cooperation (proximate or remote, necessary or unnecessary) in the wrong act of the other and the gravity of that wrong act. On the basis of these principles, it would be concluded that a physician should never perform an immoral operation, such as an abortion or sterilization, since this would be immediate material cooperation. A nurse who has a proportionate reason is justified in assisting in such procedures, since her cooperation is mediate.

"Scandal" is a sinful or seemingly sinful word, action, or omission that tends to incite or tempt another to sin. Direct scandal in which the sin of the other is intended is always wrong. Indirect scandal, in which the sin of the other is not intended but only permitted, may be allowed under two conditions: if the act giving scandal is in itself not morally wrong and if there is a sufficient reason for doing such an act. Much of the classic Roman Catholic literature of the 1950s employed these principles governing cooperation and scandal in their discussion of matters in medical ethics.[39]

Specific Questions

Obligations of Physicians and Rights of Patients. The textbooks of medical ethics in the 1950s considered many of the questions originally posed by Antoninus of Florence more than five hundred years ago—professional competence, the obligation to attend patients, selection of remedies, correction of errors, fees, and newer additions such as ghost surgery and fee splitting. Important practical questions such as the obligations of secrecy and truthfulness, especially informing the patient about death, received extended treatment. The professional secret, for example, may be divulged, but need not be, when the patient has become an unjust aggressor and is threatening harm to an innocent third party under the cover of professional secrecy.[40]

Sexuality and the Transmission of Life. The natural purpose of the sexual organs and faculties and the limited stewardship that individuals have over them constitute the basis for the condemnation of contraception and contraceptive or direct sterilization. However, Roman Catholic teaching has accepted the basic principle of responsible parenthood: While always open to the gift of life, married couples should have the number of children they can properly care for and educate as good Christians and human beings. Acceptance of responsible parenthood gradually appeared in formal Roman Catholic teaching. Pope Pius XII explicitly recognized that medical, eugenic, economic, and social indications can justify the limitation of the number of children. Official Roman Catholic teaching accepted rhythm, or the use of the infertile periods, since it involves no positive interference with the God-given purpose of the sexual faculty or act.[41]

The Roman Catholic teaching on sexuality did not rest ultimately on the primacy of procreation but on an understanding of the sexual act as both open to procreation and expressive of love union. Catholic teaching as illustrated by Pope Pius XII in 1956 opposed masturbation as a means of obtaining semen for fertility tests, even though procreation would thereby be facilitated. On three different occasions Pope Pius XII spoke about and condemned artificial insemination, even with the husband's semen (AIH), because such an act goes against the nature and finality of the sexual act. Contraception interferes with the procreative aspect of the act; AIH does not recognize the love union aspect of the sexual act.[42]

The Beginning of Life and Birth. Catholic theology acknowledges a possible theoretical doubt about when personal human life begins, but in practice all must act as if personal human life is present from the moment of conception. Since the fetus in the womb is defenseless, Catholic theology all the more feels the need to speak out in its defense. According to Pius XII and Catholic theology in this period, direct abortion is always wrong. Indirect abortion is permitted for sufficient reasons. The two most often proposed examples of indirect abortion involve the removal of the cancerous uterus when the woman is pregnant and the removal of the fallopian tube or the cervix containing an ectopic pregnancy. Caesarean sections were also still discussed in the textbooks of medical ethics. Premature delivery of a viable fetus is morally acceptable if there is a proportionate reason justifying the danger to the fetus involved in such a procedure. Inducement of labor follows the same general principle.[43]

Care for Health, Surgery, and Other Procedures. Rational human nature grounds the obligation to protect and promote our well-being in general and our health in particular. The patient has a right to use all moral means possible to overcome pain, even though in some way all will know the meaning of suffering in human existence. However, the Catholic tradition recognizes the right of the person freely to accept pain as a form of participation in the redemptive suffering and death of Jesus. The danger of habit-forming drugs is often discussed in this context of using drugs to relieve pain.[44]

The principle of totality justifies surgery and other procedures to suppress bodily organs and functions provided they are for the proportionate good of the individual. Many Roman Catholic ethicists justified cosmetic surgery, but an operation is less justifiable in relation to the danger it poses.[45]

Organ transplants raised a problem, especially when the organ was taken from another living donor. Here the one person is mutilated not for his or her own good but for the good of the other. Pope Pius XII pointed out that the principle of totality cannot justify such transplants, because the mutilation is not for the good of the individual who is harmed. Some Roman Catholic moralists, therefore, considered organ transplants among the living as immoral operations, but others justified them on the basis of the principle of fraternal charity. However, even those allowing such transplants cautioned that the donors cannot gravely endanger their lives or seriously impair their functional integrity even for the sake of helping the neighbor.[46]

Death and Dying. On the basis of the teaching that the individual does not exercise full dominion but only stewardship over life, Roman

Catholic moral teaching rejects active euthanasia. However, painkillers can be given to the dying person even though an indirect effect of these drugs might be the hastening of the death of the patient.

Clearly distinct from euthanasia is the teaching that one does not have to use extraordinary means to preserve human life. The teaching arose in the context of the positive obligation to care for health. Positive obligations do not hold in the face of moral impossibility. By the sixteenth century there was much discussion in the moral literature about the means necessary to preserve life; moral theologians Domenic Soto and Domenic Banez offered the distinction between ordinary and extraordinary means of preserving life. Generally speaking, an individual has no obligation to use extraordinary means to preserve life. A well-accepted opinion views extraordinary means as all medicines, treatments, and operations that cannot be obtained or used without excessive expense, pain, or other inconvenience, or if used would not offer a reasonable hope of benefit. From such an ethical perspective, no moral difference exists between not using an artificial respirator to sustain life for a few hours or even days or shutting off the respirator already in use.[47]

Even before recent discussions about the appropriate definition of the moment of death, Roman Catholic medical ethics treated the question. The traditional theological definition of death as the separation of the soul from the body lacks precision. To determine exactly when death occurs lies beyond the competence of the church or theology and belongs to the competency of medical science as Pope Pius XII stated in his 1957 "Address to Anesthesiologists."[48]

Other Questions. Under the heading of the spiritual care of the patient, questions concerning informing the patient about impending death and especially the celebration of the sacraments of baptism, penance, and anointing of the sick (extreme unction) were considered. On the question of medical experimentation, the textbooks generally followed the teaching of Pope Pius XII in his "Address to the Eighth Congress of the World Medical Association," September 30, 1954, in distinguishing between experimentation for the good of the individual and experimentation in the strict sense for the good of others. For the good of the individual, experimentation is allowed provided no certainly effective remedy is available, if the dubious treatment most likely to help the patient is chosen, and if the consent of the patient is at least reasonably presumed. Experimentation for the good of others (experimentation in the strict sense as opposed to therapy) may be permitted for the proportionate good of others and of science if the subject freely consents, if no experiment that directly inflicts grave injury or death is used, and if all reasonable precautions are taken to avoid even the indirect causing of grave injury or death.[49] Later, theologians and ethicists would probe these criteria more deeply and apply them to the cases of children, prisoners, and others whose ability to consent was in some way or other diminished or lacking.

Current Trends

Significant developments have occurred in Roman Catholic medical ethics since 1960. The newer technological and biomedical developments that have sparked such a broad interest in medical ethics today have also had an impact on Roman Catholic medical ethics. Changes within the Roman Catholic Church associated with Vatican II have significantly affected medical ethics in its specific characteristics of authoritative church teaching and natural law methodology.

In 1968 Pope Paul VI issued the encyclical *Humanae vitae*, reaffirming the condemnation of artificial contraception for spouses. For the first time in modern church history, many Catholic moral theologians publicly dissented from such teaching and recognized the right of all Catholics to disagree in theory and in practice with such a noninfallible teaching. These theologians maintained that the specific moral teachings on complex issues depend primarily on human reasoning, do not involve the essence of the faith, and contain very specific judgments or applications that cannot claim absolute certitude. A presumption exists in favor of the authoritative teaching, but that presumption can be overturned by evidence or for serious reasons. Subsequently, many Roman Catholic theologians have proposed dissenting positions on many specific issues in medical ethics. The hierarchical teaching and pastoral office in the church seems to tolerate some dissent in practice, but in theory does not admit the legitimacy of such dissent and has taken disciplinary action against a few theologians because of their dissent. Some Roman Catholic medical ethicists also strongly deny the legitimacy of such dissent from authoritative church teaching.[50]

A number of criticisms have been directed against the concept of natural law as proposed in the manuals of moral theology and of medical ethics. A more historically conscious approach gives more emphasis to growth, development, and change and likewise emphasizes the individual, the particular, and the contingent more than older natural law theory did. A more inductive and not so totally deductive methodology remains more tentative about its conclusions than the former deductive method. Newer approaches put more emphasis on the personal and less on the (merely) "natural" and call for a greater stress on the uniqueness of individuals. A personalist perspective objects to basing morality only on the finality and purpose of distinct physical faculties viewed in isolation from the total person.[51] Above all, revisionist Roman Catholic moral theologians disagree with the physicalism of the older approach, according to which the moral aspect of the human act is identified with the physical aspect of the act. The distinction is often proposed between physical or premoral evil, on the one hand, and moral evil, on the other. According to the theory of proportionalism, physical or premoral evil can be justified for a proportionate reason.[52]

Feminist theory has been introduced into Roman Catholic bioethics, and its insistence on the experience of women involves a newer methodological approach that criticizes the patriarchy of older approaches.[53] In practice the leadership of the Sisters of Mercy (on sterilization)[54] and some individual religious women (on abortion)[55] have challenged the positions of the hierarchical magisterium. In the light of all these developments, one can no longer speak of a monolithic natural law theory in Roman Catholic moral theology or medical ethics. A pluralism of methodological approaches now exists.

The revisionist ethicists (e.g., Richard A. McCormick,[56] Lisa Sowle Cahill,[57] Charles E. Curran,[58] Margaret A. Farley,[59] Bernard Häring,[60] Eileen P. Flynn,[61] David F. Kelly,[62] Daniel C. Maguire,[63] Thomas A. Shannon[64]) do not necessarily form a single school or agree among themselves about specific issues. A good number of Roman Catholic moral theologians challenge the theory that bases morality on the purpose and finality of the sexual faculty viewed in itself and disagree with the absolute condemnations of contraception, sterilization, masturbation for seminal analysis, and AIH (artificial insimination by husband). A few even accept AID (artificial insemination by donor) in some circumstances. Many theologians reject the principle of double-effect especially because of the condition that emphasizes the physical causality of the act by requiring that the good effect must be equally immediate as the evil effect. To a lesser extent theologians have proposed differing positions of when truly individual human life begins and how this affects abortion decisions. Much discussion centers on withdrawing life support systems from the dying and disagreement exists about the role of quality of life considerations in such cases. A few ethicists (e.g., Maguire) argue for active euthanasia in some circumstances.

A smaller but still strong number of Catholic medical ethicists (e.g., Charles J. McFadden,[65] Thomas J. O'Donnell[66]) continue to support the traditional natural law theory. Germain Grisez proposes a revised natural law theory to better support the authoritative teachings of the hierarchical magisterium.[67]

The hierarchical magisterium itself (e.g., papal addresses, declarations and letters of the Congregation for the Doctrine of the Faith, documents of national conferences of bishops such as "Ethical and Religious Directives for Catholic Health Care Facilities" approved as a national code for the United States by the National Conference of Catholic Bishops in 1971 and a later version issued in 1994, and documents from committees of that conference) continues to appeal directly and indirectly to the older monolithic natural law methodology to support its continued teaching on the immorality of contraception, direct sterilization, direct abortion, euthanasia, in vitro fertilization, and questions associated with birth and dying. Significant official documents of the hierarchical magisterium on these questions include Pope Paul VI, *Humanae vitae*, 1968, and three documents from the Congregation for the Doctrine of the Faith, whose purpose is to safeguard the truths of faith and morality—"Declaration on Procured Abortion," 1974, "Declaration on Euthanasia," 1980, "Instruction on Respect for Human Life in Its Origin," 1987.[68]

Thus, on the contemporary scene, Roman Catholic bioethics experiences tensions and pluralism concerning the role and binding force of the hierarchical magisterium, the methodology of bioethics, and the solution to many specific issues.

Notes

1. Alphonsus Bonnar, *The Catholic Doctor*, 2d ed. (New York: Kenedy and Sons, 1939); Edwin F. Healy, *Medical Ethics* (Chicago: Loyola University Press, 1956); Gerald A. Kelly, *Medico–Moral Problems* (St. Louis: Catholic Health Association, 1958); John P. Kenny, *Principles of Medical Ethics*, 2d ed. (Westminster, Md.: Newman, 1962); Albert Niedermeyer, *Pastoralmedizinische Propädeutik, Einführung in die geistigen Grundlagen der Pastoral-Medizin und Pastoral-Hygiene* (Salzburg: Pustet, 1935); Thomas J. O'Donnell, *Morals in Medicine* (Westminster, Md.: Newman, 1956); Jules Paquin, *Morale et médecine* (Montreal: L'Immaculée conception, 1955); Georges Payen, *Déontologie medicale d'après le droit naturel: Devoirs d'état et droits de tout médecin* (Paris: Bailliere, 1935); Jaime Pujiula, *De medicina pastorali: Rencentiores quaestiones quaedam exponunter*, 2d ed. (Turin: Marietti, 1953); Luigi

Scremin, *Dizionario de morale professionale per i medici*, 5th ed. (Rome: Editrice studium, 1953).

2. Charles W. Gusmer, *And You Visited Me: Sacramental Ministry to the Sick and Dying* (New York, Pueblo, 1984).
3. Richard P. McBrien, *Catholicism*, new ed. (San Francisco: Harper, 1994), 11–12.
4. For the story of Catholic healthcare in the United States, see Christopher Kauffman, *Ministry and Meaning: A Religious History of Catholic Healthcare in the United States* (New York: Crossroad, 1995).
5. For the best available treatment in English of the historical development of Catholic medical ethics, see David F. Kelly, *The Emergence of Roman Catholic Medical Ethics in North America* (New York: Edwin Mellen, 1979), 13–228.
6. John T. Noonan, Jr., *Contraception: A History of Its Treatment by Catholic Theologians and Canonists*, enlarged ed. (Cambridge, Mass.: Belknap Press of Harvard University Press, 1986), 56–106.
7. John Connery, *Abortion: The Development of the Roman Catholic Perspective* (Chicago: Loyola University Press, 1977), 33–64.
8. John Mahoney, *The Making of Moral Theology: A Study of the Roman Catholic Tradition* (Oxford: Clarendon, 1987), 5–11. See also Connery, 65–87; Noonan, 152–170.
9. For the development of canon law at this time, see James A. Brundage, *Medieval Canon Law* (New York: Longman, 1995).
10. *Decretals Gregorii IX*, l. 2, tit. 19, in *Corpus iuris canonici*, ed. Aemelius Friedberg, 2 vols. (Druck U. Verlagsanstalt, 1959), vol 1, 306–15.
11. *Decretales Joannes XXII*, XIV, *Agnum Bullarium* (Luxemburgi: Andrae Chevalier, 1927), 205–8.
12. Thomas Aquinas, *Summa theologiae*, 4 vols. (Rome: Marietti, 1952).
13. Aquinas, *Summa*, I II, q. 94.
14. Antoninus, Archbishop of Florence, *Summa theologica*, 4 vols. (Verona: Typographia Seminarii, 1740), 3, col. 278–92; Louis Vereecke, *De Guillaume d'Ockham à Saint Alphonse De Liguori: Études d'histoire de la théologie morale moderne 1300-1787* (Rome: Collegium S. Alfonsi de Urbe, 1986), 259–81.
15. Paolo Zacchia, *Quaestiones medico–legales*, 3 vols. (Lyon: Poseul, 1701).
16. Michiel Boudewyns, *Ventilabrum medico–theologicum* (Antwerp: Cornelius Woons, 1666).
17. Theophile Raynaudus, *De ortu infantium* (Lyons: G. Boissat, 1637).
18. Girolamo Florentinus, *Disputatio de ministrando baptismo* (Lyons: Claudius Chancey, 1658).
19. Francesco Cangiamila, *Sacra embryologia* (Munich: J. F. X. Gratz, 1764).

20. For essays dealing with this development, see Vereecke, *De Guillaume D'Ockham*; for a more complete history, see Louis Vereecke, *Storia della teologia morale moderna*, 4 vols., multicopied (Rome: Accademia Alfonsiana, 1979–80). These volumes are for public sale.
21. Albert R. Jonsen and Stephen Toulmin, *The Abuse of Casuistry: A History of Moral Reasoning* (Berkeley: University of California Press, 1988), 101-278.
22. Carl Capellmann, *Medicina pastoralis*, 4th ed. (Aachen: R. Barth, 1879).
23. Pierre Debreyne, *La théologie morale et les sciences medicalés*, 6th ed. (Paris: Poussielgue Frères, 1884).
24. Alphons Eschbach, *Disputationes physiologico–theologicae* (Paris: Vict. Palmé, 1884).
25. Giuseppe Antonelli, *Medicina pastoralis*, 3 vols. (Rome: Pustet, 1906).
26. Albert Niedermeyer, *Handbuch de speziellen Pastoral Medizin*, 6 vols. (Vienna: Herder, 1948–52).
27. Charles Coppens, *Moral Principles and Medical Practice* (New York: Benziger Brothers, 1897).
28. Kauffman, 252, 288–93.
29. Pius XI, *Casti connubii*, in *Acta apostolicae sedis* 22 (1930): 539–92.
30. Paul VI, *Humanae vitae*, in *Acta apostolicae sedis* 60 (1968): 481–3.
31. Kenny, 272, in the index refers to Pius XII's discussion of forty different topics in medical ethics.
32. Pius XII, *Humani generis*, in *Acta apostolicae sedis* 42 (1950): 568.
33. John C. Ford and Gerald Kelly, *Contemporary Moral Theology I: Questions in Fundamental Moral Theology* (Westminster, Md.: Newman, 1958), 19–32.
34. Kenny, 113–50.
35. Kelly, 5–8.
36. McFadden, 302–17, gives the revelant text of Pius XII. For the best available sources in English of the teachings of the hierarchical magisterium on medical moral issues, see *Medical Ethics: Sources of Catholic Teaching*, ed. Kevin O'Rourke and Philip Boyle (St. Louis: Catholic Health Association, 1989). However, their treatment of the principle of totality leaves out the very important 1958 address of Pius XII, "Address to the College of Neuro-Psycho-Pharmacology," in which the pope stated not only are individual organs subordinated to the good of the body but the body is also subordinated to the spiritual good of the person. See *Acta apostolicae sedis* 50 (1958): 693-694.
37. Healy, 11; 156–61; 171–84.
38. Kelly, 12–16; 109–12; 296.
39. Healy, 101–19.

40. Kenny, 17–66.
41. McFadden, 75–134.
42. Kenny, 89–96.
43. Kelly, 66–89; 142–48.
44. Kenny, 32–40.
45. O'Donnell, 66–90.
46. Healy, 139–42.
47. Kelly, 115–41.
48. O'Rourke-Boyle, 69–70.
49. McFadden, 293–01.
50. See *Readings in Moral Theology No. 6: Dissent in the Church,* ed. Charles E. Curran and Richard A. McCormick (New York: Paulist, 1988).
51. Charles E. Curran and Richard A. McCormick, eds., *Readings in Moral Theology No. 7: Natural Law and Theology* (New York: Paulist, 1991).
52. Bernard Hoose, *Proportionalism: The American Debate and Its European Roots* (Washington: Georgetown University Press, 1987).
53. Barbara Hilkert Andolsen, "Elements of a Feminist Approach to Bioethics," in *Religious Methods and Resources in Bioethics,* ed. Paul F. Kamenish (Dordrecht, Holland: Kluwer, 1994), 227–57; Margaret A. Farley, "Feminist Theology and Bioethics," in *Women's Consciousness, Women's Conscience: A Reader in Feminist Ethics,* ed. Barbara Hilkert Andolsen, Christine E. Gudorf, and Mary Pellauer (New York: Harper and Row, 1985), 285–305.
54. Richard A. McCormick, *The Critical Calling: Reflections on Moral Dilemmas Since Vatican II* (Washington: Georgetown University Press, 1989), 281–87.
55. Maureen Fiedler, "Dissent Within the U.S. Church: The Case of the Vatican '24'," in *Church Polity and American Politics: Issues in Contemporary American Catholicism,* ed. Mary C. Segers (New York: Garland, 1990), 303–12.
56. Richard A. McCormick, *How Brave a New World? Dilemmas in Bioethics* (Garden City, N.Y.: Doubleday, 1981); *Health and Medicine in the Catholic Tradition* New York: Crossroad, 1984).
57. Lisa Sowle Cahill, *Between the Sexes: Foundations for a Christian Ethics of Sexuality* (Philadelphia: Fortress, 1985).
58. Charles E. Curran, *Issues in Sexual and Medical Ethics* (Notre Dame, Ind.: University of Notre Dame Press, 1978).
59. Farley, "Feminist Theology and Bioethics," in *Women's Consciousness,* 285–305.
60. Bernard Häring, *Medical Ethics,* ed. Gabrielle L. Jean (Notre Dame, Ind.: Fides, 1973).

61. Eileen P. Flynn, *Human Fertilization In Vitro: A Catholic Moral Perspective* (Lanham, Md.: University Press of America, 1984).
62. David F. Kelly, *Critical Care Ethics: Treatment Decisions in American Hospitals* (Kansas City, Mo.: Sheed and Ward, 1991); Kelly, *The Emergence of Roman Catholic Medical Ethics.*
63. Daniel C. Maguire, *Death by Choice* (Garden City, NY: Doubleday, 1974).
64. Thomas A. Shannon and Lisa Sowle Cahill, *Religion and Artificial Reproduction: An Inquiry into the Vatican "Instruction on Respect for Human Life in Its Origin and on the Dignity of Human Reproduction"* (New York: Crossroad, 1988).
65. Charles J. McFadden, *The Dignity of Life: Moral Values in a Changing Society* (Huntington, Ind.: Our Sunday Visitor, 1976). This book is basically an update of his *Medical Ethics.*
66. Thomas J. O'Donnell, *Medicine and Christian Morality* (New York: Alba House, 1976).
67. Germain Grisez, *Abortion: The Myths, the Realities, and the Arguments* (New York: Corpus Books, 1970). Germain Grisez and Joseph M. Boyle, Jr., *Life and Death with Liberty and Justice* (Notre Dame, Ind.: University of Notre Dame Press, 1979).
68. O'Rourke-Boyle, 37–40, 109–10, 159–63.

~ *3* ~

The Manual and Casuistry of Aloysius Sabetti

The first two chapters have highlighted the importance of the *Institutiones theologiae moralis,* or manuals of moral theology, which came into existence in the beginning of the seventeenth century. These manuals continued in existence until Vatican II and constituted the Catholic approach to moral theology. This chapter will examine in some detail the most influential manual ever written in the United States.

The American Catholic church in the nineteenth century produced manuals of moral theology to serve as textbooks for its seminarians. These manuals prepared the future priests to serve as confessors with special emphasis on their role as judge to determine what is sinful and the degree of sinfulness. This study will focus on the manual originally written by the Jesuit Aloysius Sabetti in 1884, *Compendium theologiae moralis,* which continued to go through subsequent updatings with newer editions put out by Sabetti's successors in teaching moral theology at Woodstock College, the Jesuit Scholasticate in Maryland.[1] Sabetti's Latin manual was the most influential and long-lasting of the nineteenth century moral manuals written in the United States, with over thirty editions published.[2] In a 1935 doctoral dissertation, Theodore Heck, a Benedictine monk, examined the course of study in thirty-two seminaries training diocesan priests at that time. Ten of the seminaries reported using Sabetti as the textbook in moral theology, while the text of Jerome Noldin, an Austrian Jesuit, was the most popular textbook, used in twelve diocesan seminaries.[3]

Overview of the Work and the Author

In accord with our contemporary understanding, Aloysius Sabetti is really not the author of probably ninety percent of the book which bears his name. This transplanted Neopolitan Jesuit has merely taken the John Peter Gury manual, edited by Anthony Ballerini, and redacted it for American use at Woodstock. The excellent quality of this older manual influenced him to adapt this book to the American context rather than try to write a new volume of his own.

His redaction of Gury–Ballerini involved a number of steps. First, he eliminated from the volume those aspects dealing specifically with the French situation. Second, he updated some of the material especially on the matters of censures in the light of more recent Roman documents. Third, he included the pertinent realities from the American scene. Since moral theology deals with practical applications, one must know the diverse local conditions. Fourth, Sabetti worked to improve the practical usefulness of the Gury–Ballerini manual. Subsequent updatings had increased the notes at the bottom of the page and added to the growing size of the manual. In fact, often the footnotes took up more space on the page than the text. Our American author did away with all the footnotes and put everything into the text in the same type of print. He also shortened the book and tried to make his points as clearly and concisely as possible.[4] Sabetti indicated that he was using the third edition of the Gury–Ballerini manual, so one can readily compare the original with the adaptation made by the American Jesuit.[5] The modern reader who reads the brief preface is still unprepared for the extent to which Sabetti depended on and used Gury–Ballerini.

The contemporary American reader and scholar come from a very different perspective, where the author presents her own thought and any material taken from another must be carefully cited and noted. The American academy today is very conscious of plagiarism and looks upon intellectual work as the private property of the individual scholar. Sabetti and all the manualists came out of a different tradition. Their writing is done in and for the church. Sabetti was merely trying to hand on to his own students the best possible textbook in moral theology. He made no claim to originality but only wanted to help students from the common patrimony of the Catholic tradition. Sabetti closely follows the Gury–Ballerini manual not only in its general outline and development of particular issues but even in its ideas and very words. A fellow professor at the Jesuit theologate at Woodstock has confirmed this judgment. "He never claimed any originality for his volume; I do not mean originality of principles for that would be a very dangerous claim for any theologian to make; but not even an originality of treatment. He simply took up Gury and applied his principles to changed circumstances of time and place."[6] Another commentator points out that especially in his first fourteen years at Woodstock, Sabetti was very wary of giving his own opinions and even more so in defending them. However, after an encounter with a particularly articulate but unbalanced interlocutor, Sabetti gained confidence and began to speak more in his own voice.[7]

Sabetti's compendium fits squarely into the tradition of the manuals of moral theology. In his introduction to the work, our Jesuit author makes no specific mention of the sacrament of penance, but it is evident that his whole purpose is to prepare seminarians and priests for their role as confessors in deciding about the morality and gravity of particular actions. According to the Council of Trent, the faithful have to confess their sins according to number and species.[8] The manuals primarily focused on what was sinful and the gravity of the sin. For example, in the discussion of the obligation to hear mass on Sundays and feast days, Sabetti's very first sentence asserts that all the faithful who have the use of reason are held *sub gravi* (under grave obligation) to be present at mass as is evident from various places in canon law and from all the catechisms in which the certain precept of hearing mass on these days is declared.[9]

Although the introductory note to the reader does not mention the sacrament of penance, Sabetti clearly states the nature of his work—a brief and practical manual with the intended audience of young students in our seminaries preparing themselves for priesthood and missionaries laboring in the Lord's vineyard. The students do not need dense dissertations, nor controversies, nor doubts, nor new and strange approaches but brief and solid solutions provided by their professors. Missionaries (for Sabetti pastoral work in the United States was missionary work) will find a short treatment in which solutions that perhaps have been forgotten will at a moment's notice be perceived.[10]

Aloysius Sabetti was not an intellectual and really did not claim to be a scholar. Sabetti received the same education as other Jesuit priests and had no special graduate training in moral theology. The Italian Jesuit did not originally come to the United States to teach at Woodstock College, but to work among the Indians in New Mexico. However, after six months of preparing to go to New Mexico, he was told that he was to teach at Woodstock College. He later affectionately referred to his Woodstock students on many occasions as "his Indians."[11]

The testimony of his colleagues and students confirms the impression from his writings that Father Sabetti was not really an intellectual or original scholar. Patrick Dooley in his discussion of the early Woodstock mentions the scholarly work of Fathers Meyer, Mazzella, and De Augustinis. "It does not detract in the least from his [Sabetti's] merit to say that in point of talent he could not equal any one of the three just mentioned, yet in point of achievement he surpassed them all in winning credit for the house. . . ."[12]

His personality seemed perfectly suited for the work he did in preparing ministers for the sacrament of penance. Almost all the published material we have about Sabetti the person comes from reminiscences of colleagues and students published in *Woodstock Letters* shortly after his death. One must approach these comments written on the occasion of his death with the proper hermeneutic, for such reminiscences usually filter out the negative and accentuate the positive. However, the various commentators paint a very similar picture of Aloysius Sabetti. Above all, he was a sympathetic person. Dooley describes him as a "loving and sympathetic personality."[13] A fellow professor maintained that Sabetti had in an eminent degree the quality of sympathy.[14] In one paragraph Father Ennis used the noun "sympathy" or its adjective five times to describe Sabetti.[15] Italians have the habit of calling a person "*simpatico*," which is a term of great respect and endearment that would seem to be a most appropriate description of this transported Southern Italian.

Sympathy is a very important virtue for one who is a moralist. One must be able to appreciate and feel for the people in their predicaments. A cold detached personality too often cannot appreciate the reality and experience of others. The confessor and the moral theologian should be sympathetic in order to truly help the penitent. The Jesuit students at Woodstock recognized the sympathy of their moral professor for in times of their own doubts and problems they would go to him for help. The great majority of students chose him for their confessor rather than another member of the faculty.[16]

The term "moralist" used in a derogatory sense includes the connotation of puritanical and rigoristic. Neither Sabetti's writings nor his personality seemed to have such characteristics. There is also the tendency for moralists to take themselves and their own opinions too seriously and stress their own self-importance. Sabetti was not such a person. Sabetti was apparently an easy-going, lovable, somewhat heavy-set Italian who was interested in helping other people and well liked by all. He was if anything, somewhat naive, and was often teased by fellow faculty members and students alike. However, he enjoyed being teased and would think something awry or that he had offended someone if he were not teased.[17] Sabetti did not take himself too seriously but could often laugh at himself and others according to these reminiscences. Recall that for the first fourteen years he seldom ventured to even give his own opinions on a particular subject.[18] His humility, self-effacement, and ability not to take himself too seriously all helped him to be a good moral theologian in terms of preparing confessors for the sacrament of penance.

Another important characteristic for a good moralist is clarity. Anyone reading Sabetti's textbook can appreciate this virtue in the author. The clarity, order, conciseness, and preciseness of his written exposition indicate the same characteristics in his thinking. The testimony of his colleagues and friends underscores the clarity of his writing and of his thinking. Clarity and sympathy are the two words most used about Sabetti in the reminiscences at the time of his death. He was perfectly clear in his explanations. When a difficulty arose he was never satisfied until his questioners understood and accepted the answer.[19] Father Ennis acknowledges that there are probably works wherein questions are treated more extensively and with greater erudition, but none are clearer or of easier application than Sabetti.[20] Precision is closely allied to clarity, and Sabetti was precise in his thinking and his writing. In the latter he adapted the material of Gury–Ballerini to his students by reducing its length and sharpening its force. In the introduction to his compendium, Sabetti claims that the students do not need long disquistions but brief and solid solutions.[21] Precision in analyzing the situation, in describing what is the heart of the problem, and in proposing solutions is a most important characteristic for the manualist. Sabetti's precision is evident throughout his work.

The moral theologian following the path of Alphonsus Liguori strives to avoid the twofold extremes of rigorism and laxism. Such a person needs a good pastoral and common sense. Beware of the zealot or the one who acts too hastily. A fellow professor lauded Sabetti for his "mental stability and equipoise."[22] This clearheaded common sense comes through in his writing and helps give him his reputation.

Sabetti had no ambition to be a scholar or an original thinker but wrote for the needs of the church. As such he had to be aware of the realities that people lived and experienced in their lives. His sympathetic nature was a big help in this matter. But Sabetti knew that he had to be familiar with the problems and issues of people. He often spent his vacations hearing confessions and working in a parish so that he would be in touch with what was happening and never become one who taught but never practiced what he taught.[23]

The Moral Model

Contemporary theologians talk about three different models for moral theology—the deontological, the teleological, and the relationality–responsibility model.[24] Not all moral theologians even on the contemporary scene deal explicitly with the question of the ethical model they are using, but in reality all approaches will use one or another of these models as the primary way of understanding the moral life.

Sabetti does not explicitly consider the question of models, but he obviously follows the deontological model. The deontological model sees the moral life primarily in terms of duty and obligation. Sabetti structures his development of moral theology on the basis of a law model. This legal model common to all the manuals coheres very well with the purpose of the manuals to point out what acts are sinful and their degree of sinfulness. The manuals of moral theology first treated fundamental moral theology, discussing what was basic and common to all moral issues. The manuals then developed at much greater length special moral theology, which considered specific moral actions generally following the schema of the commandments and the sacraments.

Fundamental Moral Theology. The first three short treatises in the compendium clearly show forth the legal model at work in this manual as in all manuals. The first treatise discusses human acts; the second, conscience; and the third, laws. The very nature of the matters discussed here, as well as the fact that they are the first three matters considered, shows the legal model at work. However, Sabetti would have been even more explicit about the model he is using had he not chosen to eliminate the very first introductory paragraphs found in Gury–Ballerini in the discussion both of human acts and laws. Sabetti apparently left them out in his attempt to shorten the discussion, but they are very important short paragraphs because they explain the basic framework of the approach taken. Gury–Ballerini's first paragraph in this section maintains that since moral theology concerns the proper evaluation of human acts, both the nature of things and common custom call for the book to begin with a discussion of such human acts.[25] The introductory paragraph on law succinctly states that law is the external and remote rule of human acts, just as conscience as the dictate of reason is the internal and proximate rule of human acts.[26] Sabetti, with his penchant for clarity, might better have retained these two short introductions that explicitly give the reason for treating these three topics at the very beginning of the manual and explain the legal model employed. Sabetti himself, near the beginning of his discussion of conscience, points out that conscience is the proximate rule of the will.[27] The fourth tract treats sins and on the basis of the legal model defines sin as the free transgression of any law binding in conscience.[28]

The Commandments. This legal model dictates the basic approach taken not only in the short discussion of the fundamentals of morality but also in the consideration of particular moral acts. The major discussion of the morality of human acts common to all employs the schema of the Ten Commandments with each commandment developed on the basis of the sins opposed to the commandment. In discussing the first commandment, for example, Sabetti begins by pointing out that this commandment, insofar as it is affirmative, prescribes the acts of the virtue of religion, specifically the obligations of adoration and prayer. The purpose and model of the manual dictate how these realities are treated. Prayer must constitute an important part of the life of the Christian person, and one would expect to see both adoration and prayer as the response of the Christian to the gift of God's loving self in Jesus through the Spirit. But the one-page consideration is only interested in the legal and minimal aspects. Sabetti makes two comments about prayer. The first treats the necessity of prayer. Prayer is certainly necessary for all adults by a necessity of precept as is evident from many texts in the scriptures. In addition, according to most authorities, prayer is also necessary by a necessity of means because it is the ordinary way instituted by God for attaining graces.[29]

This first statement made by Sabetti about prayer deserves some comment. Something is necessary by a *necessity of means* if it is required by the nature of things to achieve a necessary goal. Something is required by a *necessity of precept* if one is commanded to do it by a competent authority. In this case the first reason for the necessity of prayer is the precept found in the Bible. A legal model tends to make the will of the legislator the primary source of obligation. Sabetti does mention that most authorities hold to the obligation of prayer as a necessity of means, but the emphasis here is not on the internal reasons why prayer is necessary as a means to the end, but simply that most authorities hold it to be so. The one and only reason given why prayer is considered by most to be required by a necessity of means concerns the need to obtain the necessary graces. But even at this time Catholic theology did not reduce prayer just to supplication for the necessary graces to live a Christian life. Prayer involves adoration, contrition, and thanksgiving as well as supplication. In the light of the narrow purpose of the manuals, these other aspects of prayer are not mentioned. Prayer becomes merely a means to obtain the necessary grace to obey the law.

Today one rightly rejects such an approach and understanding. The Christian life involves our loving union with a gracious God who comes to us. Prayer is an absolutely necessary means to receive, perceive, and grow in that union with God. The very nature of the Christian life calls for prayer. Prayer is not something established primarily by a precept or command coming from the outside but arises from the very nature of the Christian life itself. A legalistic approach easily becomes extrinsic and sees something to be good because it is commanded. However, prayer is commanded because it itself is good and necessary for the Christian life. The Christian life is distorted if its obligations are seen primarily as coming from an external power and not based on the intrinsic meaning and enfolding of the reality itself. Sabetti and the manualists in general put heavy emphasis on morality as obeying an external authority, who in this case is God who commands us to do certain things.

The legal model in moral theology tends to emphasize the role of human acts in salvation and forgets that salvation is primarily God's gracious gift. Historically such an approach has been identified with the heresies of Pelagianism and semi-Pelagianism. We save ourselves by our own works. According to the brief sections in this text we should do the act of human praying in order to obtain the divine grace to avoid sins and be saved. Note that the human act of prayer comes before divine graces! One thus sees in this discussion of prayer the dangers of legalism, extrinsicism, and a tendency to downplay and subordinate the divine gift and God's grace.

Sabetti's second comment about prayer records the need to pray frequently, but that does not mean without interruption, for that is impossible given human weakness. The biblical words from Luke 18 about praying always mean to pray frequently and at the opportune time. The two questions raised in this one-page discussion of prayer have to do with when the precept to pray obliges. *Per accidens*, the obligation to pray arises whenever prayer is necessary to attain a certain end. Clearly the precept to pray obliges per se often and frequently in our life. However, the experts are greatly divided over precisely when this obligation arises. In practice, one can hold the opinion maintaining that one who prays at least once a year does not commit a grave sin. Notice here the tendency to become minimalistic because of a hesitancy to convict a certain act of being a mortal sin. To his credit, Sabetti, following Gury–Ballerini, points out that the confessor should be more solicitous about inculcating in the penitent the necessity of praying frequently than in determining a grave fault when prayer is omitted. Sabetti, following his guide, also raises a question that was still common among Catholic children (and even adults) in the pre-Vatican II American church—does one sin at least venially by not saying morning and night prayers? The short, precise, and clear response is: per se, one does not sin because there is no law which prescribes determined prayers at particular times or days. Here again, the primacy is on the law as the force of obligation and law understood as something external to the lived reality.[30]

The first commandment, in addition to prescribing certain acts, also forbids certain acts which are then discussed under the two headings of superstition and irreligiosity. In keeping with the precision of the manuals these terms are first defined and the various types of superstition and irreligiosity are discussed. Superstition is, according to Aquinas, the vice opposed to the virtue of religion by excess either because it gives divine worship to someone or thing to which it is not due (the more common form) or gives divine worship in an inappropriate way or manner. Four species of superstition are succinctly defined and discussed. Idolatry is the action by which the worship due to God alone is given to a creature. Vain observance is a superstition by which means that are neither proportionate nor instituted by God are used to achieve a certain effect. The three types of vain observance are: seeking knowledge without labor, seeking health by inappropriate means, or seeking from the observance of fortuitous events that one will have good or bad luck in the future. The above is a paraphrase of Sabetti but shows the clear mind at work and the concise and precise way in which the material is discussed. These same attributes are present in the discussion of the nature and gravity of vain observance. Vain observance is a grave sin because it gives divine honor to a creature while expecting from the creature what one should expect from God alone and because it is based on an implicit pact with the devil. However, often it will only be a venial sin because of the imperfection of the act, simplicity of the person, or a certain ignorance or timidity as often happens among uneducated people.[31] Here the author prudently recognizes the many factors that in practice diminish culpability and make this only a light or venial sin. In a similar way Sabetti discusses divination and magic.[32] The contemporary reader is struck by the frequency with which these considerations involve the work of the devil. Belief in good and evil spirits still retains an important role in Sabetti's manual in the late-nineteenth-century United States.

The entire elaboration of the Ten Commandments, consuming almost one hundred pages, follows the legal model and clearly illustrates this method at work. After discussing the Ten Commandments, Sabetti employs a similar customary manual treatment for the commandments or precepts of the church. Sabetti mentions in the beginning that different enumerations of these commands binding on all the faithful are found in different sources, but that there is not that much difference with regard to substance. Sabetti here follows the number and wording of the commandments of the church that had been formally adopted by the Third Plenary Council of Baltimore in 1884. The six precepts of the church are: (1) to hear mass on Sundays and feast days; (2) to observe fasting and abstinence on certain days; (3) to confess sacramentally at least once a year; (4) to receive the eucharist (communion) in paschal time; (5) to contribute to the fitting support of the pastor; and (6) to abstain from the celebration of marriage in those circumstances forbidden by the church.[33] This discussion takes up almost twenty pages, but the material about marriage is discussed in the later section on the sacraments and not here.[34] The legal model certainly encouraged the development of such a list of commandments of the church to go along with the Ten Commandments of God. These commandments then become the means that the faithful use to examine their consciences before going to the sacrament of penance.[35]

The tenth and last tract before the long discussion of the sacraments continues to flesh out and illustrate the legal model by discussing particular obligations. The first part, comprising eight pages, deals with the particular obligations of lay people.[36] Sabetti notes that he will treat primarily those obligations relating to the public good and especially legal matters. Other roles of the laity such as workers, merchants, and teachers are discussed elsewhere in the book. Thus he discusses the obligations of judges, lawyers, defendants, and witnesses. A final short section discusses the obligations of doctors. Here again, for example, he states the general obligations of doctors clearly and concisely and then develops further ramifications. Doctors are held above all under grave obligation to have sufficient knowledge and skill and to use diligence proportionate to the gravity of the matter. If doctors are deficient in these things, they are held to all the damage that follows from their acts. In addition, doctors are to help gratuitously the poor who are in need.[37] Much of the discussion focuses on the obligations of clerics and religious.[38] The short discussion given to the particular obligations of the laity in comparison to clerics and religious indicates the greater importance and emphasis given to the clerical and religious life as well as the tendency of the manuals to emphasize church laws which are quite numerous with regard to religious and clerics.

Other Treatises. Apart from the treatment of the sacraments, there are two tracts in the entire book which do not at first sight seem to follow from and be structured by the legal model. The fifth tract deals with the virtues. "Virtue" is defined as the habit of acting according to right order. Theological virtues (faith, hope, and charity) have God as their immediate formal object, whereas the moral virtues have the correctness of the action as their immediate formal object. The moral virtues can be reduced to the four cardinal virtues of prudence, justice, fortitude, and temperance. This section, however, discusses only the theological virtues because the moral virtues are discussed throughout the other parts of the compendium.[39] In the beginning of the discussion of faith, Sabetti mentions that he will not consider the many things treated about faith in dogmatic theology but will discuss only the necessity of faith, the material object of faith, and the vices opposed to faith. Thus the treatise is not at all about the virtue of faith but about the acts of faith. The necessity of faith discusses both the internal and external acts of faith that are required. The material object again deals with the act of faith. The vices opposed to faith are the two acts of infidelity and heresy.[40] Thus the discussion of the virtue of faith is really a discussion of the acts of faith, precisely under the legal rubric of what is required and when, as well as the acts opposed to faith. Sabetti discusses hope and charity in the same way.[41] So despite the title dealing with virtue, the tract considers only acts in the light of what is prescribed or prohibited. The legal model has totally influenced the way that Sabetti treats the theological virtues.

Tract VIII, on justice and rights, constitutes the longest discussion on strictly ethical matters, prescinding from the sacraments.[42] The discussion begins with the definition of justice and a description of the four kinds of justice. Legal justice inclines one to render to society what is required for the common good. Distributive justice regulates how the honor, offices, and common burdens are to be distributed among the members of the society according to a due proportion of merits and abilities. Vindictive justice inclines the ruler for the good of society to inflict on the guilty appropriate punishments (Sabetti here has not made the transition to the American scene but merely repeats the word *princeps,* used by Gury–Ballerini,[43] which is not accurate in the American scene). Commutative justice inclines the will to render a strict right to a private individual observing a strict arithmetic equality. By that is meant that commutative justice deals with the inherent arithmetic equality, which is the same for all no matter who the persons are. After this brief mention of the four kinds of justice, Sabetti concludes that his book will treat only commutative justice because in the strict sense commutative justice alone merits to be called justice.[44]

The reason proposed by Sabetti for treating only commutative justice is traditional within Catholicism. Commutative justice involves a strict mathematical equality of what is due and what is given. The other types of justice aim at a proportional equality and therefore in theory are not strict justice. However, the real reason for not treating the other aspects of justice comes from the very nature of the manuals. They are geared to the confessor and the penitent and hence deal primarily with individual morality. The entire aspect of social ethics as distinguished from individual ethics is missing in these textbooks. Thus in Sabetti there is no discussion of the state, the political order, the economic order, or the cultural realities. All these aspects lie outside the parameters of the manuals of moral theology.

This individualistic orientation coheres very well with a legal model. The law determines what the individual should and should not do. Thus the discussion on justice does not consider all the ramifications of justice, especially in terms of the relationship of society to the individual. For all practical purposes the discussion on the virtue of justice really amounts to a discussion of the seventh and tenth commandments. Sabetti signaled this reality earlier in his treatment of the Ten Commandments. He skips the seventh and tenth commandments because the tract on justice and rights will discuss the "various sins of injustice" concerning property and possessions.[45]

The Sacraments. Sabetti devotes over three hundred pages to the discussion of the sacraments. The opening tract on the sacraments in general introduces separate tracts on each of the seven sacraments—baptism, confirmation, Eucharist, penance, extreme unction, orders, and matrimony. The fundamental definitions are developed on the basis of a legal model. A sacrament is a sign permanently instituted by Christ to sanctify and confer grace.[46] The very definition is geared to examine the validity of the sacrament from a legal perspective. The primary question concerns what is required to truly constitute the sign. Contemporary theologians often speak of sacraments as encounters with God and the community, but such understandings are difficult to analyze from a legal perspective.

The basic questions concern what is required for a valid sacrament (what is required so that the church acknowledges this reality as a true sacrament) and a licit or lawful sacrament (what is in keeping with the laws of the church, but not affecting the basic validity of the sacrament). For example, the wearing of certain vestments might be required for liceity or the lawfulness of the sacrament but not for its validity. The discussions of the sacraments in general and of each of the individual sacraments follows the same general outline. The role of the sacraments in the life of the community and of the individual Christian is not mentioned. The whole spirituality of the sacramental life is missing. The legal perspective by definition deals with the minimum and with the minimum understood primarily in the light of visible external criteria. Sabetti and the manualists first discuss the matter and form of the sacraments. The matter is the sensible reality determined by its form to become a sacrament. The form which determines the significance of the matter regularly consists in the words of the minister.[47] Thus, for example, in baptism the matter is the ablution with water, and form involves the words spoken by the minister, "I baptize you in the name of the Father and of the Son and of the Holy Ghost." The questions raised in this section concern what words are required for validity (e.g., is "I christen" a valid form?) and what material is truly water (e.g., what about snow?).[48]

The discussion next considers the minister of the sacrament, who in general must have the proper attention (the attention required for a truly human act which is compatible with some distractions) and intention (a virtual intention but not an habitual or interpretive intention suffices for validity). Under this heading Sabetti repeats the general teaching that neither faith, nor probity of life, nor the state of grace is required on the part of the minister for a valid sacrament, although they are required for a licit administration at least if the minister is consecrated to confer the sacrament and confers it solemnly in accord with the prescribed ritual.[49] Sabetti earlier mentioned the famous reason why the sacrament is valid without faith or the state of grace in the minister—the sacraments are said to work *ex opere operato*—by the very fact that the work or the sacrament has been done.[50] Thus if the matter and the form are present, with the necessary attention and intention, there is a valid sacrament. The discussion of each sacrament goes more specifically into the question of the minister of that particular sacrament. For example, the ordinary minister of confirmation is the bishop, while a simple priest is the extraordinary minister.[51]

This section in general then treats the subject of sacraments in terms of both validity and lawfulness. In penance, for example, the discussion of the subject treats the three acts of the penitent—contrition, confession (with the requirement of the integral confession of sins according to number and species), and satisfaction.[52] The last part of the sacraments in general discusses the ceremonies in the administration of the sacraments.[53] Thus the discussion of the sacraments in general and that of each individual sacrament both follow the same basic approach about the requirements of validity and lawfulness with regard to matter and form, the minister, the subject of the sacrament, and the ceremonies.

The legal influence on the understanding of sacraments is even more pronounced with regard to marriage. Marriage is both a contract and a sacrament. As a contract, marriage is an agreement by which a man and a woman legitimately give to each other dominion over their bodies for acts that are per se apt for the generation of offspring and obligate themselves to an indivisible partnership of life. As a sacrament, marriage is a sacrament of the new law conferring grace for sanctifying the legitimate union of husband and wife and for faithfully undertaking progeny and educating them piously and virtuously.[54] However, the sacrament is understood primarily as a contract, and the concept of contract pervades the whole treatise.

The Catholic Church has developed an elaborate legal system to deal with marriage, and the centrality of the concept of contract underscores this legal approach. What is required for a valid contract? Church law developed a long list of impediments. Prohibitive impediments render the marriage contract unlawful but not invalid. Diriment impediments render the marriage null and void and include substantial error, consanguinity, and so forth. Note that one can attain a dispensation from some impediments.[55] The church court system has been developed to deal with annulments of marriage. The official Catholic position then and now holds to the indissolubility of marriage thus forbidding divorce and remarriage, but marriage can be declared null and void if there is no true contract from the very beginning.

After the long treatment on the sacraments, Sabetti has two tracts (XIX and XX) on censures (spiritual and medicinal penalties) and irregularities (impediments to the reception or exercise of Holy Orders). By definition these are legal realities discussed in canon law and developed accordingly by Sabetti and all the manualists.[56]

Thus Sabetti, in keeping with all the manualists, emphasizes a legal model and consistently and coherently develops the entire book on that basis. From the ethical perspective, some of the negative aspects of such an approach have been mentioned—the emphasis on the minimal, the extrinsic, and human effort as distinguished from divine grace. The legal model also distorts the understanding of God and of the church. God is seen primarily as the lawgiver. The love, mercy, and forgiveness of God are mentioned, but they are subordinated to the role of God as lawgiver. God the lawgiver also provides the reward and sanction for the law. Often the fear of the sanction becomes more important than our love for God. The justice of God assumes a greater significance than the mercy of God. God's grace, the primary reality in the Christian life, is reduced to a means to obey the law. The legal model coheres well with the ultramontanist ecclesiology that stresses the church as a hierarchical society with the pope enjoying the fullness of power. Such a model downplays the church as the people of God or even the body of Christ.

Positive features of the legal model also deserve mention. The legal mind at work in Sabetti and other manualists results in a very precise and concise approach. Definitions and concepts are clearly given. Important distinctions are delineated so that one can classify the different types of actions. Principles are enumerated in a very accurate and concise manner. The manuals stand out for their clear and orderly presentation. Such an approach has much to recommend it, especially to the beginning student who is trying to learn a discipline for the first time.

Specific Moral Reasoning about Human Acts

Human reason occupies a central place in the approach of Sabetti and the manualists to evaluate the morality of particular acts. Sometimes this reason will employ arguments from scripture and church authority, but these fit within the larger framework of human reason enlightened from other sources going about its work. The legal model influences how reason goes about its task of evaluating human actions. This section will discuss how Sabetti develops his casuistry or moral analysis of particular cases.

The Method of the Compendium. Every consideration begins with a definition which is characterized by a very precise and concise formulation. For example, "scandal" is defined as a word or deed less upright, giving to another the occasion of a spiritual fall. These terms are then briefly explained. "Word or deed" includes also omissions. "Less upright" refers to both something which is evil in itself or has the appearance of evil. "Giving the occasion" recognizes that the proper cause of sin is the will of the primary agent. "Spiritual fall" includes either mortal or venial sin.[57] "Dominion," for example, is defined as the right of disposing of a certain thing as one's own in every use which is not prohibited by law or agreement.[58] Another example: "drunkenness" is voluntary excess in drinking to the point of losing reason.[59] Such succinct definitions clearly delineate what is being talked about.

After the definition, Sabetti ordinarily strives for precision and further classification by presenting the important distinctions or types of what is being considered. Such classification enables the student to discern precisely what is involved in a particular case. Sabetti, for example, accepts the classical distinction of lying as speech against what is in the mind. There are three types of lies: a *malicious lie* inflicts unjust harm on another; an *officious lie* is told for the advantage of oneself or another; a *jocose lie* is told for the sake of a joke or amusement. This threefold distinction obviously paves the way for the judgment about the morality and the gravity of lying. A lie differs from a *mental reservation*, which is an act of the mind distorting or restricting the words of a certain proposition to a meaning different from the natural and obvious meaning. There are two types of mental reservations. A *pure mental reservation* occurs when the true meaning of what is spoken can in no way be perceived by the hearer. A *broad or improper mental reservation* means that the true sense of the speaker can be perceived from the circumstances. Sabetti illustrates a broad mental reservation with the classical case of the servant who tells a caller that the master is not home when in reality the master is home. People generally understand such speech to mean that the master is not home for the purpose of visiting or talking.[60]

Such careful distinctions help the student and the priest in the confessional to sort out and classify the matter under discussion. These distinctions supply one with a grid of classifications so that one can determine exactly what is the particular reality under discussion. Is this a lie, a pure mental reservation, or a broad mental reservation? If it is a lie, what kind of lie is it? The legal approach tends to classify, compare, contrast, and differentiate. All this abets an orderly and clear process. The first step in ethical analysis is to determine what is occurring. What is the reality that must be morally analyzed?

The example of almsgiving also illustrates this method.[61] A true precept of giving alms to the needy exists as is proved from the general law of charity, obliging us to love our neighbor, and from scripture, which is supported by two proof texts—Eccl 4:1 and Mt 25:42. The precept of giving alms includes two presuppositions—indigence or necessity on the part of one receiving the alms and a superfluity on the part of the giver. Necessity can be of three different types: *extreme necessity* means that the danger of death or of another evil almost equal to death is so proximate that it cannot be avoided except with the help of another. *Grave necessity* renders one's temporal existence very burdensome. *Ordinary and common necessity* is that state in which one is able to provide for oneself without grave difficulty. Poor beggars on the street generally fall into this category, for their life, according to their condition, is not too burdensome or miserable. Superfluous goods are of two types: *superfluous for life* are those goods which one is able to live without; *superfluous to one's state in life* are those goods which are not necessary for honestly and decently living according to one's state in life; e.g., having servants, entertaining guests. (This discussion well illustrates the class differences found throughout Sabetti.)

Three practical and succinct rules follow. (1) I am obliged to come to the assistance of my neighbor in extreme necessity certainly and only with goods necessary for my own state in life. Certainly, because the right order of charity demands that the life of the neighbor take precedence over my own far inferior good; only, however, because my life is nearer to me than the life of my neighbor, and therefore I do not have to sacrifice what is necessary for my life. (2) In grave necessity which comes close to extreme necessity, I should help my neighbor with goods that are somewhat necessary for my state in life or with a slight harm to my state in life. Notice the attempt to find another category between the categories of extreme and grave. In a grave necessity which is not bordering on the extreme, it is enough to assist my neighbor from those goods which are superfluous for my state in life. (3) In common necessity, although there is no obligation of giving alms to this or that person in particular, the common opinion of theologians maintains that the person having goods superfluous to one's state and never giving any alms cannot be excused from sin.

What about the gravity of this precept to give alms? Almsgiving, like the precept of charity, per se constitutes a grave obligation, but it does not oblige gravely in every necessity. In extreme and grave necessity touching on the extreme, the obligation is grave. Theologians are divided not only about whether there is a grave obligation to give alms to a particular poor person who labors under a simply grave necessity, but whether there is a grave obligation for helping poor people in general who are in common need.

How much should be given to the poor? In extreme need or grave touching on extreme, one must give what suffices to take away the need here and now unless there are others willing to help. No one is held, however, to give a large sum of money for freeing a poor person from the danger of death or for obtaining extraordinary and very expensive remedies. In common need, a determined quantity cannot be assigned, but more probably it suffices to give fifty percent of the goods which are superfluous to one's state.

The discussion of killing an unjust aggressor moves in the same direction. After justifying the killing of an unjust aggressor in order to save one's own life, Sabetti proposes four legitimate instances of killing an unjust agressor: if the aggressor of my life is out of her mind or drunk, for such a person is a materially unjust aggressor; in defense of material goods of great value; a woman in defense of her chastity; and killing the unjust aggressor to save the life of a neighbor. Sabetti gives a negative response to the case of killing an unjust aggressor of one's honor. Such a position is in keeping with the condemnation of Innocent XI. If the injury is already done, then the act is not defense. If the injury is in the process of being done, it can be repelled by means less than the death of the attacker. In this example of killing in self-defense, one sees how the case of defense of honor differs from the other cases and therefore is not permitted.[62]

In the context of the compendium, Sabetti approaches particular cases by going from principles to rules to the cases. However, this method is obviously dictated by the very purpose, method, and approach of the manuals themselves. The compendium does not pretend to be solving cases for the first time. The compendium's format comes from its pedagogical purpose of preparing seminarians and priests for the ministry of the confessional. Logically, the cases are seen as applications of principles and rules to the particular issue, but is this how Sabetti would deal with the morality of a case when it is first presented to him?

The Logic of Sabetti's Casuistry. We know that bishops, priests, and others frequently consulted him about moral cases. He discussed a case of conscience each week at Woodstock. Before he fell ill near the end of his life, he apparently was planning on putting together a book on cases of conscience based on his previous work.[63] Sabetti published a number of solutions to cases of conscience in the *American Ecclesiastical Review*. However, the vast majority of these cases do not deal with moral issues as such but with canonical issues such as baptismal cases, marriage and its invalidity, confession, nuptial blessing, generic confession, matrimonial impediments, and the sanation of marriages.[64] A few moral issues are discussed, but the most in-depth discussion concerns ectopic pregnancy. An examination of this discussion should shed some light on his casuistry.

The *American Ecclesiastical Review* presented a discussion among many doctors and some theologians on the question of ectopic pregnancy beginning in 1893. Three theologians took part in the discussion—August Lehmkuhl, the German Jesuit; Joseph Aertnys, a Dutch Redemptorist; and Sabetti. The original case had a number of parts dealing with different ways of removing the ectopic pregnancy which was threatening the life of the mother. Sabetti and Lehmkuhl both agreed that the ectopic pregnancy (i.e., the immature fetus outside the womb) which is threatening the life of the mother could be removed, but they gave very different justifications for it.[65]

Sabetti himself begins his discussion with a reference to his own methodology in solving cases: It is easier and more intelligible to proceed from the certain to the uncertain.[66] The discussion also illustrates how his case method involved trying to find parallels with other aspects and why parallels did not exist in certain cases. One might speak here of what some contemporary authors call paradigm cases.[67] The crux of the method was to show whether or not the case was permitted by comparing it with principles and other cases.

Parameters of the discussion must be kept in mind. Sabetti had always opposed craniotomy to save the life of the mother and after the Congregation of the Holy Office's condemnation, he maintained that all Catholic theologians would agree. Direct abortion, including craniotomy, was always wrong even if it was done to save the life of the mother. Sabetti strongly insisted on the principle that the end does not justify the means and cited this axiom at the end of his discussions of abortion and craniotomy.[68]

Sabetti clearly recognizes he has to prove two points to make his argument that the ectopic fetus threatening the life of the mother can be killed to save the mother.[69] First, it is licit to kill even directly a materially unjust aggressor against one's life. In its own way this constitutes an exception to the principle that one can never directly kill another human being and somewhat modifies the principle that the end does not justify the means. But Sabetti does not go into these aspects. Sabetti understands "direct" as that which is a means to obtain the end. "Killing the fetus" is the means by which the mother is saved. "The right to life" implies that the individual has all the means necessary for protecting that right provided the means do not in some way contradict nature or the natural law. Since the aggressor is acting unjustly, he cannot claim any rights. Since the aggressor has lost the right to life by what he does unjustly, the one who kills him in self-defense does nothing wrong. But is this also true of the materially unjust aggressor, that is, the one who does not knowingly and willingly do the injustice against another's life? The ultimate reason why it is permitted to kill an unjust aggressor, observing the proper limits, does not come from the actual malice of the aggression but from the right to defend one's self which is the same whether the aggression is formal or material. The classic example here concerns the aggressor who is drunk or insane.

Second, is the ectopic fetus threatening the life of the mother a materially unjust aggressor? The presupposition of its threatening the life of the mother proves it is an aggressor. But is it unjust? Yes, the fetus is disturbing the order of nature by being present where it should not be. The ectopic fetus, by being where it should not be, is disturbing the course of nature and severely endangering the certain and persisting right of an innocent party.

Sabetti accepts as a general principle that whenever we find something unnatural and strange, one cannot say that removing it goes against the law of nature because nature does not contradict itself. Thus if a person is born with two noses or six fingers one can legitimately cut off the extra members. The person in this case does not commit a forbidden mutilation against the fifth commandment because the body is not deprived of its natural integrity. Since the fetus is acting against nature by being where it should not be, it is unjust in its aggression and, therefore, can be directly removed. But Sabetti recognizes an objection that can be raised against him. Logically, if the head of the fetus is too large and cannot be removed from the mother whose life is being threatened, one then can do a craniotomy to save the life of the mother. But the size of the head is not the same unnaturality as two noses, six fingers, or a fetus outside its natural place in the womb. The greater size of the head is an accidental and not a substantial unnaturality. Sabetti recognizes that his approach would justify a craniotomy in this one case if necessary to save the life of the mother threatened by an ectopic pregnancy. But such is his fear and horror of craniotomy that he would repudiate his position in the case of the ectopic pregnancy if the proponents of craniotomy in other cases were to use it to justify themselves.[70] Precisely because Sabetti justifies direct killing of the unjust aggressor, it makes no moral difference to him if the fetus is killed in the womb or outside the womb. In fact, he maintains the decision of what means to use belongs in this case to the doctor and not to the theologian.[71]

While defending his own position, Sabetti strongly rejects the justifying position proposed by Lehmkuhl. Lehmkuhl rightly points out that the primary difference between them is whether the removal of the fetus is a direct or indirect killing and secondarily whether or not the ectopic fetus is an unjust aggressor. Lehmkuhl argues that the removal of the fetus in this case is indirect and not a direct killing. Unlike Sabetti, Lehmkuhl does not allow the fetus to be killed in the womb. Lehmkuhl maintains that the removal of the fetus comes first and with it comes the saving of the mother. The death of the fetus comes only later. Hence the killing is indirect. The death of the fetus is not the means by which the mother is saved. This differs from craniotomy, since the death of the fetus is the means by which the mother is saved. Lehmkuhl appeals to other similar cases to show that the killing here is indirect. His main analogy comes from two shipwrecked people holding onto a plank to save themselves. Knowing that the plank cannot hold both, one person willingly gives up the plank even though she can't swim and will soon drown. Many prominent theologians agree with this approach. Lehmkuhl also appeals to the famous cases of Eleazar and Samson in the Hebrew bible. Eleazar (1 Mc 6:43 ff.) walked under the elephant carrying the enemy king and slew the elephant, which fell on him and killed him, but the king died too. Many theologians see that as an indirect killing. His action killed the elephant and equally immediately Eleazar and the king died. The death of Eleazar was not the means by which the king was killed.[72]

Sabetti admits the three other examples given by Lehmkuhl. In the case of the shipwreck, Eleazar, and Samson the killing is indirect. The action is good or indifferent, and from this action there follows equally immediately the good effect and bad effect. But the removal of the fetus is not a good or indifferent act. You are depriving the fetus of what is absolutely necessary for its life. This is directly killing. Sabetti appeals to the analogy of taking a fish out of water or cutting off a human being's supply of air. The removal of the fetus is a death-bearing means which brings about the good effect. The killing act is the means by which the good is accomplished. In Sabetti's mind there is an even more important factor at work in this analysis. Sabetti correctly recognizes that the theory proposed by Lehmkuhl would permit the acceleration of birth of an immature fetus which is not ectopic, in order to save the life of the mother. The American Jesuit steadfastly opposes such an action.[73]

Who is correct on this point? In accord with the understanding of the meaning of "direct" and of the condition of the double-effect—that the good effect must occur equally immediately as the evil effect and the evil cannot be the means by which the good effect occurs—I think the case could be made for Lehmkuhl. If there were an artificial womb available, the fetus would not have to die. This shows the good effect of saving the mother is not achieved by means of the bad effect of the death of the fetus. However, this position would definitely have resulted in a different approach to conflict situations involving abortion. The problem revolves around how you define the object of the act. Here the object of the act is the removal of the fetus. The act itself does not kill the fetus. Sabetti adds a circumstance to the object of the act. However, Lehmkuhl's argument has weaknesses of its own. For example, he maintains that one can think of certain actions which in ordinary circumstances are directly killing or the equivalent of it, but in extraordinary circumstances there is no malice and the death is only permitted.[74] Logically, Lehmkuhl should not say that circumstances change the object. The act would be the same, that is indirect killing in all circumstances, but in the normal circumstances no proportionate reason justifies the indirect killing.

At the end of the nineteenth century, both authors agreed on what was meant by direct and the conditions of the principle of the double effect. Direct is referred to both the intention of the agent and to the nature of the act, especially the causality of the act. You could not directly intend and directly do the evil deed. Sabetti saw the act as directly killing because the act takes away what is absolutely essential for the life of the fetus. Lehmkuhl understood the causality and the object of the act to be the removal of the fetus and not the death which would follow later.

Although Sabetti recognizes that the removal or killing of an ectopic pregnancy in the womb is a direct killing, he still wants to justify such an action when the life of the mother is threatened. He appeals to the principle that one can directly kill a materially unjust aggressor. His argument here is somewhat weak. The ectopic pregnancy is not where nature wants it to be. Therefore, it is an unjust aggressor because it is disturbing the course of nature and threatening the life of the mother. The fetus should not be doing what it is doing just like the drunk or mentally deranged attacker.[75] One could argue, as Lehmkuhl does, that the ectopic fetus is really not an unjust aggressor, because unlike the drunk or deranged person, the fetus is doing nothing. The fetus' own condition is not caused by itself but by its parents and natural causes.[76]

The hierarchical magisterium soon condemned both Lehmkuhl's defense of indirect abortion and Sabetti's defense of direct abortion in the case of the ectopic pregnancy threatening the mother's life.[77] Later Catholic theologians developed the understanding that the tube or organ containing the fetus becomes infected and hence one could remove the infected tube or organ which happens to contain the fetus. The action does not constitute a direct killing because the act is directed at the diseased or infected organ even though the fetus is contained in it and will die.[78]

The extended debate on the ectopic pregnancy sheds some light on the nature of Sabetti's casuistry. Sabetti's approach to solving moral cases was more complex than the compendium's approach of seeing it as the application of principles and norms to particular cases. This case history shows a comparative and contrasting analysis with other cases to determine the morality of the case under discussion. Lehmkuhl and Sabetti make different claims in this area even though they come to somewhat the same conclusion.

Another important factor is also at work in Sabetti's casuistry. Sabetti seems to have a basic intuitive moral judgment that the action is good or bad. This intuitive or nondiscursive judgment is part of the whole process. A positive judgment about a particular act looks for a way, if possible, to justify such a conclusion. In this case Sabetti used the principle of repelling a materially unjust aggressor to justify aborting the ectopic pregnancy. One of his students indicated the very significant role of intuitive and nondiscursive judgments in Sabetti's approach which cannot be found or discovered in the manual itself. When asked a question in class he would often give an answer without seeing clearly the intermediate steps. On several occasions he replied, "Here is the answer, I'll give the reasons tomorrow; I don't see them clearly now." The student reporting this noted that such a jump to a solution with the frank recognition that Sabetti could not now give his reasons increased rather than decreased one's confidence in him.[79] Such testimony sheds light on how Sabetti's mind worked, but even the genre of cases of conscience does not reveal this factor at work. Sabetti's casuistry certainly recognizes a great role for principles and norms and their applications; but a comparative and contrasting analysis with other cases takes place, and also the intuitive judgment about the morality of the act plays a significant role.

The question arises: Can the judgment about a particular case through this more inductive approach ever cause the theologian to modify or change a very specific principle or norm? Sabetti never recognizes this in any of his cases. For him the insistence on eternal, immutable principles and norms appears to argue against such a modification. This more inductive approach to principles also goes against the heavy emphasis on deduction throughout his work. His classicist approach with little or no historical consciousness would not be open to such changes or modifications in principles and norms. However, in reality such changes have occurred in the history of Catholic moral theology, and John B. Hogan, a French-born American contemporary of Sabetti, recognized the possibility of such modifications.[80]

Another important factor in casuistry for Sabetti and the Catholic manualists of the time was the intervention of the hierarchical teaching office. Sabetti believed that once Rome had spoken, even through a curial congregation, the debate was finished. Sabetti not only did not resent this Roman involvement but warmly welcomed it.[81] The nineteenth century witnessed the growing emphasis on the power, authority, and prerogatives of the role of the papacy in the church. In the case of morals the papal teaching office intervened more than ever before to settle disputes among theologians as well exemplified in the case of direct abortion, craniotomy, the acceleration of birth, and ectopic pregnancy.[82] Aloysius Sabetti, in the tradition of the Neapolitan Jesuits and the Woodstock faculty, was a staunch ultramontanist in his support of the papacy.[83]

Here again one notices an extrinsicism at work. The practical cases deal with what Sabetti in theory called the somewhat distant and remote conclusions from the first principles of the natural law, where different positions exist and theologians often held different sides. But Roman authority could intervene and decide the case once and for all despite this apparent lack of certitude. Where does that certitude come from?

Sabetti's casuistry recognized a role for comparisons with other cases and for intuitive, nondiscursive moral judgments, but these were always subordinated to and controlled by the accepted principles and rules. No matter how strong and sharp the debate about particular cases, the papal teaching office through the Roman congregations could and should intervene to solve the question and put an end to all debate.

Aloysius Sabetti was not an original thinker, nor did he make significant contributions to moral theology. However, his work well illustrates the general approach, method, and casuistry of the teachers of moral theology at the end of the nineteenth century.

Notes

1. Aloysius Sabetti, *Compendium theologiae moralis* (Woodstock, Md.: Woodstock College Press, 1884). In 1882 Sabetti published one hundred copies of a trial edition which he used with his students at Woodstock and submitted to others for their evaluation and responses. See Edmund G. Ryan, S.J., "An Academic History of Woodstock College in Maryland (1869–1944): The First Jesuit Seminary in North America" (Ph. D. diss., Catholic University of America, 1964), 64. Thirteen editions were published in his lifetime. This chapter uses the seventh edition published by Fr. Pustet in Germany and New York in 1892. References will be given to the paragraph numbers (n.) which are basically the same in the earlier editions as well as to the page number of this particular edition used here.
2. Francis J. Connell, "The Theological School in America," in *Essays on Catholic Education in the United States,* ed. Roy J. Deferrari (Washington: Catholic University of America Press, 1942), 224. Paul E. McKeever, "Seventy-Five Years of Moral Theology in America," *American Ecclesiastical Review* 152 (1965): 19–20; John P. Boyle, "The American Experience in Moral Theology," *Proceedings of the Catholic Theological Society of America* 41 (1986): 26.

3. Theodore H. Heck, *The Curriculum of the Major Seminary in Relation to Contemporary Conditions* (Washington: National Catholic Welfare Conference, 1935), 46–47.
4. Sabetti, *Compendium*, v–vii.
5. Ibid., facing 1.
6. "Father Aloysius Sabetti: A Fellow Professor's Reminiscences," *Woodstock Letters* 29 (1900): 216.
7. Patrick J. Dooley, *Woodstock and Its Makers* (Woodstock, Md.: The College Press, 1927), 87.
8. Sabetti, *Compendium*, nn. 741–43, pp. 535–38.
9. Ibid., n. 240, p. 179.
10. Ibid., vii.
11. "Father Aloysius Sabetti," *Woodstock Letters* 29 (1900): 215–17; Dooley, *Woodstock and Its Makers*, 86–89.
12. Dooley, 86.
13. Ibid.
14. "Father Aloysius Sabetti," *Woodstock Letters* 29 (1900): 216.
15. "Father Aloysius Sabetti: Reminiscences of Father Ennis," *Woodstock Letters* 29 (1900): 221
16. "Father Aloysius Sabetti: A Pen Picture of Father Finn," *Woodstock Letters* 29 (1900): 223; also 217.
17. "Father Aloysius Sabetti," *Woodstock Letters* 29 (1900): 221, 213. Dooley, 86.
18. Dooley, 87.
19. "Father Aloysius Sabetti," *Woodstock Letters* 29 (1900): 217.
20. Ibid., 219.
21. Sabetti, *Compendium*, vii.
22. "Father Aloysius Sabetti," *Woodstock Letters* 29 (1900): 218.
23. Dooley, 87–88.
24. For my approach, see my *Directions in Fundamental Moral Theology* (Notre Dame, Ind.: University of Notre Dame Press, 1985), 11–14, 188–90.
25. Ioannes Petrus Gury et Antoninus Ballerini, *Compendium theologiae moralis*, 10th ed., 2 vols. (Rome: Typographia Polyglatta, 1879), above n. 1., p. 1.
26. Ibid., above, n. 81, p. 77.
27. Sabetti, *Compendium*, n. 30, p. 21.
28. Ibid., n. 124, p. 85.
29. Ibid., n. 202, p. 143.

30. Ibid., nn. 202–03, p. 143.
31. Ibid., nn. 204–06, pp. 144–45.
32. Ibid., nn. 207–11, pp. 146–50.
33. Ibid., n. 326, p. 233.
34. Ibid., nn. 326–44, pp. 233–51.
35. Ibid., n. 757, p. 552.
36. Ibid., nn. 558–66, pp. 365–73.
37. Ibid., nn. 565–66, pp. 372–73.
38. Ibid., nn. 567–627, pp. 374–417.
39. Ibid., n. 151, p. 107.
40. Ibid., nn. 152–61, pp. 107–15.
41. Ibid., nn. 162–99, pp. 115–39.
42. Ibid., nn. 345–557, pp. 252–364.
43. Gury-Ballerini, *Compendium*, n. 518, p. 475.
44. Sabetti, *Compendium*, nn. 345–46, pp. 252–54.
45. Ibid., n. 309, p. 220.
46. Ibid., n. 628, p. 418.
47. Ibid., n. 631, p. 420.
48. Ibid., nn. 654–57, pp. 438–41.
49. Ibid., nn. 634–36, pp. 421–23.
50. Ibid., n. 628, p. 418.
51. Ibid., n. 672, p. 454.
52. Ibid., nn. 729–67, pp. 523–62.
53. Ibid., nn. 649–50, pp. 432–33.
54. Ibid., n. 852, p. 653.
55. Ibid., nn. 867–928, pp. 668–722.
56. Ibid., nn. 944–1061, pp. 738–840.
57. Ibid., n. 182, p. 128.
58. Ibid., n. 350, p. 256.
59. Ibid., n. 147, p. 104.
60. Ibid., nn. 310–13, pp. 221–23.
61. Ibid., nn. 175–77, pp. 124–25.
62. Ibid., nn. 268–89, pp. 200–02.
63. "Father Aloysius Sabetti," *Woodstock Letters* 29 (1900): 228.
64. "Sabetti, S. J., The Rev. Aloysius," *American Ecclesiastical Review Index, Vol.*

1–50, 283.

65. Augustinus Lehmkuhl, Josephus Aertnys, Aloysius Sabetti, "*Solutiones theologorum*," *American Ecclesiastical Review* 9 (1893): 347–60.
66. Sabetti, *American Ecclesiastical Review* 9 (1893): 354.
67. Albert R. Jonsen and Stephen Toulmin, *The Abuse of Casuistry: A History of Moral Reasoning* (Berkeley, University of California Press, 1988), 251–53, 321–25.
68. Aloysius Sabetti, "*Animadversiones in casum*," *American Ecclesiastical Review* 9 (1893): 433; Aloysius Sabetti, "The Catholic Church and Obstetrical Science," *American Ecclesiastical Review* 13 (1895): 132.
69. Sabetti, *American Ecclesiastical Review* 9 (1893): 354–57.
70. Aloysius Sabetti, "*Animadversiones in controversia de ectopicis conceptibus*," *American Ecclesiastical Review* 11 (1894): 434.
71. Sabetti, *American Ecclesiastical Review* 9 (1893): 358.
72. Augustinus Lehmkuhl, "*Excisio foetus atque eius directa occisio*," *American Ecclesiastical Review* 10 (1894): 64–67.
73. Sabetti, *American Ecclesiastical Review* 10 (1894): 131–34.
74. Lehmkuhl, *American Ecclesiastical Review* 10 (1894): 65.
75. Sabetti, *American Ecclesiastical Review* 9 (1893): 356.
76. Lehmkuhl, *American Ecclesiastical Review* 10 (1894): 67.
77. Decree of the Holy Office, May 5, 1902 in T. Lincoln Bouscaren, *Ethics of Ectopic Operations*, 2d ed. (Milwaukee: Bruce, 1943), 22.
78. Bouscaren, *Ethics of Ectopic Operations*.
79. "Father Aloysius Sabetti," *Woodstock Letters* 29 (1900): 218–19.
80. John Hogan, "Clerical Studies: Moral Theology III: Casuistry," *American Ecclesiastical Review* 10 (1894): 1-12. This article and others in the series published in the *American Ecclesiastical Review* appeared later as a book—John B. Hogan, *Clerical Studies* (Boston: Marlier, 1898), 223–35.
81. Sabetti, *American Ecclesiastical Review* 6 (1892): 165-166; 7 (1895):130–31.
82. For the story of these interventions, see Bouscaren, *Ethics of Ectopic Operations*.
83. John L. Ciani, "Metal Statue, Granite Base: The Jesuits' Woodstock College, Maryland, 1869-1891," a paper delivered at the Cushwa Center of Notre Dame University in 1993.

~ 4 ~

The Role of the Laity in the Thought of John Courtney Murray

John Courtney Murray (1904–1967) was the most outstanding Catholic theologian in the United States in the twentieth century. This Jesuit priest is best known for his pioneering work on religious freedom. Murray's research and publications paved the way for Vatican II to accept the principle of religious freedom. Before 1965 Catholic teaching held in thesis (the ideal order) the need for union of church and state, with the state forbidding the external practice of false religions. Murray rejected the older Catholic approach and showed the compatibility between the American understanding of the separation of church and state and Catholic teaching. However, Murray strongly resisted any attempts to privatize the spiritual and deny it a role in public life. He strenuously insisted on both the primacy of the spiritual and the autonomy of the temporal.[1]

This chapter will analyze Murray's understanding of the role of the laity as making the spiritual present in the temporal. His writings on this subject all predate Vatican II, and the final section of this chapter will criticize some aspects of his approach in the light of the theology of the church developed at Vatican II. Such a criticism underlines anew the deep changes that Vatican II brought about in Catholic theology. Even a theologian of Murray's greatness and creativity could not anticipate all the developments sanctioned by

Vatican II. Chapter eight, however, will build on Murray's pioneering understanding of the relationship between law and morality that was intimately connected with his approach to religious freedom.

An overall view of Murray's work, especially from the perspective of hindsight and history, helps to understand better his position on the role of the laity. Murray's life work centered on the problem of the proper relationship between the spiritual and the temporal. From the early 1940s until his death in 1967, the American Jesuit vigorously opposed any type of monism which would not respect the proper roles of both the spiritual and the temporal in human affairs. Monism opposes what Murray calls the "dyarchy"—the two powers, the two societies, the church and the state. In his early writing and throughout his life, Murray strongly opposed secularism and continental liberalism. *Secularism* drives the spiritual out of human life and contributes in its own way to many of the crises facing our world because these crises often come from a spiritual cause. *Continental liberalism* enshrines individual reason as autonomous and reduces religion to the private sphere, thus opening the door for an omnicompetent and totalitarian state. The spiritual has a role to play even in the temporal order which the state cannot deny. On the other hand, John Courtney Murray rejected the older Catholic position on church and state in the name of the dyarchy and in opposition to a different type of monism, this time coming from the side of the spiritual. The church cannot take away the legitimate autonomy of the state, but such autonomy must not deny the primacy of the spiritual.[2]

Two realities—natural law and the role of the laity—serve as important mediating factors between the spiritual and temporal and sustain both the primacy of the spiritual and the autonomy of the temporal. This chapter will deal with the role of the laity. Murray discusses the role of the layman in three different specific contexts, each illustrating the mediation between the spiritual and the temporal—Catholic Action and the role of the laity in general, intercreedal or interconfessional cooperation in the temporal order, and church–state relations.[3]

Murray himself recognizes a logical relationship among the three contexts beginning with the role of the layman in Catholic Action and the apostolate of the laity. Our author explicitly recognizes analogies between this understanding and the role of the layman in intercreedal or interconfessional cooperation in the temporal order and in the proper understanding of the church–state relationship. This chapter will now analyze Murray's understanding of the laity in these three contexts.

Catholic Action and the Apostolate of the Laity

John Courtney Murray did not write extensively on the apostolate of the laity, but his whole corpus and explicit footnotes in the earlier writings testify to his knowledge about and interest in the issue. In deliberating about his own future in the 1940s, Murray mentioned his interest in this matter. In 1941 Murray had become editor of the new Jesuit theological quarterly, *Theological Studies*, but also later became religion editor of *America*, the more popular Jesuit journal of opinion. According to his biographer, Donald Pelotte, Murray's correspondence with his provincial superior in April 1946 and other events at the time showed his concern for and interest in questions about the laity. In his letter Murray pointed out the need for two full-time people to serve the two quite different roles of editor of *Theological Studies* and religion editor of *America*. Murray indicated his own work was moving more in the direction of the *America* job. His primary interest had become religion and society. His interest in the theory of Catholic Action sparked his interest in and involvement with the international student movement. He also cooperated with the National Catholic Welfare Conference in a number of different projects.[4]

Murray never wrote on Catholic Action or the apostolate of the laity in a distinct, in-depth manner, but he was very familiar with the theory of Catholic Action and most interested in some of its practical involvements. His most concentrated discussion of Catholic Action and the apostolate of the laity comes in two early articles (1944) in *Theological Studies* dealing with a theology for the layman.[5] The very fact that Murray recognizes the need for such a theology indicates his interest in supporting and strengthening the role of the laity in the church.

The question of a theology for the layman involves much more than rhetoric or just reducing to more popular language the scholastic theology of the seminary or theologate. True to his natural law background, Murray insists on a teleological approach to the question. He gives the article the subtitle—"The Problem of Its Finality." The preparation of the priest and the preparation of the laity are two distinct realities because of their different finalities. To determine an appropriate theology for the layman, one must first examine the function or purpose of the laity, which has been defined with new clarity and completeness in our present age.[6]

Murray develops his understanding of the lay priesthood and the lay apostolate in light of the papal teaching of Pope Pius XI and Pius XII on Catholic Action. Pius XI desired as an ideal that Catholic Action involves the organized participation of the laity in the apostolate of the hierarchy governed by specific norms. However, one can legitimately interpret the papal approach in a broader sense that does not involve such a juridical organization but still requires its own real organization. Murray calls this second reality Catholic action (without the capital) or the apostolate of the laity.

The present emphasis on the role of the laity comes from the great social transformations of our time that have affected the secularization of modern life. Separation and opposition exist between the spiritual and the temporal, between the church and human society. The masses have become de-Christianized and demoralized. The Catholic Church cannot just withdraw from such a situation and live in its own world. The saving mission of the church includes a necessary but secondary task of furthering the common good of humankind.[7]

Elsewhere Murray gives a further elaboration of this necessary but secondary part of the saving mission of the church. Christians live in the world and the conditions in which they live must be favorable to their eternal life and salvation. These external conditions are not absolutely necessary, but they can and should facilitate our saving relationship with God. In addition, human life here and now constitutes an object of God's will, for God desires a world of unity, peace, and justice.[8]

But in carrying out its own mission to spiritualize the temporal order, the church must safeguard and respect two essential freedoms. Her own spiritual freedom demands that the church must not be compromised by engagement in the uncertainties of the political and economic order. Also the temporal order and the state must be free and autonomous in their own order. How can the spiritual crisis in the temporal order be overcome if both the church and the temporal order, especially the state, are to retain their true freedom?

The specific finality of the laity consists primarily in their mediation of the spiritual to the temporal. The laity receive the word of life, the Holy Spirit, and the command to act from the hierarchy. The church affects the temporal order not directly through the hierarchy or by direct immersion in the political arena but indirectly through the involvement of the laity. The ministerial and hierarchical priesthood mediates grace and the Holy Spirit to human beings which is the divinizing mission of the church. The laity mediate the Christian spirit to the institutions of civil society which is the humanizing mission of the church. (In the light of what he has said elsewhere at the same time, Murray could have strengthened his position on the role of the laity by pointing out that in the human and temporal sphere they act in accord with the principles of natural law.) Thus the autonomy and freedom of the temporal order are respected and preserved because the church does not enter directly into the temporal order. Murray admits that he and the church herself sharpen the distinction between the spiritual and the temporal in order to unite them better and more organically without danger of confusion.[9]

Murray insists on one important characteristic of lay action in modern times—its social nature. Pope Pius XI has pointed out that the personal apostolate no longer suffices if indeed it ever did. The aim is to change a milieu and a situation. A one-on-one type of approach is not sufficient to meet the challenges of the present.[10]

To examine the theology Murray proposes for the laity lies beyond the scope of this chapter, but two brief comments are in order. First, Murray's exposition shows that in the 1940s he is well aware of and supportive of many of the developments in the educational, catechetical, liturgical, and social apostolates that would have such a great impact on Vatican II. Second, Murray's call for a different theology for laity indicates even at this early stage an incipient historical consciousness which will become so central in his later development.[11]

Intercreedal and Interconfessional Cooperation

From 1942 to 1945 Murray was involved with the question of the cooperation of Catholics with people of other religions in the same organizations to overcome the crisis in the social order. Murray himself worked in collaboration with others to draft "The Declaration of World Peace," a common statement on peace with separate Catholic, Protestant, and Jewish introductions issued simultaneously by leaders of these three religious groups.[12] In addition Murray delved more deeply into the theoretical and practical aspects of this cooperation in three articles in *Theological Studies* and one in *American Ecclesiastical Review*. The latter article responded to criticism raised against Murray's position by Paul Hanly Furfey.[13]

In this whole matter, our Jesuit author insists that the first and most important step involves the recognition of the problem—the grave spiritual crisis that confronts us in the temporal order. The need for greater justice and true peace based on the recognition and observance of God's law should be obvious to all. This problem serves as the reason for the urgent call of Pope Pius XII for the collaboration of all people of good will in an organized way to work for the temporal common good.

Pope Pius XII's Christmas Allocutions from 1939, 1941, and 1942 called for a crusade to bring about true justice and peace in the world. These allocutions were made in the midst of World War II but also looked forward to the peace after the war and a new world order. According to Murray's analysis of Pius, the nature of this collaboration between all people of good will, including Catholics, is compassionate charity; the goal is peace, the work of justice; and its basis rests on four truths of the natural order: (1) a religious conviction as to the sovereignty of God over nations as well as institutions; (2) a right conscience about the essential demands of the moral law for social life; (3) a religious respect for human dignity for all people because the human being is an image of God; and (4) a religious conviction as to the essential unity of the human race.[14]

This collaboration cannot involve an ecclesial or church unity. The members of the churches are working together, but the unity cannot be ecclesiastical. Catholics believe that they are the true church of Christ and there can be no *communicatio in sacris* (sharing in holy things) with those who are not Catholics. Murray points out that many Protestants view such cooperation as a matter of church unity and as a bond of faith uniting all in a common enterprise. According to Murray, there cannot be and is not in the present movement an ecclesial union based on a common faith.[15]

What is the nature of this collaboration and the union of different people involved in it? The cooperation and collaboration to deal with the crisis involve a middle position between interconfessional worship, which implies doctrinal and ecclesiastical unity with non-Catholics, and cooperation with non-Catholics in the Chamber of Commerce. The crisis is a spiritual crisis in the temporal order. Murray calls the collaborative response to this crisis "Religio-Civic Action."[16]

The problem is Religio-social with two possible approaches to solving it. The Catholic takes hold of the social order and looks for agreement on the natural religious and moral principles of social unity and peace. Protestant liberals take hold of the religious end of the problem and look for agreement on certain fundamentals of Christianity and seek unity on the religious or ecclesiological plane. The Catholic position calls for a religio-social unity in the natural order, not an ecclesiastical unity.[17]

To explain his point further, Murray brings in an analogy with Catholic Action understood now in the strict papal sense. Such an analogy constitutes an analogy of proportion which involves similarities and differences. The similarities concern the organized way whereby the spiritual can get a grip on the temporal; both are also the work of laymen. Both are social apostolates, for belief in God imposes a personal responsibility for human society. But there are differences. The basis of Catholic Action is the supernatural divine unity of the hierarchical church; the basis of Religio-Civic Action is the natural spiritual unity of the human race whose affective bond is belief in God. Catholic Action in the strict sense is organized confessionally under the mandate of the Catholic bishops; the other is organized interconfessionally under the universal mandate of conscience as obedient to the Author of the moral law.[18]

Murray admits that both Catholic Action and Religio-Civic Action are difficult to understand.[19] In my judgment Murray's own explanation of Religio-Civic Action, while clear in its general differentiation from an interconfessional church unity because of its appealing to the natural order, still contains some lack of clarity. The terms "spiritual" and "religious" are sometimes used ambiguously. Perhaps Murray might have added to the clarity by insisting that faith and charity (from the supernatural order) exist as motivation for what is done in the natural order.

In Murray's understanding of intercreedal cooperation, natural law and the laity again serve as mediators in the process between the spiritual and the temporal. The question is similar to the role of the lay apostolate in the broad sense—how does the church which exists on the supernatural level relate to the temporal order which has its own autonomy and finality? Here again the answer rings loud and clear: the laity. But in this cooperation a complicating element appears. The laity work in concert with other Christians and other people of good will and not just as a Catholic group. Murray solves the problem by adding another layer to the mediational process. Religio-Civic Action involves the participation of all people of good will and the apostolate of the Catholic laity. Such involvement is a type of Catholic Action twice removed—removed from any roots in the organic unity of the visible church and removed from organic relationship to the pastoral authority of the hierarchy.[20]

Murray envisions this organized action for the temporal common good as involving both the masses and an elite body of trained specialists with the technical expertise to bring about a more just society. The Catholic Church's contribution involves the role of these dedicated and technically competent Catholic laity who will work together with all others for the temporal common good. Behind this body of Catholic laity working together with all people of good will stands the organization of Catholic Action, which inspires them and educates them for their mission. Behind Catholic Action stands the total sacramental reality of the church that powerfully deploys its sacerdotal action in prayer and sacrifice so that the whole body of the church may be filled to all the fullness of God and flow over in beneficient actions for the temporal common good of all. Note again the two ends of the church (divinization and humanization) and the corresponding different roles of the hierarchical priesthood and the laity. The Roman Catholic Church's contribution is multiple—spiritual, theological, programmatic, and in the order of personnel. The personnel are the Catholic laity who form a part of this organized approach. From the church they receive their holiness and grace. The theological contribution is the church's understanding of the human being. The programmatic contribution comes from the teaching of the popes on humanity's problems which is based on the natural law.[21]

In the course of this discussion between 1942 and 1945 Murray briefly indicates two aspects about the role of the laity that will assume much greater importance in his approach to the church–state problem. The first concerns how the church relates to this interconfessional cooperation. First, the hierarchy, which for Murray at this time means the church, relates to these organizations only indirectly and not directly. The church directly influences or, in Murray's word, "controls" the Catholic members of the group but only indirectly touches the interconfessional organization itself through the influence of the Catholic members.[22] The point of mediation is the conscience of the Catholic believer who is also a member of the interconfessional organization or institution working for the temporal common good. No opposition exists for Murray between authority properly understood and conscience. The indirect influence of the Catholic Church on these interconfessional groups in the process of mediating the spiritual to the temporal becomes the paradigm that our Jesuit author employs later to develop the power of the church with regard to the state.

Second, Murray, in an offhand comment in the present discussion, describes the basic issue in a way that he will further develop in the church–state discussion. The relationship between church and society can better be described as the relationship between the Catholic (who is at once Catholic and citizen) and a religiously pluralistic and de-Christianized society.[23] The layman thus becomes the link between the church and temporal society. Putting these two points together we come to the conclusion that the church indirectly touches and affects both interconfessional organizations and the temporal society or the state (Murray had yet to distinguish between society and state) through the conscience of the Catholic layman who is both Catholic and citizen. These two ideas will play a prominent role in Murray's ultimate solution to the church–state question.

One final point deserves elaboration. Murray emphatically stresses the need for organized and institutional activity because individuals alone cannot bring about the necessary change. This activity attempts to create a new ethical spirit and to incorporate this spirit into a new set of social institutions supporting instead of crushing the moral conscience as well as the temporary happiness of humankind. Such a purpose requires organization. The exemplary moral life of an individual has great inspirational value, but it will not create an ethos in society. Murray mentions that a great will for peace on the part of individual nations will not insure an international order of peace unless it is institutionalized in an international organization. The principle is clear and needs no great elaboration: action for social peace and justice must itself be social and organized.[24]

Murray confirms this rationale for organized social action by appealing again to the analogy with Catholic Action. Pope Pius XII rightly insisted that Catholic Action entails a firmly structured organization. The ultimate agent as the ultimate beneficiary of all social change remains the free human person. However, the individual conscience receives its education and illumination within an organization and the action of the personal apostolate becomes an agent for social change only when the powerful social force of organizational solidarity supports and strengthens the responsible individual. The papal methodology of both Catholic Action and of the broader cooperation calls for organized social action as alone able to bring about the required societal and institutional effects.[25] Murray's position here coheres with his strong and continual condemnation of individualism.

Church–State

John Courtney Murray often described the nub of the problem of church and state as how to maintain both the primacy of the spiritual and the autonomy of the temporal. The mediating role of the lay person who is both Catholic and citizen enabled Murray to maintain the primacy of the spiritual (the church) and the autonomy of the temporal (the state). This important concept came to the fore in three different but related questions that Murray discussed as he wrestled with the problem of religious liberty and the relationship between the church and state. Our discussion will proceed in Murray's chronological sequence dealing first with the First Amendment to the United States Constitution, then the indirect power of the church over the temporal, and finally the ordered harmony between the two societies.

The First Amendment. In a number of articles in the mid 1940s, Murray developed his understanding of the First Amendment which differs from many Protestant approaches and also from continental liberalism's understanding of the separation of church and state.[26] Protestants often see the First Amendment as a theological statement that all churches are voluntary societies of human origin and of equal value. Catholics cannot accept such a theological understanding. Continental liberalism understands the separation of church and state to mean that religion has no public role in society, and the state is basically omnicompetent. For Murray the First Amendment is not a theological document but a political document. Later Murray describes the First Amendment as articles of peace and not articles of faith.[27]

The First Amendment arose in the midst of the religious pluralism existing in this country at its origin, but the First Amendment is not merely a pragmatic document. The ethical basis of the amendment recognizes the dualism inherent in the human being. Every individual is a civic person, a member of organized society, subject to the authority of government, and ordained to its earthly end. Every individual is likewise a religious person, a creature of God, subject to the authority of conscience, and ordained to an end transcending time. The First Amendment recognizes a dual set of rights flowing from this dual nature. Government cannot interfere with the religious conscience of the individual.[28]

According to Murray writing in 1949, the terms of the dyarchy present in the First Amendment are not church and state but state and human person, "*civis idem et christianus*," to adopt the phrase of Leo XIII. (Note that Murray has found this important phrase in Leo XIII's *Immortale Dei*, which reinforces and gives added strength to his own understanding.[29] Perhaps Murray had been familiar with the quote from Leo XIII before, but in his own earlier references to the person who is both Catholic and citizen there is no citation of Pope Leo XIII.) The First Amendment recognizes a spiritual power that stands as it were not only over against it but above it—the religious conscience whose demands are acknowledged as relevant to the political order, whose right of moral judgments on all the processes of government is likewise acknowledged, guaranteed free expression, and provided with institutional channels for it. By acknowledging and safeguarding the religious conscience of the one person who is both citizen and Christian, the First Amendment recognizes the primacy of the spiritual without injury to the due autonomy of the temporal and the legitimate independence of the state. The citizen is free and safeguarded in working in the temporal order on the basis of one's religious conscience which is formed by the church.[30]

The Indirect Power of the Church (1948–1949). Murray, in his analysis of the power of the church over the temporal order, came to the same conclusion about the primacy of the spiritual and the autonomy of the temporal through the dyarchy of the individual who is both citizen and Christian and whose religious conscience is both safeguarded and allowed to influence the temporal. Murray recognized the cardinal question concerns the spiritual authority of the church over the temporal and went about investigating this subject in 1948.[31]

In this context Murray analyzes three different theories in church history about the relationship of the two powers (the church and the state)—the theory of direct power, the indirect power theory of Robert Bellarmine, and the indirect power theory of John of Paris. The *theory of direct power* interprets the primacy of the spiritual power to mean that the temporal power is included in it as an emanation from it. The church possesses and has dominion over the two swords but ordinarily delegates the temporal sword to the prince. However, if the prince is delinquent or recalcitrant, the pope recovers the power for the superior interest of Christendom. This theory rests on a concept of Christendom as a religio–political entity in which the unity and good of the state (in reality there really was no state) was identical with the unity and good of the church. This was the relationship of the church (*sacerdotium*) and the Roman Empire (*imperium*). Such a theory obviously violates the autonomy of the state.[32]

Robert Bellarmine's theory of indirect power represents a transitional approach from the era in which people lived in one society that was both church and, what we would call today, state, to the era in which we live in two societies—the nation–state and the church. Bellarmine properly wants to underline the spiritual character of the church's power and to develop a sane middle position between the extremes of hierocratic theory and the regalist theory both of which from different extremes really deny the existence of the dyarchy of the two powers or the two societies. Bellarmine refutes the theory of direct power and insists that the power of the church is exercised only for a spiritual end. But the power that the church uses for its spiritual end constitutes a truly temporal power which accomplishes temporal effects for a spiritual purpose. Thus, for example, the pope could depose unjust rulers or directly produce other effects in the temporal order if this were done for the spiritual ends of the church. Murray maintains that Bellarmine's theory of indirect power really involves a direct power limited to exceptional use and truly denies the autonomy of the state.[33]

Murray strongly agrees in principle with *the indirect power theory of John of Paris* (d. 1306).[34] The theologian succeeded in proposing a theory that recognizes the primacy of the church but keeps the autonomy of the temporal intact: he insists that the state is a natural institution for human and temporal ends and the unity of the church is supernatural with its power being exclusively spiritual. The state and the power of the prince are not mediated by the church but are of divine origin, since the state is an exigence of human nature independent of both sin and grace. The civil prince is not the instrument of the church for the ends or purposes of the church. Murray understands John of Paris to hold that the civil power is subordinate to the spiritual power in the sense that the whole order of the terrestrial is subordinate to the order of the transcendent spiritual destiny to which the church guides us. The primacy of the spiritual does not involve a feudal lordship but a spiritual reign respectful of all human freedoms in the temporal order. The normal and ordinary exercise of the primacy of the spiritual concerns the right of the church to teach princes to rule their political activity by the norms of Christian justice. The church does not teach the prince his politics. Here the power of the church is magisterial, terminating at conscience and its Christian formation—an action that is truly spiritual in nature but indirectly may and should have effects in the temporal order.

Our Jesuit theologian applies the basic theory of the indirect power of the church to the changed conditions of political life today. The agent and bearer of the political power is no longer the Christian prince. The relationship today does not involve *sacerdotium* (church) and the *regnum* (the prince). Today, in the midst of democratic principles, the relationship involves the church (*sacerdotium*) and the human person who is citizen and Christian (*civis idem et Christianus*). The church instructs and forms the conscience of the citizen who is free then to conform the life of the city to her conscience. The spiritual power of the church is directed at the conscience of the believer who is also a citizen and is free to bring her conscientious beliefs to bear on the life and structures of the temporal sphere. The action of the church is purely spiritual and indirectly affects the temporal order through the person who is both citizen and Christian. The principle of freedom brings together the freedom of the church and the freedom of the citizen.[35]

Murray directly and explicitly makes the link between John of Paris and Pope Pius XI's theory of Catholic Action. Pius XI sees the lay person as the mediator between the church and the temporal world and the way in which the church ultimately touches the temporal.[36] Thus the theory of the indirect power of the church espoused by John of Paris continues to have validity today because the spiritual power of the church touches conscience and indirectly reaches the temporal order through the mediation of the conscience no longer of the prince but of the democratic citizen.

The Orderly Relationship and Harmony between Church and State. According to Murray, Leo XIII in his entire corpus never develops the theory of indirect power. However, Leo does address the central question of the primacy of the spiritual and true autonomy of the state in terms of the orderly relationship (*ordinata colligatio*) and the harmony between the two powers or societies.[37]

According to Murray, Leo XIII followed in the Gelasian tradition of the dyarchy. The orderly relationship between the church and the state requires full respect for the nature of both. Leo was fighting against state encroachments in the religious sphere and insisted on the church's right to deal with the sacred elements in the temporal sphere (such as the family and the institutions of marriage and education) by maintaining that the spiritual power has consequences on the political, legal, social, and economic aspects of the temporal order. Leo clashed with the upholders of continental liberalism who wanted to keep the church in the sacristy. Leo solved this clash by his definitive establishment of the principle that the church's action in the temporal order is purely spiritual.

Murray points out that in the modern context the autonomy of the temporal order requires that its spiritual direction and correction come from within the temporal order itself through the agency of its own institutions. Leo finds the key to the orderly relationship between the two societies in the fact that the rule of both powers is over the same person (*utriusque imperium est in eosdem*). Once again the pivot is the *civis idem et Christianus*. The starting point for Leo consists in the dualism within the human person who is both a believer and a citizen. The orderly relationship between the two calls for the primacy of the spiritual which implies the right to have the two powers to which the individual is subject in harmony with each other. The human person and her integrity as citizen and Christian constitute the end and object of the harmony between the two societies. The human person is the artisan of the harmony through the free exercise of her civic rights under the guidance of her Christian conscience. Once again Murray sees the connection between this and Pius XI's teaching on Catholic Action whereby the church touches the temporal through the work of the laity. Our author in this context quotes with great approval the description of Catholic Action as the "modern form of relations between church and state."[38]

Little did Murray realize in the early 1940s how significant and helpful his knowledge of and personal involvement with the role of the laity would become in his later life. This knowledge gave him an important key to help solve the troubling issues of interconfessional or intercreedal cooperation and the relationship between church and state.

Evaluation

Has there been any development in Murray's understanding of the role of the laity in these three contexts? The basic theory has remained constant. The laity are the bridge between the spiritual and the temporal which gives specification to the basic principle of the primacy of the spiritual and the autonomy of the temporal.

Some significant development has occurred within this continuing overall understanding. One aspect concerns the relationship of the activity of the laity to the hierarchy or the church as Murray understood it in his earlier writings. Catholic Action is immediately related to the church (the hierarchy) and has roots in the organic society of the visible church. Religio-Civic Action (intercreedal cooperation) and the working together of Catholics with all others for the temporal common good are removed from any organic relationship with the visible Catholic church and the pastoral authority of the hierarchy.

More importantly, in the church–state discussions the Catholic laity, included in the civic people have a greater role to play in the very formulation of the natural law in contrast to the role given them in Catholic Action. In the church–state discussions Murray has accepted and developed the Thomistic social authorization principle according to which the people are the ultimate judges of the king's justice. In the contemporary situation the Thomistic social authorization principle means that the people have the responsibility for formulating the public consensus. In the latest of the essays published in his 1960 collection *We Hold These Truths*, Murray very explicitly says, "It is not the function of the church as such to elaborate the public consensus, which is a body of rational knowledge, a structure of rational imperatives, that sustain and direct the action of the People Temporal and of their secular rulers."[39]

The church continues to instruct the conscience of the Catholic laity but they with all other people have a greater role in determining the concrete requirements of natural law itself. Following Aquinas, Murray distinguishes two types of natural law conclusions. Some human actions such as perjury, theft, murder, and adultery are readily perceived as evil on grounds of the common and first principles of the natural law. Other matters, because of the complexity of the circumstances, require careful consideration and reflection, which according to Aquinas is the province of the wise. This second type of conclusion relates to the public consensus, whose elaboration belongs to the *studium* and the wise and not to the church. Today the wise are the wise and honest people who care for society. In general, reasonable people can grasp the reasonableness of these conclusions which have first been reached by the wise.[40] Murray's position remains somewhat elitist, but the point is clear—the public consensus is not the work of the church but of the people helped and instructed by the wise. Thus in Murray's development the laity have come to play a much greater and more independent role not only in the temporal life of society but even in the formulation of aspects of the natural law. J. Leon Hooper has perceptively pointed out and studied this significant development in Murray's thought.[41]

If one were to judge Murray's understanding of the laity solely on the basis of his discussion of the lay person in the church–state problematic of maintaining the primacy of the spiritual and the autonomy of the temporal, a serious criticism could be lodged against his approach. *Civis idem et Christianus* appears almost as a refrain in the church–state writings. The church reaches the temporal only through the person who is both citizen and believer. The believer in conscience freely accepts the teaching and sanctification of the church and applies this teaching in working for the good of the temporal order. Such a view is decidedly individualistic and smacks of the very continental liberalism which Murray so strenuously opposed.

However, Murray's earlier writings refute the charge of individualism in his understanding of the role of the laity. Catholic Action in the strict sense called for an organization. The whole thrust of Murray's defense of interconfessional cooperation in the temporal sphere comes from the insufficiency of individual action. Organization is required to change social institutions and structures. Even organizations of Catholic laity alone under the hierarchy are not enough to change society. To bring about change in the pluralistic temporal order all people of good will must work together in an organized and institutional manner. Interconfessional cooperation is necessary in order to be effective in the temporal order. At this time Murray was also calling for an international organization as necessary to help bring about peace and justice in the world.[42] Anyone familiar with Murray's earlier writings knows that the American Jesuit is no individualist but sees the role of the laity in terms of organized and institutional efforts.

But why did Murray not say more about the lay person touching the temporal in and through the various groups and organizations including interconfessional groups when he was discussing church and state? He leaves out a very important part of his understanding of the laity in this discussion.

Murray himself is not unaware of the problem. In one of his *Theological Studies* articles discussing Leo XIII in 1953, Murray defends Leo XIII against the charge of individualism because of his seeing the dyarchy in terms of the right order and harmony within the one person who is a member of two societies and subject to the laws of each—the *civis idem et Christianus.* According to our author, Leo's "one man, Christian and citizen" does not defend the atomistic individual of rational theory. Murray simply asserts that Leo is thinking in terms of the human being's nature as not only personal but also social, and social in two directions in as much as the Christian human being is a civil and also an ecclesiastical individual. Pius XI, according to Murray, will complete this understanding with an institutional theory of society and by his insistence that the reform of society—the harmonization of the church and society—can only be achieved by institutional and organized action.[43]

Murray, in his church–state writings before 1955, was not attempting to develop a full theology of the lay person nor a full theology of the role of the church in the temporal order. His primary concern focused on religious liberty and the church–state relationship. Murray in the course of his writing came to realize the key importance and significance of the distinction between society and the state. He was concerned then primarily with the state and not with the whole of the temporal order or of society.

The concept of the person who is both believer and citizen and the lay person as the link for the church between the spiritual and temporal orders fit perfectly with the restricted problematic Murray considered. Both John of Paris and Leo XIII emphasized the spiritual action of the church with regard to the conscience of the believer who then acted in the temporal order in accord with one's own conscience. The generally accepted Protestant understanding at the time proposed the same basic approach—the church works in the temporal order through the conscience of individuals.[44] Murray used this understanding for his interpretation of the First Amendment whereby he could hold together the primacy of the spiritual, the freedom of the church, the freedom of the individual citizen, and the autonomy of the temporal.

Perhaps Murray would have gone on to develop a full-blown understanding of the role of the laity with regard to the church–state issue and the temporal order if he had not been silenced before even finishing the publication of his long analysis of Pope Leo XIII. One can only conjecture, but I do not think he would have done so because the explanation of the church–state and religious liberty issues did not necessarily call for a full-blown theology of the laity and their role.

One might conjecture that other reasons influenced Murray in not developing the role of the laity and of the church in the temporal order at this time. Some analogy exists with what Murray himself had written earlier about interconfessional cooperation in the temporal order. The theory is clear and presents no particular difficulty, but the practical organizational aspect remains more difficult and problematic.[45] The same could be said here. The theology about the person who is both Christian and citizen is clear, but the organization of their efforts in the concrete is much more difficult. Remember that Murray not only did not develop how the believer part of the dyarchy should act in the temporal sphere, but also he did not develop how the citizen part of the dyarchy should act. The development of both aspects was definitely beyond his immediate concern, but also these organizational issues were so complex and difficult that he might not have wanted to get into them even in the slightest way.

Perhaps another consideration also influenced Murray. Our author obviously had no problem with general hierarchical statements about the moral principles governing the temporal order. He commented extensively, for example, on the statements of many popes about the temporal good of society and in his writings gave special importance to the statements on peace and war. As a theologian he worked with other religious leaders to produce the joint statement "The Declaration of World Peace" in 1943.[46] In earlier contexts Murray had discussed the organized temporal role of the laity and their relationship to the hierarchy. If he had gone into the question of how the laity carried out their role in the 1950s, he would have to discuss those organized and institutional ways in which the church and the laity functioned. Such consideration at that time could give fuel for the fire of people like Paul Blanshard who were continually worried about the power and influence of the Catholic Church in American society. However, Murray never shied away from what he thought to be the truth because of the fear of hurting the feelings of others. Murray stingingly attacked Paul Blanshard, accusing him of a new nativism.[47] Especially in his earlier writings some of his comments about Protestant thinkers are biting and sarcastic.[48]

Whatever the truth of these conjectures, the fact remains that Murray did not develop the specific role of the laity in his discussion of the narrower question of church–state relations, but in his earlier writings he emphasized more than anything else the need for organized, social, and institutional action in order to be effective in working for the temporal common good. Murray cannot be criticized for having an individualistic understanding of the role of the laity in the temporal sphere.

My major negative criticism of Murray's understanding of the role of the lay person stems from his theological understanding of the lay function and his consequent failure to recognize the role of the total church as such in the temporal realm. However, the contemporary commentator must take a page from Murray himself and recognize here the important role of historical consciousness. Murray's most complete development of the role of the laity occurs in his writings before 1945. In fact at that time Murray was in the forefront of the newer understandings of the role of the laity. Even in the 1940s Murray, as already noted, knew about important developments in the catechetical, liturgical, lay, and social action fields that would have such an impact on Vatican II. However, in the light of the broad theological developments at Vatican II, Murray's understanding of the laity and the role of the total church in the temporal sphere needs to be criticized and changed. These criticisms have often been made of the older theology of the laity in more recent theological literature and will just be summarized here.[49] Three areas in particular merit some attention—ecclesiology, the distinction or separation between the spiritual and the temporal, and the grounding and understanding of the social mission of the church.

Ecclesiology. Vatican II stressed the fact that the church is the people of God and not just the hierarchy. The hierarchical role exists in service of the total church, but the church as such remains the people of God.

Our author explicitly recognizes that at times the church includes the laity, but his early writings also understand the church in the restricted view of just the hierarchy. The hierarchical role takes place on the supernatural or spiritual level, whereas the lay role involves mediation between the spiritual and the temporal, between the supernatural and the natural. Murray emphasizes a sharp and clear distinction between the two roles with the hierarchy's being superior and the laity's inferior. The hierarchical role mediates the grace and teaching of the church to the laity who then mediate this to the world. Murray refers to the genial metaphor of the Christian laity as a vast Tarcisius (the famous Roman layman who brought the Eucharist to Christians in prison) receiving Christ from the hands of the priest and communicating him to the modern world.[50] The work of divinization and sanctification belong to the hierarchy and the ministerial priesthood, whereas the work of humanization belongs to the laity.[51]

Murray also accepts the strong distinction and separation between the hierarchy as the *ecclesia docens* (the teaching church) and the laity as the *ecclesia discens* (the learning church). Murray forcefully maintains this distinction but allows some communication between the two. Our author cites with approval Etienne Gilson's insistence that the teaching church and not the church taught chooses the principles, organizes the course, and gives the course in lay theology to those she judges worthy of it. If the church taught may not by any means pretend to teach, it can at least submit its demands and make known its needs.[52] The last two sentences in Murray's second article on a theology for the lay person underscore in a remarkable way the separated roles and subordination of the laity to the hierarchy. "By divine constitution the sheep are not the shepherds. And it is hardly fitting that we should either invite the sheep to draw up a chair to the shepherd's table, or ask the shepherds to crawl about cropping grass with the sheep."[53]

A people of God ecclesiology strongly disagrees with such an approach and emphasis. The whole people of God, hierarchy and laity, in accord with their own proper roles contribute to the sanctifying and teaching work of the church and to its social mission. The role of the laity cannot be restricted only to the temporal order and the hierarchy only to the spiritual order.

The Separation between the Spiritual and the Temporal Orders. This naturally brings to the fore the question of the distinction between the two orders—the spiritual and the temporal, which is so significant for Murray. This distinction is central to Murray's understanding of the issues he was most concerned with—the laity, intercreedal cooperation, and church–state. In his discussion of the laity, Murray points out that his formulas may perhaps sharpen the distinction. However, in these latter days according to Murray the church itself has wished to sharpen the distinction between the spiritual and the temporal in order to unite them better and more organically without danger of confusion.[54] In discussing church and state, Murray recognizes that the development of the understanding of church–state relationships has been conditioned by the sharpening of the distinction between the spiritual and the temporal orders.[55]

However, post-Vatican II theology in general cannot agree with such a sharp separation. Grace, the gospel, and Jesus Christ directly touch and affect the world and the temporal order. Murray has used this sharp distinction and almost dualism to distinguish the various roles of the hierarchy and the laity and to diminish the role of the church as such in the temporal order. The separation between the supernatural order and the natural order grounds Murray's restriction of the laity to the natural realm and of the hierarchy to the supernatural realm. But the whole church is active in both orders although the hierarchy and the laity have their proper and distinctive roles.

SOCIAL MISSION OF THE CHURCH. In the light of the sharp distinction between the spiritual order and the temporal order, Murray distinguishes two different missions of the church—divinization and humanization, with humanization being important but secondary. This humanizing mission in the temporal order is important for two reasons. First, the conditions of the temporal order have some influence, but not a strict causality, on one's supernatural life. Second, God's plan or law for human existence is to be obeyed in the temporal order.

Such an approach was very much in keeping with the best of the 1940s theology of the laity, but today, especially in the light of a closer relationship between the supernatural and the natural, Catholic thought generally refuses to speak of these two different missions. The often quoted statement from the 1971 Synod of Bishops maintains, "Action on behalf of justice and participation in the transformation of the world fully appear to us as a constitutive dimension of the preaching of the gospel, or, in other words, of the church's mission for the redemption of the human race and its liberation from every oppressive situation."[56] In the light of this one mission of the total church touching all reality the distinction between hierarchy and laity, based on two different missions no longer makes sense.

In conclusion, Murray's understanding of the role of the laity played an important part in his theological endeavors throughout his life especially in the issues of intercreedal cooperation and church–state relations. However, the American Jesuit never really developed or changed his understanding of the general role of the laity after 1945.

Although the writings on church–state center on the individual person who is both citizen and believer, this study concludes that one cannot justly accuse Murray of individualism. However, the theological developments which came to the fore at Vatican II point out the inadequacy of Murray's ecclesiology and his approach to the role and function of the laity.

A different understanding of the church will not change Murray's conclusions about intercreedal cooperation and church–state in general, but will definitely affect his portrayal of the social mission of the church.[57] Many contemporary thinkers are grappling with this issue today. However,

Murray's distinction between society and the state, which he never explicitly incorporated into his understanding of the role of the laity in the temporal order, remains most helpful in trying to structure the social mission of the church as such.

Notes

1. This aspect of Murray's project is developed by Robert W. McElroy, *The Search for an American Public Policy: The Contribution of John Courtney Murray* (New York: Paulist, 1989).
2. See, for example, Edward A. Goerner, "John Courtney Murray and the Problem of Church and State," (Ph.D. diss., University of Chicago, 1959); Thomas T. Love, *John Courtney Murray: Contemporary Church–State Theory* (Garden City, N.Y.: Doubleday, 1965); Faith E. Burgess, *The Relationship between Church and State According to John Courtney Murray, S.J.* (Düsseldorf: Rudolf Stehle, 1971); Richard J. Regan, *Conflict and Consensus: Religious Freedom and the Second Vatican Council* (New York: Macmillan, 1967).
3. This chapter will generally use Murray's term *layman* which today is both inaccurate and sexist.
4. Donald E. Pelotte, *John Courtney Murray: Theologian in Conflict* (New York: Paulist, 1976), 7–13.
5. John Courtney Murray, "Toward a Theology for the Layman: The Problem of Its Finality," *Theological Studies* 5 (1944): 43–75; "Toward a Theology for the Layman: The Pedagogical Problem," *Theological Studies* 5 (1944): 340–76.
6. "Toward a Theology for the Layman I," *Theological Studies* 5 (1944): 46–47.
7. Ibid., 64–68.
8. John Courtney Murray, "The Roman Catholic Church," *Catholic Mind* 46 (1948): 580 ff.
9. "Toward a Theology for the Layman I," *Theological Studies* 5 (1944): 71–75.
10. Ibid., 72–73.
11. For differing evaluations of Murray's historically conscious hermeneutic of Leo XIII's teaching, see my *American Catholic Social Ethics: Twentieth Century Approaches* (Notre Dame, Ind.: University of Notre Dame Press, 1982), 223–32; and Thomas Hughson, *The Believer as Citizen: John Courtney Murray in a New Context* (New York: Paulist, 1993), especially 40–56.
12. John Courtney Murray, *The Pattern for Peace and the Papal Peace Program*, Catholic Association for International Peace, Pamphlet No. 34 (New York: Paulist, 1944), 11.
13. John Courtney Murray, "Current Theology: Christian Cooperation," *Theological Studies* 3 (1942): 413–31; "Current Theology: Cooperation: Some

Further Views," *Theological Studies* 4 (1943): 100–111; "Current Theology: Inter-Creedal Cooperation: Its Theory and Its Organization," *Theological Studies* 4 (1943): 257–86; "On the Problem of Cooperation: Some Clarifications," *American Ecclesiastical Review* 112 (1945): 194–214.

14. *The Pattern for Peace*, 3–15.
15. "Cooperation: Some Further Views," *Theological Studies* 4 (1943): 102–03.
16. "Inter-Creedal Cooperation," *Theological Studies* 4 (1943): 258–61.
17. Ibid., 273–74.
18. Ibid., 260–61.
19. Ibid.
20 "Inter-Creedal Cooperation," *Theological Studies* 4 (1943): 260–61.
21. Ibid., 276-279.
22. "On the Problem of Cooperation," *American Ecclesiastical Review* 112 (1945): 212–14.
23. "Inter-Creedal Cooperation," *Theological Studies* 4 (1943): 265.
24. Ibid., 262.
25. "On the Problem of Cooperation," *American Ecclesiastical Review* 112 (1945): 195–98; "Inter-Creedal Cooperation," *Theological Studies* 4 (1943): 261–63.
26. John Courtney Murray, "Current Theology: Freedom of Religion," *Theological Studies* 6 (1945): 85–113; "Religious Liberty: An Inquiry," *Theological Studies* 7 (1946): 151–63; "Separation of Church and State," *America* 76 (Dec. 7, 1946): 261–63; "Separation of Church and State: True and False Concepts," *America* 76 (Feb. 15, 1947): 541–45.
27. John Courtney Murray, *We Hold These Truths: Catholic Reflections on the American Proposition* (New York: Sheed and Ward, 1960), 45–78. This essay first appeared as part of "The Problem of Pluralism in America," *Thought* 24: (Summer 1954): 165–208.
28. "Separation of Church and State," *America* 76 (1946): 261–263.
29. Pope Leo XIII, *Immortale Dei*, n. 19, in *The Papal Encyclicals 1878–1903*, ed. Claudia Carlen (Washington: Consortium, 1981), 111.
30. John Courtney Murray, "Contemporary Orientations of Catholic Thought on Church and State in the Light of History," *Theological Studies* 10 (1949): 188–91.
31. John Courtney Murray, "St. Robert Bellarmine on the Indirect Power," *Theological Studies* 9 (1948): 491.
32. John Courtney Murray, "Governmental Repression of Heresy," *Proceedings of the Catholic Theological Society of America* 3 (1948): 39–42.
33. "St. Robert Bellarmine," *Theological Studies* 9 (1948): 491–535; "Governmental

Repression," *Proceedings of the Catholic Theological Society of America* 3 (1948): 42-52.

34. "Contemporary Orientations," *Theological Studies* 10 (1949): 177–234; "Governmental Repression," *Proceedings of the Catholic Theological Society of America* 3 (1948): 52–70.
35. "Contemporary Orientations," *Theological Studies* 10 (1949): 188–227.
36. "Governmental Repression," *Proceedings of the Catholic Theological Society of America* 3 (1948): 52.
37. "Contemporary Orientations," *Theological Studies* 10 (1949): 215–27.
38. Ibid., 224.
39. *We Hold These Truths*, 121.
40. Ibid., 114–23.
41. J. Leon Hooper, *The Ethics of Discourse: The Social Philosophy of John Courtney Murray* (Washington: Georgetown University Press, 1986), 82–120.
42. "Inter-Creedal Cooperation," *Theological Studies* 4 (1943): 262.
43. John Courtney Murray, "Leo XIII: Separation of Church and State," *Theological Studies* 14 (1953): 211.
44. Robert Wuthnow, *The Struggle for America's Soul: Evangelicals, Liberals, and Secularism* (Grand Rapids, Mich.: William B. Eerdmans, 1989), 30–31.
45. "Inter-Creedal Cooperation," *Theological Studies* 4 (1943): 257.
46. *The Pattern for Peace*, 31–32.
47. John Courtney Murray, "Paul Blanshard and the New Nativism," *The Month* 5 (1951): 214–25.
48. In speaking about religious liberty in 1946, Murray mentioned, "As a matter of fact the Protestant mind is itself natively confused, endemically unclear in this whole matter." "Separation of Church and State," *America* 76 (1946): 261.
49. See, for example Rémi Parent, *A Church of the Baptized: Overcoming Tension Between the Clergy and the Laity* (New York: Paulist, 1989); Leonard Doohan, *The Lay-Centered Church: Theology and Spirituality* (Minneapolis, Minn.: Winston, 1984); Joseph A. Komonchak, "Clergy, Laity, and the Church's Mission in the World," *The Jurist* 41 (1981): 433–47.
50. "Toward a Theology for the Layman I," *Theological Studies* 5 (1944): 69.
51. Ibid., 73–74.
52. Ibid., 45–49.
53. "Toward a Theology for the Layman II," *Theological Studies* 5 (1944): 376.
54. "Toward a Theology for the Layman I," *Theological Studies* 5 (1944): 74.
55. "Contemporary Orientations," *Theological Studies* 10 (1949): 191.

56. 1971 Synod of Bishops, "Justice in the World," in *Catholic Social Thought: The Documentary Heritage*, ed. David J. O'Brien and Thomas A. Shannon (Maryknoll, NY: Orbis, 1992), 289.

57. In this context one can raise a hypothetical question: Would Murray have approved of church statements such as the recent pastoral letters of the United States Catholic bishops that make more specific judgments about the temporal order? Murray's theory as developed well before Vatican II supplies strong reasons supporting a negative answer to the question. Murray insisted that the public consensus was not under the competency of the church, and he also feared that the freedom of the church would be jeopardized by too concrete an involvement in the temporal order. His sharpening of the distinction between the spiritual and the temporal as well as between the role of the hierarchy and the role of the laity also supports such a negative response to the question. In my judgment this would simply be another case in which the ecclesiology developed at and since Vatican II would have to change Murray's understanding of the social mission of the church.

~ 5 ~

Catholic Moral Theology in the Past Forty Years

Catholic moral theology involves the systematic, thematic, and critical scientific reflection on the Christian moral life from the Roman Catholic perspective. The Catholic Church has always been interested in how Christians should act and from earliest times has reflected on the implications of faith and the gospel for Christian life and actions. As chapter one points out, a truly systematic and scientific theology as such arose in the twelfth and thirteenth centuries as illustrated in the work of Thomas Aquinas (d. 1274). Moral theology as a discipline separated from dogmatic theology began in the seventeenth century with the manuals of moral theology which continued in existence until Vatican II.[1]

Despite the significant changes and developments in recent Catholic moral theology, distinctive characteristics of the Catholic tradition continue to shape Catholic moral theology today—mediation, catholicity with a small *c*, opposition to individualism, and the relationship to the life of the Catholic Church. The emphasis on mediation sees the divine as mediated in and through the human, with the acceptance of a fundamental goodness of the human and of human reason as illustrated in the traditional acceptance of natural law understood as human reason directing us to our end in accord with our human nature. To discover what God is asking, one does not go immediately and directly to God but to the reason and creation made by God. Catholicity with a small *c* involves a concern for all aspects of human life in this world and for a catholic and universal perspective that deals with the good of humankind as a whole. The Catholic approach rejects any sectarianism which sees the church as cut off from the rest of society. Mediation and catholicity ground the Catholic emphasis on a "both–and" approach rather than an "either–or." The Catholic tradition insists on faith and reason, grace and works, scripture and tradition, Jesus and the church. The distinctive Catholic approach opposes individualism by insisting that the person is by nature social and political, called to live in political society and striving for the common good and not merely one's own individualistic good. The relationship to the church sees the moral life in the context of the church with special emphasis on the life of the sacraments such as penance and in relation to the hierarchical teaching office with its authoritative teaching role in matters including morality.

Chapters one and three have discussed and analyzed the manuals of moral theology which were the textbooks of the discipline before Vatican II. An important aspect of Catholic moral theology in the twentieth century concerned the increased role of the papacy in determining and authoritatively deciding the morality of particular acts, especially in the area of sexual and medical morality. Pope Pius XII spoke out on many issues in medical ethics such as abortion, anesthesia, conflict situations, death and dying, sterilization, or selling blood. Whenever the pope spoke out, the issue was closed.[2]

The popes in the late nineteenth and twentieth centuries insisted that Catholic philosophy and theology follow the teaching and method of Thomas Aquinas. Neoscholasticism became the Catholic approach. Although the manuals of moral theology claimed to be following the approach of Aquinas, their narrow focus and legal model were not Thomistic. Catholic philosophers (e.g., Jacques Maritain) developed and applied the ethical approach of Thomas Aquinas. In the course of the twentieth century, some Thomists and some followers of the Tübingen school (emphasizing a life-centered and biblically oriented approach) criticized the manuals of moral theology, but these textbooks remained basically unchanged and were used in Catholic seminaries until Vatican II.[3] This council and the 1968 encyclical *Humanae vitae* significantly affected the development of Catholic moral theology in the contemporary era.

Vatican II and Its Aftermath

Vatican II did not devote a specific document to moral theology (although the Pastoral Constitution on the Church in the Modern World dealt with aspects of social ethics), but the basic approach of the council deeply affected moral theology in a number of important areas—focus, model, method, integration of scripture and theology, emphasis on the person, ecumenism, and dialogue with the world and others.

Vatican II insisted on the universal call of all Christians to holiness.[4] Christians must take a greater responsibility for their world and work in all areas to bring about a better human condition. Thus the scope of moral theology could no longer be limited to the training of judges in the sacrament of penance with the emphasis on the minimal and what is sinful. Moral theology became life-centered and not sin-centered.

Bernard Lonergan, a very significant Catholic systematic theologian and philosopher, maintained the primary change effected by Vatican II was a shift from classicism to historical consciousness. Classicism tends to see reality in terms of the eternal, immutable, and unchanging, and often uses a deductive approach as illustrated in Sabetti's manual. Thus a pre-Vatican II theology began with the definition of terms (e.g., what is a human being, what is political society) which was true for all times and all places and deduced moral considerations from these premises. Vatican II proposed a historically conscious approach which gives more emphasis to the particular, the contingent, and the changing, while still insisting on continuities with the past and employing a more inductive approach.[5] The Pastoral Constitution on the Church in the Modern World began its discussion of important social areas not with an abstract definition true in all circumstances but with the signs of the times (nn. 47; 54–56; 63; 73; 77). Without abandoning the Catholic emphasis on universality and catholicity, this method greatly transformed Catholic theology. Such a move made it easier for later developments to begin with the experience of the poor and the marginalized or with the experience of women. The emphasis on a more inductive approach means that the discipline will not expect as firm and great a certitude with regard to its moral decisions and conclusions as with a deductive approach for historical developments might also bring about new situations and changes.

Vatican II insisted on the need to overcome the split between faith and daily life.[6] The council also stressed the need to make scripture the soul of theology and to give the scripture a very significant place in the liturgy and in the spiritual lives of Catholics.[7] The earlier natural law approach to moral theology so emphasized the roles of reason and nature that scripture was reduced at best to a proof text which was occasionally used to prove a conclusion that had been based on natural law reasoning. Since that time Catholic theologians in dialogue with others have been discussing the proper role and function of the scriptures in moral theology, with many recognizing a significant role of the scripture in forming the personal and communal identity of Christian people and in describing the attitudes and virtues of the Christian. On specific issues the direct involvement of the scriptures is much less significant since these issues depend heavily on reason and contemporary realities. The need to make moral theology more theological responded to the Council's call for faith to have a more immediate effect on daily life in the world. However, in keeping with the traditional Catholic emphasis on mediation, most Catholic moral theologians recognize that scriptural and theological concepts must be mediated in and through the human.[8]

The recognition of the need to incorporate scripture and theology into moral theology raised a question that has been widely discussed in the subsequent years: What is distinctive or unique about Catholic ethics and morality? I maintain there are many distinctive aspects about Catholic morality, but Catholics or Christians in their daily lives in this world are not called to act in ways which no other human beings are called to act in working for a better society. There is no unique Christian moral content for life in the social, political, and economic orders of human existence in this world.

Vatican II gave greater emphasis to the person and the subject as distinguished from the natural and the objective. However, in keeping with the traditional Catholic "both–and" approach the emphasis on the subject does not do away with a proper role for the objective. The Declaration on Religious Liberty of Vatican II (n. 1) based its acceptance of religious freedom, which represented a significant change from past teaching, on the dignity of the human person which has been expressing itself more and more deeply on the consciousness of contemporary human beings (note also the shift to historical consciousness). The older denial of religious freedom rested on the objective nature of truth, but the shift to the person and the subject resulted in a different approach to religious freedom.

The emphasis on the person together with a call to holiness had a significant effect on moral theology's emphasis on the moral growth and development of the person. Bernard Häring, the primary international figure in the renewal of moral theology before and after Vatican II, insisted on the importance of conversion (note the biblical influence). Conversion calls for a fundamental change of heart and the need to deepen and grow through continual conversion.[9] Karl Rahner, probably the most significant Catholic theologian in the twentieth century, developed an anthropology that distinguished the core freedom of the person from categorical freedom. His theory of *fundamental option* insisted on the basic orientation of the person in the depths of one's core freedom which is expressed and developed through concrete categorical actions. The goodness of the human being as distinguished from the rightness of the act comes from this basic orientation.[10]

Such emphasis on the subject and the person changed the understanding of the important Catholic distinction between mortal sin and venial sin and the understanding of the sacrament of penance. Mortal sin breaks one's relationship with God and makes one deserving of eternal damnation in hell whereas venial sin offends God but does not break the basic relationship. The pre-Vatican II approach saw sin primarily as an act against the law of God. Thus many different moral acts were often described as grave sins, although in reality they should have been called grave matter. In the perspective of the fundamental option sin involves the changed fundamental option or orientation and cannot be reduced just to the external act itself.[11] Some, including Pope John Paul II in his encyclical *Veritatis splendor*, have criticized the fundamental option for downplaying the importance and significance of the external act.[12] Chapter eleven will show that the proper response to these objections appeals to an important distinction. The particular or categorical act can be described as morally right or wrong, but whether or not mortal sin is present depends on the fundamental orientation or the conversion of the person.

The Vatican II shift to a life-centered, rather than a confessional- and sin-oriented, moral theology in conjunction with the emphasis on the person and subject resulted in a renewed recognition of the role of the virtues in moral theology. The Catholic tradition as illustrated in Thomas Aquinas gave great importance to the virtues, but the manuals of moral theology with their emphasis on acts and sins neglected the virtues. While in theory Catholic moral theologians today recognize the primary importance of the virtues in the moral life, the virtues have not received the attention they deserve because of the more disputed areas in contemporary moral theology.

Vatican II's Decree on Ecumenism encouraged ecumenical dialogue with Christians and other religions. Before the council the Catholic Church saw itself as the one true church of Christ primarily in opposition to and distinguished from Protestantism. The initial ecumenical enthusiasm of the council has waned and institutional ecumenism has not really developed, but ecumenism deeply influences Catholic moral theology today. Catholic theologians read and dialogue with Protestant theologians. One cannot properly do Catholic theology today without such a dialogue. Ecumenical societies of moral theology exist in which Protestants and Catholics together discuss the aspects of their discipline.

Vatican II especially emphasized dialogue with the modern world and purposely avoided any condemnations.[13] Such an approach contrasted strongly with the pre-Vatican II era with its defensive position with regard to modern culture frequently resulting in a ghetto posture. Subsequently many have criticized Vatican II for being too optimistic about the modern world, but the Catholic Church cannot become a sect cut off from the world. The emphasis on dialogue has greatly affected Catholic theology in general and moral theology in particular. In the late nineteenth and early twentieth century, the popes insisted on Thomism as the Catholic theology and philosophy in an attempt to prevent dialogue with other contemporary methods and approaches. Since Vatican II moral theology has been open to learn from and utilize many different philosophical approaches. No longer can one speak of a monolithic method in Catholic moral theology, but certain traditional Catholic moral emphases continue to be present.

Humanae Vitae and Its Aftermath

Humanae vitae, the 1968 encyclical letter of Pope Paul VI reiterating the Catholic teaching condemning artificial contraception in marriage, constitutes a second very significant event that shaped the development of Catholic moral theology in the last three decades.

Before 1963 there had been no article in a theological journal calling for a change in the Catholic teaching on artificial contraception. In the church atmosphere of the early twentieth century this teaching was not questioned. The changed atmosphere brought about by Vatican II occasioned the questioning of this teaching both by Catholic couples and by theologians. In June 1964, Pope Paul VI publicly called attention to a special commission appointed earlier by John XXIII to study the question of artificial contraception and took the issue out of the competency of the council in the light of this commission. However, during the council there were some discussions which touched on contraception. The long fifth session of the commission showed that the vast majority favored a change in the teaching and some documents were leaked to the press in 1967.[14] However, on July 29, 1968, Paul VI publicly issued his encyclical. "(T)he church, calling men back to the observance of the norms of the natural law as interpreted by their constant doctrine, teaches that each and every marriage act must remain open to the transmission of life. . . . Indeed, by its intimate structure, the conjugal act, while most closely uniting husband and wife, capacitates them for the generation of new lives, according to laws inscribed in the very being of man and woman."[15]

The papal encyclical has continued to echo in the life of the Roman Catholic Church and basically set the future agenda for moral theology in four important areas—sexual ethics, natural law, the existence and grounding of norms, and dissent from authoritative hierarchical teaching.

The papal and hierarchical teaching have continued to employ in sexual ethics the basic criterion found in *Humanae vitae* that the nature and purpose of the sexual faculty call for sexual acts that are both open to procreation and expressive of love union. On this basis the hierarchical magisterium has continued to condemn masturbation, homosexuality, and pre- and extramarital sexuality, as well as artificial contraception.[16] The majority of Catholic moral theologians reject the teaching on artificial contraception. Roman Catholicism has witnessed the same debate over homosexual genital acts which has transpired in other Christian churches and in the broader society. The papal teaching and some theologians continue to condemn homosexual genital acts even within the context of a loving union striving for permanency. Other theologians justify these acts on the basis of the loving commitment of the two parties. A third position justifies such acts in this context but sees them as falling short of the ideal. Chapter seven will discuss the morality of homosexual relationships in greater detail. Sexuality has continued to be an area of strong disagreements within Roman Catholicism.[17]

Humanae vitae has also touched off a continuing discussion about natural law.[18] From a theological perspective, natural law refers to the fact that the Catholic approach has traditionally recognized human reason and not just revelation as a source of ethical wisdom for the discipline. The philosophical aspect of the question refers to how one understands the meaning of natural and the meaning of law. The papal teaching follows the older Thomistic understanding that human reason discovers the three levels of basic human inclinations—those shared with all living things (the inclination to continue in existence); those shared with all animals (procreation and the education of offspring); and those proper to humans as rational beings (to know God and to live together in human society). These inclinations are morally normative.[19]

Catholic revisionist moral theologians object to this understanding from two different perspectives.[20] First, they accuse *Humanae vitae* and this approach to natural law of physicalism, which makes the physical or biological morally normative and forbids human reason to interfere in these physical and biological processes. The human can and should interfere in the physical process if this is for truly human good. The physical is just one aspect of the human and at times can and must be sacrificed for the good of the total human. In other areas, e.g., killing, the moral aspect of the act (murder) is distinguished from the physical aspect of the act (killing). Not all killing is murder. The anthropology of the encyclical makes the physical or the animal aspect morally normative in conformity with an anthropology that sees the human being as a rational animal.

Second, the revisionist understanding rejects the faculty approach to natural law which makes the nature and purpose of the faculty the moral criterion. Rather the faculty must be seen in relationship to the person and to the marital relationship. Thus for the good of the marriage or the good of the person, one can and should interfere with the purpose of the faculty. Notice here the effect of giving greater emphasis to the person as the ultimate moral criterion.

More radical criticisms of the manualistic natural law approach have also arisen coming especially from the recognition of historicity and historical consciousness. The emphasis on history and God working through history contrast with the view that God works through nature. An historically conscious approach will also be more inductive than the deductive approach of the manuals of moral theology. The older natural law approach did not give enough importance to diversity and pluralism. Emphasis on praxis and starting with the experience of the oppressed and marginalized have also challenged the more universal and neutral starting place of natural law. Even those in the Catholic tradition who challenge natural law still recognize such basic realities in the Catholic tradition as the role of reason, the need for mediation, and the possibility of some type of universal ethic permitting a dialogue among all people.

Whereas most revisionist approaches to natural law or challenges to it support positions often at odds with hierarchical teaching in the sexual area, Germain Grisez and John Finnis have been proposing a modified natural law theory which strongly supports the papal teaching on artificial contraception. This newer approach to natural law denies that the natural teleology of human functions demands absolute moral respect. They likewise appear to reject the basic teleology of the Thomistic approach in general with their insistence on the role of practical reason with its self-evident knowledge of certain basic human goods which one can never go against but which can be ordered in different ways. Procreation is one of these basic human goods which one can never directly go against.[21] Thus the discussion about natural law continues with different approaches—some strongly defending the view found in Aquinas and in the hierarchical teaching, others modifying this understanding of natural law, and others rejecting Thomism and proposing a different methodology.

Humanae vitae also set the stage for the ongoing debate in Catholic moral theology about the existence and grounding of moral norms which is sometimes described as the debate about intrinsically evil acts.[22] Dissenters from *Humanae vitae* point out the fallacy of physicalism in the encyclical, which identifies the human moral act with the physical or biological structure of the act. Revisionist Catholic theologians thus distinguish between moral evil and premoral evil (also called ontic or physical). By its very nature something that is described only in terms of the physical structure or aspect of the act cannot ipso facto be morally normative. In this light, revisionist theologians disagree with the hierarchical teaching on contraception, sterilization, artificial insemination, and the principle of the double effect, which has been employed in the Catholic tradition to solve problems in which one act has effects that are both good and bad. The crucial condition of the principle of double effect is that the good effect must follow equally immediately as the bad effect, or in other words that the bad effect cannot be produced by means of the good effect. Thus one could not abort a fetus (presumed to be a living human being) in order to save the life of the mother. One could, however, remove a cancerous uterus which was pregnant because the physical act does not immediately target the fetus as a means to save the mother but targets the diseased uterus itself. In this approach the physical causality or physical structure of the act is morally normative.

In the light of the problem of physicalism many revisionist Catholic moral theologians have developed a theory often called proportionalism. One may do a physical or premoral evil if there is a proportionate reason. However, these proportionists also want to avoid the opposite danger of a total consequentialism or utilitarianism. Thus in weighing the good against the bad they propose various ways of avoiding such a total consequentialism. The Catholic proponents of proportionalism generally hold on to the condemnation of bombing cities or civilian targets in order to shorten the war. Disagreement about the exact meaning of a proportionate reason necessary to do a premoral evil remains, but all attempts strive for a middle way between the older Catholic approach and total consequentialism or utilitarianism.

Pope John Paul II, in his encyclical *Veritatis splendor* (nn. 71–83) strongly condemns proportionalism. Some Catholic theologians agree with the condemnation. Grisez and others also oppose proportionalism on the basis of their theory of certain basic human goods which one can never directly go against and thereby agree with the particular positions taken by the hierarchical magisterium.[23]

A fourth issue precipitated by *Humanae vitae* concerns the legitimacy of dissent from papal teaching and the proper relationship between the hierarchical teaching authority in the church and theologians. Before Vatican II the Roman Catholic church had become more centralized and authoritarian than ever before in its history. Recall the many pronouncements of Pope Pius XII (1939–58) on moral issues which ended any further theological discussion. Vatican II in theory called for a less authoritarian understanding of the church and its teaching office and saw the hierarchical magisterium in service of the total people of God. In the light of these developments some Catholic theologians openly dissented from the teaching of *Humanae vitae* condemning artificial contraception.[24]

The dissenters then and now justify their action by appealing to the nature of authoritative noninfallible teaching.[25] This term only came into existence in the latter part of the nineteenth century after the definition of papal infallibility. In the light of the circumstances of twentieth-century Catholicism with its defensiveness and authoritarianism (recall the condemnations of Americanism and modernism at the turn of the century) dissent had never been discussed in any depth. Authoritative noninfallible teaching does not belong to the core of faith. Most of the moral teachings or issues involved (contraception, principle of double effect) are based on reason and not on faith and the gospel. Also the moral issues involve a great deal of complexity and specificity in the light of which one cannot claim a certitude that excludes the possibility of error. These teachings on specific moral issues might be wrong. The assistance of the Holy Spirit given to the hierarchical magisterium does not mean that the hierarchical teaching authority does not have to do all the homework in striving to arrive at moral truth. History also shows that many such specific moral teachings (e.g., slavery, the rights of the accused, usury, religious freedom, the justification for the marital act) have all changed over the years. Even early proponents of the nineteenth-century terminology of authoritative noninfallible teaching admitted the possibility of error in such authoritative noninfallible teaching.

However, the papal teaching office has never publicly and explicitly acknowledged the legitimacy of such dissent. The hierarchical magisterium has not changed its teaching on any of the controverted issues and has taken action against some dissenting theologians. John Paul II wrote his encyclical *Veritatis splendor* (n. 5) to address the crisis in the church constituted not by occasional limited dissent but by an overall and systematic calling into question of traditional moral teachings on the basis of certain ethical and anthropological presuppositions. The discussion within the Roman Catholic Church continues with regard to dissent from such authoritative noninfallible teaching and about the proper roles of theologians and the hierarchical magisterium.

A very few Catholic theologians (e.g., Grisez) have maintained that the teaching on contraception is infallible on the basis of the ordinary infallible magisterium of pope and bishops always and everywhere teaching something as a matter of divine faith to be held definitively by the faithful.[26] The vast majority of Catholic theologians disagree because such issues were not taught as a matter of faith to be held definitively by all the faithful. However, Pope John Paul II in his encyclical *Evangelium vitae* of 1995 condemns murder, direct abortion, and euthanasia by using a formula that some could interpret as claiming these teachings are infallible by reason of the ordinary magisterium of pope and bishops.[27]

All recognize that a restorationist approach in recent actions of the hierarchical magisterium wants to tighten things up in the Roman Catholic Church especially with regard to moral theology. In my judgment, this attempt cannot and will not be successful in the long run, but the tensions are very prevalent at the present and for the immediate future. Many of the subsequent chapters will deal with specific instances of these tensions. I appeal to the traditional Thomistic and Catholic understanding of an intrinsic morality—something is commanded because it is good and not the other way around. The hierarchical magisterium must conform itself to what is good and true and by itself it can never make something good which is not good.

Within Roman Catholicism those, like myself, who dissent from some of the past papal sexual and medical moral teachings generally are quite supportive of the hierarchical social teachings. At the same time some who disagree with the social teachings as being too liberal are in agreement with the papal sexual and medical teachings. In my judgment this points to a difference in approach between the two areas of papal teaching.

Almost by definition the social teachings as found in the papal social encyclicals dealing with political, economic, and cultural aspects of existence in national and global society are not troubled by the problem of physicalism. Such a problem comes to the fore only in personal moral issues of sexual and medical ethics.

In addition, much change and development has occurred in papal social teaching even in the twentieth century. Pope Leo XIII at the end of the nineteenth century downplayed freedom, equality, and participation, whereas Paul VI made these important aspects of his social teaching. Nineteenth-century papal social teaching strongly condemned individual freedom, whereas twentieth-century evaluations of such freedom were much more positive. In the light of the growth of totalitarianism in the twentieth century, papal social teaching defended the dignity, freedom, and rights of the individual. John XXIII in 1963 for the first time in papal social documents developed a Catholic understanding and defense of human rights.[28]

Papal social teaching shows a definite development toward the emphasis on the person, historicity, and historical consciousness. The acceptance of religious liberty by Vatican II well illustrates these developments. The underlying and perhaps more significant issue in the religious liberty debate of Vatican II centered on change or development in church teaching. The nineteenth-century papal teaching strongly condemned religious freedom. How could the church now accept this teaching? The historical circumstances changed so that what was true in the nineteenth century is no longer true in 1965.[29] As a result the papal social teaching has an historical hermeneutic to justify change and development which is not present in the sexual and medical teaching. In order to support its teaching in the sexual and medical areas, the papacy continues to cite the older teachings of Pius XII, which emphasized the more classicist approach not open to development and change. Thus significant methodological differences exist between the papal approach to sexual and medical morality and to social morality. Chapter twelve will explore some of these differences in the more recent teachings of John Paul II.

However, Vatican II's acceptance of an historical hermeneutic to explain the changed teaching on religious liberty is quite problematic. Such an approach is inadequate. One has to recognize at least somewhere along the line that the older teaching was in error. The council fathers were unable and unwilling to admit that previous church teaching had been wrong. If the council had clearly faced the possibility and reality of error in authoritative noninfallible teaching, there might never have been a *Humanae vitae*. Paul VI in 1968 recognized that the primary reason for reiterating the condemnation of artificial contraception was the past teaching proposed with constant firmness by the hierarchical magisterium.[30] Sooner or later, and hopefully the former, the hierarchical magisterium must recognize error in its teachings.

Two Other Publics: Society and the Academy

This chapter has considered Catholic moral theology in the twentieth century in terms of its relationship to the Catholic Church. In addition, moral theology also relates to two other publics—society as a whole and the academy. These relationships have also influenced the development of Catholic moral theology.

In many ways society and developments within society propose the agenda for moral theology. The discussions about sexuality mentioned above came from societal developments emphasizing planned parenthood and the so-called sexual revolution. The global population problem has increased the pressure on the hierarchical teaching on contraception. In the whole area of sexuality, however, the disciplinary actions taken by the Roman authorities against Catholic theologians writing on these topics has obviously influenced many other Catholic theologians not to write in these areas.

The last twenty-five years have witnessed the growth of a new discipline—bioethics. Chapter two showed that before 1965 Catholic moral theologians were about the only ones who were interested in medical ethics going back to such concerns as the professional obligations and responsibilities of doctors and the important distinction between impotence and sterility in marriage legislation. Since medicine and morality before 1965 had the same basic criterion; that is, what is for the good of the individual patient, there was no need for a special discipline. However, new technological developments raised significant new questions and also for the first time posed the possibility of harming the individual person to help others as in questions of experimentation or transplantation. The Catholic tradition has made a significant contribution to the broader bioethical discussions with its teaching in a number of areas such as the obligation to use only ordinary means to conserve life. Abortion has been a controversial area in society in general and also within the Catholic Church with some Catholic theologians dissenting from the hierarchical position. Without doubt, the discussion over euthanasia will become more heated in society in the immediate future.

In terms of social issues in the world, the plight of the two-thirds world has come to the fore. Catholic theologians in South America (e.g., Gustavo Gutiérrez, Juan Luis Segundo, Leonardo Boff), writing from a praxis perspective and not an academic setting, have developed a theology of liberation with emphasis on a preferential option for the poor. Some have accepted a Marxist sociological analysis to develop such a theology. The Vatican has twice addressed the issue of liberation theology, pointing out some problems, but this remains the most widespread theological development since Vatican II.

The emphasis on a *preferential* option for the poor coheres with the traditional Catholic emphasis on inclusivity and universality so that others are not excluded. Note that liberation theology involves a different methodological approach to theological ethics and not just another area of theological study.[31] Significant relationships exist between liberation theology, which has spread from Latin America across the globe, and black liberation theology, which emerged from the black Protestant experience in the United States.

In economic ethics the Catholic tradition has historically disagreed with both socialism and capitalism. The papal social encyclicals in this century have moved from espousing a third way to a critical approach to existing economic structures. The popes condemned the atheism, materialism, and sacrifice of the person to the totality in Marxism. Although official Catholicism was a strong opponent of communism, dialogue superseded condemnation from the time of John XXIII and Vatican II. Perhaps Catholics could find a Marxist sociological analysis to be helpful.[32]

Catholicism has moved from a rather blanket condemnation of liberalism and the Enlightenment in the nineteenth century to an appreciation of some of its emphases on freedom, equality, and human rights. However, the papal approach in particular and the Catholic tradition in general will always oppose a one-sided individualism based on its more communitarian and social understanding of the human person. The traditional Catholic emphasis on the common good calls for limits on capitalism and the need for all to work together for the good of humankind and the environment. Although Catholicism has learned important aspects from the Enlightenment, it can never accept individualism.[33]

In the United States the Roman Catholic bishops in 1986 published a pastoral letter on the economy insisting on economic rights as well as political rights and seeing the fulfillment of the basic needs of the poor as of the highest priority.[34] However, some American Catholics (e.g., Michael Novak, George Weigel, and lately Richard John Neuhaus) have taken a different tack by insisting that the Catholic tradition has not given enough importance to the productivity of wealth and have adopted a much more positive view of the American economy.[35] In the political sphere, as mentioned earlier, as the twentieth century progressed the official Catholic teaching became more open to basic political rights and to recognize democracy as the best form of government.

In many parts of the globe, including the United States, questions have arisen about the best way for the church and the Christian to address the issues facing our pluralistic societies. Before Vatican II the Catholic approach generally used a natural law method based on human reason and human nature, which Christians share with all humankind, thus facilitating dialogue with everybody. The Vatican II insistence on relating faith more directly to daily life has resulted in more theological and Christian symbols and concepts. However, in using such distinctively Christian approaches in a pluralistic society, one must try to make them understandable to others who do not necessarily share these beliefs.

A particularly divisive topic in many countries concerns the relationship between law or public policy and morality.[36] With the acceptance of religious liberty, the Catholic Church recognized that the freedom of individuals in society be recognized as far as possible and curtailed only when necessary.[37] The debate about abortion laws has erupted in many countries. Many Catholic theologians, together with the pope, insist that civil law must protect the rights of the unborn, the most vulnerable of people in society. However, I have reasoned that because of the existing doubts and debates in society at large about the personhood of the fetus, law should give the benefit of the doubt to the freedom of the mother.[38] Chapter eight will discuss public policy and gay rights.

Ecological and environmental concerns have come to the fore in the last few decades. These significant issues and reflection upon them have called on moral theology to change and adjust its own method and self-understanding. Moral theology after Vatican II moved to an emphasis on the subject and historicity, but environmental ethics reminds us of the need not to forget the objective and the natural. Post-Vatican II moral theology has become too anthropocentric and needs to develop more its older emphasis on creation and nature to deal more adequately with environmental issues.[39]

Feminism constitutes an important social issue that has received much attention in the academy. Feminist thought in general and feminist ethics have challenged the perspective of a disinterested neutral observer approach and insisted on beginning with the experience of women in a patriarchal society. Likewise, the differences between feminist, womanist, and mujerista approaches have surfaced. Catholic women have strongly and rightly attacked the patriarchy in the church which is seen today especially in its denying women access to priesthood and leadership. Despite their strong protests about existing structures in church and society and their insistence on starting with the experience of the oppression of women, Catholic feminists generally insist on the need for an inclusive morality that involves all. Here their catholicity with a small *c* comes through despite the starting point of their ethical considerations.[40]

Especially in the United States the academy has become the primary home of moral theology as distinguished from the seminary in the pre-Vatican II period. Catholic colleges and universities include moral theology as an academic discipline to be treated the same as other disciplines. This shift in location grounds the emphasis—especially in the United States—that academic freedom protects the rights and responsibilities of Catholic theologians in the academy. Chapter nine will show that Vatican officials have been wary about accepting the academic freedom of Catholic theologians in United States colleges and universities precisely because of losing control over these academics.[41]

The academic standards of the academy have improved the discipline of moral theology. More articles and books are being written now than fifty years ago. Especially in the United States, with its large number of Catholic colleges and universities, there are many more moral theologians today than in the past. The shift of the locus of moral theology to the academy as contrasted with the seminary has had beneficial results for the discipline.

The complexity of the matter to be studied and the academic nature of the enterprise call for specialists in specific particular areas. No longer will one person be able to claim competency in the many different areas of moral theology. Thus individuals specialize in moral theology and bioethics, social, political and economic ethics, business ethics, legal ethics, the ethics of the professions, or environmental ethics. However, despite or perhaps somewhat because of inclusion in the academy, the interdisciplinary aspect of moral theology has not developed as much as it should have.

Without doubt, philosophical ethics remains the primary dialogue partner for moral theology because of sharing the same subject matter and many of the same methodological concerns. This dialogue takes place in many different ways. The debate over the existence and grounding of exceptionless norms has brought moral theology into dialogue with contemporary deontological and teleological theories. The dialogue between Catholicism and liberalism has already been mentioned. Philosophers often distinguish different approaches to ethics; e.g., principled, virtue, or casuist approaches. Catholic moral theology in its historical development and by virtue of its distinctive inclusive character has tended to see these approaches as complementary. All three aspects belong to moral theology in my judgment, although one approach might receive greater emphasis from a particular author.

At the present time postmodernism has become prominent in philosophical circles. The Catholic tradition shares some of its problems with modernism, but the traditional Catholic commitment to human reason and its insistence on a catholic, small *c*, morality embracing all humankind resists some of the more decentering aspects of postmodernism. In this connection some postmodernist ethicists reject foundationalism according to which all ethics is grounded in one foundational reality. The Catholic natural law theory with its basis in human anthropology well illustrates a foundational approach. Catholic theologians are just beginning to grapple with these issues with some theologians accepting the criticism of foundationalism and employing a more pragmatic approach.[42] Here again the Catholic tradition stands for the need to have some type of possible dialogue and criticism among all human beings on our planet.

It is impossible to predict the future development of moral theology, but it will occur in moral theology's relationships with its three publics—the church, the academy, and society. By its very nature the relationship with the church has been and will continue to be the most significant. In addition, the distinctive aspects of the Catholic moral theology tradition—mediation, catholicity with a small *c*, and opposition to individualism—will continue to direct the discipline.

Notes

1. No definitive history of moral theology exists. For the best available study, see Louis Vereecke, *Storia della teologia morale moderna*, 4 vols. (Rome: Accademia Alfonisiana, 1980). These volumes are mimeographed notes provided to students but are available to the general public. For a very helpful study in English, which does not claim to be an exhaustive history, see John Mahoney, *The Making of Moral Theology: A Study of the Roman Catholic Tradition* (Oxford: Clarendon, 1987).
2. Mahoney, 22–36, 156–64.
3. John C. Ford and Gerald Kelly, *Contemporary Moral Theology I: Questions in Fundamental Moral Theology* (Westminster, Md.: Newman, 1958), 42–103.
4. Dogmatic Constitution on the Church, nn. 39–42, in *Vatican Council II: The Conciliar and Post-Conciliar Documents*, ed. Austin Flannery, rev. ed. (Collegeville, Minn.: Liturgical Press, 1992), 396–402. Subsequent references in the text will just give the paragraph numbers of the documents cited.
5. Bernard Lonergan, "A Transition from a Classicist Worldview to Historical Mindedness," in *Law for Liberty: The Role of Law in the Church Today*, ed. James E. Biechler (Baltimore: Helicon, 1967), 126–33.
6. Pastoral Constitution on the Church in the Modern World, n. 43, in *Vatican Council II*, 943.

7. Dogmatic Constitution of Divine Revelation, nn. 21–26, in *Vatican Council II*, 762–65.
8. William C. Spohn, *What are They Saying About Scripture and Ethics?*, rev. ed. (New York: Paulist, 1995).
9. Bernard Häring, "La Conversion," in *Pastorale du péché*, ed. Ph. Delhaye. (Tournai: Desclée, 1961), 65–45; see also Walter Conn, *Christian Conversion: A Developmental Interpretation of Autonomy and Surrender* (New York: Paulist, 1986).
10. Josef Fuchs, a very prominent figure in contemporary moral theology who taught in Rome, has developed and employed the Rahnerian approach in his moral theology. For an early discussion of fundamental option, see Josef Fuchs, *Human Values and Christian Morality* (Dublin: Gill and Macmillan, 1970); for more recent illustrations of his use of fundamental option, see Josef Fuchs, *Christian Morality: The Word Becomes Flesh* (Washington: Georgetown University Press, 1987).
11. Timothy E. O'Connell, *Principles for a Catholic Morality*, rev. ed. (San Francisco: Harper and Row, 1990), 89–102.
12. John Paul II, *Veritatis splendor*, nn. 65–70, in *Origins* 23 (1993): 316–18.
13. John W. O'Malley, *Tradition and Transition: Historical Perspectives on Vatican II* (Wilmington, Del.: Michael Glazier, 1989).
14. For the historical development, see Robert Blair Kaiser, *The Problem of Sex and Religion: A Case History in the Development of Doctrine* (Kansas City: Sheed and Ward, 1985).
15. Pope Paul VI, *Humanae vitae* (Washington: United States Catholic Conference, 1968), nn. 11–12, pp. 7–8.
16. Congregation for the Doctrine of the Faith, "Declaration on Certain Questions Concerning Sexual Ethics," *Catholic Mind* 74, no. 1302 (April 1976): 52–65; Pope John Paul II, *Familiaris consortio: The Role of the Christian Family in the Modern World* (Boston: St. Paul Editions, 1981).
17. Anthony Kosnik et al, *Human Sexuality: New Directions in American Catholic Thought* (New York: Paulist, 1977), 99–239. This book was the report of a committee established by the Catholic Theological Society of America. The board of directors of the Society "received" the report. For the negative Vatican response to the book, see "Congregation for the Doctrine of the Faith on Anthony Kosnik et al, *Human Sexuality*, July 13, 1979," in *Readings in Moral Theology No. 8: Dialogue About Catholic Sexual Teaching*, ed. Charles E. Curran and Richard A. McCormick (New York: Paulist, 1993), 485–90.
18. Charles E. Curran and Richard A. McCormick, eds., *Readings in Moral Theology No 7: Natural Law and Theology* (New York: Paulist, 1991). This series, now consisting of nine volumes, has dealt with the primary moral considerations in contemporary Catholic thought.

19. Thomas Aquinas, *Summa theologiae* (Rome: Marietti, 1952), I II, q. 94. The manuals of moral theology understood Thomas' inclinations as absolute norms and not merely as direction-giving principles.

20. For my approach, see Curran, *Directions in Fundamental Moral Theology* (Notre Dame, Ind.: University of Notre Dame Press, 1985), 119-72.

21. Germain Grisez, *The Way of the Lord Jesus I: Christian Moral Principles* (Chicago: Franciscan Herald Press, 1983), 3–274; John Finnis, *Natural Law and Natural Rights* (Oxford: Clarendon, 1980). For an accurate condensation of the Grisez position, see Germain Grisez and Russell Shaw, *Fulfillment in Christ: A Summary of Christian Moral Principles* (Notre Dame, Ind.: University of Notre Dame Press, 1991).

22. For an overview of the debate that is favorable to the revisionist position, see Bernard Hoose, *Proportionalism: The American Debate and Its European Roots* (Washington: Georgetown University Press, 1987). For studies of Richard A. McCormick who has been the foremost American contributor to this discussion, see Paulinus Ikechukwu Odozor, *Richard A. McCormick and the Renewal of Moral Theology* (Notre Dame, Ind.: University of Notre Dame Press, 1995); *Moral Theology: Challenges for the Future: Essays in Honor of Richard A. McCormick, S.J.*, ed. Charles E. Curran (New York: Paulist, 1990).

23. Grisez and Shaw, 60-74.

24. For the reaction to *Humanae vitae*, see Joseph A. Selling, "The Reaction to *Humanae Vitae*: A Study in Special and Fundamental Theology," (S. T. D. diss., Catholic University of Louvain, 1977).

25. For the recent discussion on dissent in Roman Catholicism, see *Readings in Moral Theology No. 6: Dissent in the Church*, ed. Charles E. Curran and Richard A. McCormick (New York: Paulist, 1988).

26. Germain Grisez, "The Ordinary Magisterium's Infallibility," *Theological Studies* 55 (1994): 720–32.

27. Pope John Paul II, *Evangelium vitae*, nn. 57, 62, 65, in *Origins* 24 (1995): 709–11, 712.

28. See my *Directions in Catholic Social Ethics* (Notre Dame, Ind.: University of Notre Dame Press, 1985), 5–69.

29. Richard J. Regan, *Conflict and Consensus: Religious Freedom and the Second Vatican Council* (New York: Macmillan, 1967), 38–48.

30. Paul VI, *Humanae vitae*, n. 6.

31. Alfred T. Hennelly, ed., *Liberation Theology: A Documentary History* (Maryknoll, N.Y.: Orbis, 1990).

32. Arthur F. McGovern, *Marxism: An American Christian Perspective* (Maryknoll, N.Y.: Orbis, 1980).

33. R. Bruce Douglass and David Hollenbach, eds., *Catholicism and Liberalism: Contributions to American Public Philosophy* (Cambridge: Cambridge University Press, 1994).

34. National Conference of Catholic Bishops, *Economic Justice for All: Pastoral Letter on Catholic Social Teaching and the United States Economy* (Washington: National Conference of Catholic Bishops, 1986).

35. For a position different from that of the United States bishops and espousing a more conservative position, see *Toward the Future: Catholic Social Thought and the U.S. Economy: A Lay Letter* (New York: Lay Commission on Catholic Social Teaching and the U.S. Economy, 1984).

36. Mary Segers, ed., *Church Polity and American Politics: Issues in Contemporary American Catholicism* (New York: Garland, 1990).

37. Declaration on Religious Liberty, n. 7, in *Vatican Council II*, 805.

38. Curran, *Directions in Catholic Social Ethics*, 127–45.

39. Kevin W. Irwin and Edmund D. Pellegrino, eds., *Preserving the Creation: Environmental Theology and Ethics* (Washington: Georgetown University Press, 1994).

40. Charles E. Curran, Margaret A. Farley, and Richard A. McCormick, eds. *Readings in Moral Theology No. 9: Feminist Ethics and the Catholic Moral Tradition* (New York: Paulist, 1996).

41. George S. Worgul, ed., *Issues in Academic Freedom* (Pittsburgh, Pa: Duquesne University Press, 1992).

42. Francis Schüssler Fiorenza, "Systematic Theology: Task and Methods," in *Systematic Theology: Roman Catholic Perspectives*, ed. Francis Schüssler Fiorenza and John P. Galvin, 2 vols. (Minneapolis: Fortress, 1991), vol. 1, 1–87.

• Part Two •

Contemporary Issues

~ 6 ~

Fertility Control

This chapter will discuss fertility in a broad historical and contemporary perspective, but it will give special attention to the Catholic understanding. Fertility control gives people the power and the means to limit and prevent the procreative aspects of human sexuality. Older terminology prior to the mid-twentieth century often refers to birth control and family planning to describe the same basic reality. This chapter deals with fertility control in the light of the three means most often used—contraception, sterilization, and abortion. Technological developments and contemporary theories blur the absolute distinction among these three means, but the ethical perspectives both in the past and in the present recognize important differences among them.

Contraception

Contraception in the strict sense interferes with the sexual act to prevent conception. In the broad sense contraception includes all the means that can be used to prevent conception after sexual intercourse, including sterilization, which interferes with the sexual faculty or power. A close logical connection exists between the ethical evaluation of contraception and of contraceptive sterilization. Judgments about the morality of contraception have traditionally distinguished between contraception within marriage and contraception outside marriage, although some contemporaries reject the importance of this distinction.

CONTRACEPTION WITHIN MARRIAGE. Today popular morality, philosophical ethicists, religious ethicists, and religious bodies generally accept the morality of contraception within marriage, often appealing to the need for family planning. Most recognize a relationship between marital sexuality and procreation, but marital sexuality also has other significant purposes, especially expressing and enhancing the love union of the partners and thereby the good of the marriage. Unlimited procreation, or at times any procreation, could be harmful to one of the spouses, the marriage relationship itself, the good of already existing children, or the needs of the broader society. No perfect contraception exists, but most ethical reasoning sees no significant moral differences among the various means, provided they are not harmful to the individuals who use them or to others. Logically one could justify contraception on the basis of an absolute autonomy, giving the individual control over her body to make whatever decisions she wants, but most justifications of family planning, which by definition concerns more than the individual, avoid such a radical individual autonomy. The hierarchical teaching of the Roman Catholic Church constitutes the strongest and the primary contemporary moral opposition to the use of contraception for spouses.

The widespread moral acceptance of contraception is recent and has taken place well within the twentieth century. Individuals do not make human moral judgments in the abstract but in the concrete situation. A number of very significant social factors have influenced the near unanimous acceptance of contraceptive practices within marriage—the increased life expectancy of all human beings; massive improvements in infant and child health care; the realities of an increasingly urban and industrialized society; the changing role and function of women in society; the wider and more accurate understanding of the physiology of human reproduction; the recognition of the population explosion and the need to limit population; the development, and the ready availability, and active promotion of newer, more effective forms of contraception.[1]

The Christian religion and more popular morality played the most significant role in the ethical approach to contraception in the West. John T. Noonan's writings constitute the best source for the historical development of moral approaches to contraception in Catholicism, in Christianity in general, and in the West.[2]

The ancient world of both East and West knew the reality of contraception either by avoiding insemination in the female vas or by using potions or magic. In the Greco-Roman world some philosophers (Plato, Aristotle) and some gynecologists (e.g., Soranos of Ephesus) apparently accepted contraception. The Roman Empire, however, tended to encourage childbearing. The influential Stoic philosophers insisted that procreation constituted the only purpose of sexual intercourse and thus logically condemned contraception.[3]

The Hebrew scriptures contain no law condemning contraception, but the emphasis on Israel as God's people, the descendants of Abraham and Sarah, emphasized the need for procreation and fertility. Thus Israel was generally negative toward contraception. Onan merited God's punishment by spilling his seed and by failing to provide his brother's widow with offspring (Gn 38:10). Onan's wrongdoing did not involve contraception as such but the refusal of family responsibilities, although some later Jewish writings used Onan's punishment to vindicate the wrongness of coitus interruptus. Other later Jewish authorities recognized some limit on procreation and in certain cases even approved a woman's using root potions as a contraceptive.[4]

The Christian approach to contraception developed in this milieu and also in the context in which contraception was associated with prostitution and extramarital sexuality, which Christians strongly opposed. In addition, the potions used for contraception could not clearly be differentiated from abortifacients. The Christian condemnation of contraception followed from its understanding of human sexuality. Clement of Alexandria (d. 215?) and following him, the Christian tradition, adopted the Stoic rule that marriage and sexuality exist for the purpose of procreation—proposed as a middle position between the Gnostic right, opposing all use of sex in imitation of Jesus, and the Gnostic left, celebrating the freedom to use sexuality in any manner. The influential St. Augustine of Hippo (d. 430), in opposition to his earlier acceptance of Manicheanism that excluded procreation but accepted sexual intercourse and contraception, strongly asserted the procreative rule condemning contraception. Augustine's negative view of sexuality (common to many in the early church and perhaps even stronger in others such as Jerome) strengthened his support of the Stoic procreative rule. According to Augustine, sexual intercourse transmits original sin since concupiscence as the disordered inclination to sexual pleasure always accompanies sexual relations.[5]

Medieval theologians (e.g., Thomas Aquinas) and their successors maintained that procreation did not constitute the exclusive lawful purpose for marital sexuality. The church, for example, accepted the marital sexuality of the sterile and those no longer able to procreate. The procreation of offspring also included the well-being and education of the children. However, the condemnation of contraception remained, with emphasis on its violation of the order of nature calling for the depositing of male seed in the vagina of the female. This rationale based on nature also served as the basis for the condemnation of sodomy, oral and anal intercourse, and masturbation.[6] The split between Eastern and Western Christianity in the eleventh century and the Protestant Reformation in the sixteenth century did not change the universal Christian condemnation of contraception within marriage. This teaching continued well into the twentieth century.

The impetus for change came not from religious bodies or philosophical ethicists in general but from popular morality and especially people committed to improving the human condition. In France, for example, the use of contraception brought about a precipitous drop in the birth rate between 1750 and 1800. At the end of the eighteenth century, Thomas Malthus wrote his famous *Essay on the Principle of Population*, recognizing the problem created by overpopulation and calling for restraints on procreation but not contraception. Francis Place, in England in 1820, first advocated birth control as a solution to the problem of economic and family conditions. In the United States, Robert Dale Owens in 1830 advocated the use of contraception. A Malthusian League came into existence in England in 1878, proposing contraception as a solution to the problems connected with large families, and similar groups sprang up in many other parts of the Western world.[7]

Early proponents of contraception and family planning ran into strong popular opposition. In the United States, Anthony Comstock (d. 1915), a Protestant moral reformer and crusader, succeeded in influencing Congress to pass the law bearing his name prohibiting the use of the mails for obscene materials, including contraceptives. Many states passed even more restrictive laws, and the Comstock-inspired legislation had some effect in the United States until 1965. Early proponents of family planning included many urban radicals and anarchists. Margaret Sanger, who truly merits the title of mother and founder of the family planning movement, came from such a background but soon made common cause with the medical profession and middle-class women. Sanger publicized family planning and set up clinics to educate and provide contraceptive help for the community at large, especially poorer women. The movement gained considerably from the amalgamation of rival factions into the American Birth Control Federation in 1939 which changed its name in 1942 to the Planned Parenthood Federation. Some charitable foundations (e.g., Rockefeller and Ford) became more interested in family planning and population problems. By 1970 family planning had become a successful popular movement enjoying widespread public support. People in general wholeheartedly accepted the morality of family planning and contraception.[8]

Although some Protestant lay people were involved in the early birth control movements in the Anglo–Saxon countries, the Christian churches remained firm in their condemnation of artificial contraception, as distinguished from abstinence, well into the twentieth century. The Church of England became the first Christian church to accept officially the morality of artificial contraception for spouses. Although the Lambeth Conferences of 1908 and 1920 (official meetings of the bishops of the Anglican church) condemned birth control, some Anglican statements supportive of birth control appeared in the 1920s. In 1930, the Lambeth Conference by a vote of 193 to 67 adopted a resolution recognizing a moral obligation to limit or avoid parenthood and proposing complete abstinence as the primary and most obvious way while also accepting other methods.[9]

In the United States in March 1931, the Committee on Marriage and Home of the United States Federal Council of Churches issued an influential statement in which the majority of its members accepted the careful and restrained use of contraception by spouses. However, the Federal Council of Churches did not act upon this report. Subsequently, the major Protestant churches and the most significant Protestant theological ethicists (e.g., Karl Barth, Reinhold Niebuhr) accepted contraception as a way to ensure responsible parenthood. The social, cultural, and historical conditions mentioned earlier obviously influenced this massive change in church teaching, but the proponents of change also pointed to aspects in the Christian tradition supporting such a move. Christians had gradually come to recognize the loving or unitive aspect of marital sexuality in addition to the procreative aspect. The procreative aspect itself included not only the procreation but also the education of offspring. The very possibility of procreation and education called for the good health of the parents. In this light Protestantism in general justified the use of contraception as a way for spouses to realize responsible parenthood.[10]

Roman Catholic hierarchical teachings steadfastly opposed artificial contraception within marriage. In 1930 Pope Pius XI in his encyclical *Casti connubii,* in obvious reaction to the Church of England's moral stand, strongly reiterated the condemnation of artificial contraception. Some Catholic theologians even before that time had been advocating the use of the infertile period or the so-called rhythm method. In a 1951 address to the Italian Catholic Union of Midwives, Pope Pius XII taught that serious medical, eugenic, economic, and social indications can justify the use of the sterile periods even on a permanent basis. In July 1968 Pope Paul VI issued his encyclical *Humanae vitae,* reiterating the condemnation of artificial contraception. Pope John Paul II has continued to insist upon the same teaching.[11]

As mentioned in chapter five, Vatican II and *Humanae vitae* were the two events that have significantly shaped and influenced Catholic moral theology in the last few decades. The conciliar experience exerted a great influence on the debates about *Humanae vitae*. Before Vatican II no Catholic theologian had ever written against the church's condemnation of artificial contraception. The climate created by the discussions at Vatican II and by developing cultural, social, and scientific factors made possible the first public questionings of the church's teaching by her own theologians. In 1963 John Rock, a Catholic doctor who had helped to develop the contraceptive pill, published *The Time Has Come*, which argued for the moral legitimacy of such pills for Catholic spouses wanting to practice responsible parenthood.[12] About this same time four articles appeared written by theologians who maintained that the church should change its teaching—Louis Janssens of Belgium;[13] Louis Dupré, a lay philosopher at Georgetown University;[14] Josef Maria Reuss, a German theologian and auxiliary bishop;[15] and William van der Marck, a Dutch Dominican theologian.[16]

On June 23, 1964, Pope Paul VI publicly revealed the existence of a commission, popularly known since as the birth control commission, which was studying the contraception issue. Pope John XXIII had established a small commission before he died in June of 1963. The small committee first met in October of 1963. Three other meetings with an enlarged membership took place before the final, long meeting in the spring of 1966. In the light of the work of this commission, the pope kept the issue off the agenda of Vatican II. In April of 1967, some documents from the commission were published unofficially and without approval. These revealed that the majority of the commission strongly favored a change in the teaching on contraception. Many Catholics expected change, but the change did not come.[17]

Humanae vitae sets forth the rationale for the condemnation of artificial contraception.[18] The natural law "teaches that each and every marriage act must remain open to the transmission of life" (par. 11). The pope refers to "the inseparable connection, willed by God and unable to be broken by man on his own initiative, between the two meanings of the conjugal act: the unitive and the procreative meaning" (par. 12).

According to official hierarchical Roman Catholic teaching, couples can and at times should limit their family in the name of responsible parenthood. Although artificial contraception is morally wrong, *Humanae vitae* implies that in practice, because of all the pressures couples experience, their use of artificial contraception might not always involve grave sin. Rhythm (or natural family planning) is acceptable because it does not interfere with the natural act. The pope explicitly mentioned that he could not accept the conclusions of the commission because "they departed from the moral teaching on marriage proposed with constant firmness by the teaching authority of the church" (par. 7). Thus the question of church authority was primary.

The day after the encyclical was made public, I acted as the spokesperson for a group of eighty-seven theologians and scholars who issued a statement (ultimately signed by over six hundred Catholic scholars and theologians) disagreeing with the condemnation of artificial contraception as well as the ecclesiology and natural law explicitly and implicitly found in the encyclical. The statement concluded that in theory and in practice Catholics could dissent from the teaching of the encyclical.[19] As mentioned in the last chapter, the vast majority of Catholic theologians reject the particular teaching on artificial contraception, the understanding of natural law on which it is based, and accept the legitimacy of dissent from such teaching. However, some Catholic theologians strongly support the encyclical and the subsequent reiterations made by John Paul II.[20]

Humanae vitae and its continuing reaffirmation have had very significant ramifications not only for moral theology but for the life of the Catholic Church. Andrew Greeley concludes that the encyclical "seems to have been the occasion for massive apostasy and for a notable decline in religious devotion and belief."[21] Catholic bishops recognize that the vast majority of Catholic spouses practice artificial contraception.[22] In pastoral practice the teaching is no longer an issue. The issue only arises in questions of public policy when the hierarchical church in some parts of the globe comes out against attempts to control population. However, from a symbolic perspective the teaching is most important. If the Catholic Church changes its teaching here it recognizes that it can change in other areas as well. In this context the issue of artificial contraception continues to be all important in the life of the Catholic Church as a sign that the present pope will not change any authoritative teachings.

Other religious bodies today generally support artificial contraception in the context of responsible parenthood. The Eastern Orthodox Church today accepts responsible contraception while condemning abortion and infanticide. The multiple purposes of marriage, the lack of any definitive statement against contraception by the church, a synergistic cooperation between God and humans, and the need for responsible parenthood serve as the basis for the responsible use of contraception in marriage.[23]

Orthodox Judaism gives a limited acceptance to some forms of contraception, based on the early Talmudic acceptance of the woman's using root potions. Jewish law puts the duty of procreation on the male, and this obligation militates against the use of condoms or coitus interruptus. The most acceptable contraception interferes the least with the natural sexual act. Conservative and Reform Judaism fully accept and endorse contraception provided it is not harmful to the parties involved.[24]

Islam accepts contraception if it does not entail the radical separation of procreation from marriage. All forms of contraception are acceptable provided they are not harmful and do not involve abortion. Justification for contraception in Islam rests on reports that the Prophet Mohammed did not forbid the contraceptive practices of some of his companions.[25]

Ancient Hindu medicine and Hindu tradition did not contemplate contraception, but did sanction means to enhance conception. In time, medical texts such as the sixteenth century *Bhavaprakasha* took the step toward contraception by advising a few oral preparations to prevent conception. When India embarked on a national family planning program at its independence in 1947, the discussions accepted the morality of contraception but centered on the relative population sizes of the higher and lower castes.[26]

Western philosophers today generally do not discuss in great detail the morality of contraception within marriage primarily because the basic issue is not controversial. Ethicists generally recognize at times an obligation for spouses not to procreate, but not all would agree on the reasons for such an obligation.

Concerns of feminist thought have greatly influenced the contemporary discussion about fertility control in general and contraception in particular. The growing equality and full participation of women in marriage in the global context has definitely given impetus to a wider use of contraception. Feminist ethics starts from the experience of the oppression of women and seeks to unmask and do away with the patriarchical structures of society. Feminists see an important connection between the personal and the political. The practice of medicine involves patriarchical structures and practices that have oppressed women in general and especially in the matter of reproduction which ordinarily takes place within the woman's own body. Feminists stress the need for women to control their own fertility and reproduction and to have the requisite freedom and autonomy to do so.[27]

Contemporary popular morality, philosophy, theological ethics, and religious bodies, with the major exception of Roman Catholicism, accept the morality of contraception for spouses in carrying out their call to responsible parenthood. General agreement exists on the microlevel of the family that the decision about contraception should be made by the spouses themselves in the light of their own health, the good of their marriage, the education and formation of their children, and population and environmental needs, both local and global. Population ethics deals with the question of what means individual governments can and should take in educating, persuading, encouraging, and perhaps even coercing citizens in the light of the population situation of the particular country.

Efficient and effective contraception has been a boon to human existence by giving spouses the means to control their procreation. Like any human good, contraception can be abused, but such abuse does not cancel out the great good that contraception has provided for humankind. Contraception as a power has been used by the strong against the weak. Population ethics deals with how contraceptive power has been used against the poor, the lower classes, and people of color, both within and across national boundaries. Feminists and others recognize the victimization of women by contraceptive power. Society has often forced women to bear the burden of contraception and especially to live with the medical risks of contraception. The contraceptive pill and the intrauterine device (IUD) definitely involve medical risks for women.[28]

Contraception outside Marriage. Judgments about the ethical use of contraception outside marriage depend on one's understanding of the morality of extramarital sexual activity. As a matter of fact, many nonmarried people are sexually active. Truly there has been a sexual revolution. The majority of adolescents in the United States have had sexual intercourse by the time they are nineteen years of age. The problem of teenage pregnancies continues to grow.[29] In addition to adolescents our society today includes many single people of all ages who are sexually active.

The society at large in the United States no longer views all extramarital sexuality as immoral and irresponsible, although the mainline churches and religions still generally maintain the immorality of sexual relations outside marriage. Contraception enters into the discussion of extramarital sexuality not only because of the desire to prevent procreation, but also to prevent the spread of AIDS and sexually transmitted diseases (STDs), as condoms have been known to do to some degree.

If one believes that extramarital sexual relations are morally responsible, then the use of contraception to prevent unwanted procreation is morally acceptable.

Problems arise when one believes that such extramarital sexual relations, especially among adolescents, are morally wrong. Two different positions exist. One maintains that readily available contraception itself facilitates such morally wrong behavior and that encouraging the use of such contraception contributes to this immorality. A second position holds that these people are going to have sexual relations no matter what, so that it is better to make sure that they do not conceive and do not transmit diseases. Many ethicists have accepted the general precept of counseling the lesser of two evils when one is determined to do the wrong in the first place. It is a lesser evil to have sexual relations in a way that prevents procreation and/or avoids the transmission of harmful diseases.[30]

In this context a sharp division arose within the body of Catholic bishops in the Unites States. In December 1987, the Administrative Board of the United States Catholic Conference issued a statement which, in the context of explaining Catholic teaching, maintained that in a pluralistic society the bishops would not object to educational programs providing factual information about the ways of preventing AIDS. They also recognized the possible application of the principle of counseling the lesser of two evils in these circumstances.[31] Some powerful bishops strongly disagreed with this part of the statement.[32] As a group the bishops decided not to withdraw the original statement, but to issue a new one. The new document did not mention these aspects.[33] I do not think the bishops would have any problem in accepting the principle of counseling the lesser of two evils in other situations (e.g., it is better to steal one hundred dollars from a woman than to kill her). The neuralgic reaction by some bishops in the context of contraception shows how defensive they are on this issue.

The provision of contraception to adolescents involves other moral issues, especially parental consent. Parents have the responsibility for their children and the right and the obligation to teach their children morality. Some maintain that the rights and obligations of parents mean that no contraception should be dispensed to adolescents without the permission of the parents. Others maintain that contraception can be provided without parental consent and propose a variety of reasons: some children do not and cannot communicate with parents about sexuality; some are going to be sexually active anyway, and it is better for them to use contraception than not to use it; and some are mature enough to make their own decisions in this area.

The Committee on Adolescence of the American Academy of Pediatrics issued a statement (1990) that tries to balance off the different ethical responsibilities. According to the statement, pediatricians should actively work to relieve the negative consequences of adolescent sexual activity. Preventive measures involve counseling on responsible sexual decision making, including abstinence, and providing contraceptive services for sexually active patients. A general policy guaranteeing confidentiality to the adolescent patient should be clearly stated to the patient and the parent at the time of the initiation of the professional relationship. The goal is to enhance conversation between the adolescent and the parent and to enlist parental support for the adolescent's responsible sexual behavior, including contraceptive use, whenever possible.[34]

Sterilization

Sterilization in the narrow sense is the procedure that takes away one's capacity to procreate. In this sense sterilization differs from contraception, which interferes with the sexual act and not with the sexual capacity or faculty. According to this understanding, which was standard in Roman Catholic medical ethics and accepted by others, sterilization can be either temporary or permanent. The anovulant pill technically constitutes a temporary sterilization because the pill temporarily suppresses ovulation.[35] This chapter employs the broader description of sterilization as the permanent (or somewhat permanent because of some possibility of reversal) removal of procreative capacity. Older forms of sterilization included hysterectomy and castration, but tubal ligation and vasectomy, procedures that are less than one hundred years old, have become comparatively simple and fairly common procedures today. The primary ethical distinction concerns voluntary and nonvoluntary sterilization.

Voluntary Sterilization. Religions and religious ethicists generally recognize that individual human beings have stewardship over their bodies and they should make the medical decisions that affect their life and health. Philosophers usually recognize the primacy of the person as the decision maker in matters affecting one's human good. Voluntary consent in general has become a primary canon in medical ethics. Some feminists and others insist on the total autonomy of the individual with regard to one's reproductive capacity to make whatever decisions one wants. Religious approaches in general and most philosophers as well as medical codes recognize that the individual makes the decision but that justifying reasons are required to make the decision for sterilization a good and morally acceptable one. Sterilization is proposed for either contraceptive or therapeutic reasons.

Contraceptive sterilization has become increasingly common both in the United States and in the world. As the very name indicates, contraceptive sterilization logically follows the same moral judgments as contraception. The one significant difference concerns the somewhat permanent nature of the procedure, because of which many ethicists require a more serious and permanent reason to justify it. A basic maxim of medical ethics insists that one should never do more harm than is necessary to overcome the problem. Those who accept contraception logically also accept the morality of sterilization. With a similar consistency, the hierarchical teaching of the Roman Catholic Church strongly opposes contraceptive sterilization.[36] Again, many Roman Catholics dissent in theory and in practice from this hierarchical teaching.

Therapeutic sterilization is done for the good of the individual and not for contraceptive reasons. The general literature does not frequently discuss therapeutic sterilization as such because the same standards govern therapeutic sterilization as govern other therapeutic interventions—the procedure must ultimately be for the good of the person and the evil or loss involved must be proportionate to the good attained. Official Roman Catholic teaching and ethics have treated therapeutic sterilization at length and developed an elaborate casuistry in distinguishing the morally accepted therapeutic sterilization from the morally condemned contraceptive sterilization. Since sterilization has two different effects—the sterilizing of the procreative power and the protection of the health of the individual—Roman Catholic medical ethics traditionally has applied the principle of double effect, according to which direct sterilization is always wrong, but indirect sterilizations may be justified for a proportionate reason. Direct sterilization is that which aims at making procreation impossible either as a means or as an end. Therapeutic or indirect sterilization aims directly at the health or good of the individual. Thus a cancerous uterus can be removed, but sterilization to prevent harm to the woman coming from a pregnancy involves a direct and morally wrong sterilization.[37]

The issue of informed consent, a basic principle in contemporary bioethics, arises in different circumstances. Feminist literature, with its emphasis on reproductive rights and women's control over their bodies, in the light of many abuses, strongly insists on informed consent. Until recently women have borne the burden of sterilization much more than men, even though female sterilization was a more difficult and risky procedure than male sterilization. Some poor women have been sterilized immediately after childbirth, having been "informed" about the sterilization just before the delivery of their child. Most people would also object to employers demanding that people, especially women, become sterilized as a precondition for certain types of employment.[38]

Many writings deal with the sterilization of the mentally retarded who are somewhat incapacitated or even totally incapable of giving informed consent.[39] The Committee on Ethics of the American College of Obstetricians and Gynecologists (1988) produced a statement on "Sterilization of Women Who are Mentally Handicapped," which urges all possible attempts to communicate with the person involved on whatever level is possible. In case the individual is mentally incompetent, the decision should be made by the appropriate proxy, based on the best interests of the patient after considering alternative methods of dealing with the situation.[40]

Nonvoluntary sterilization. Can some other purpose or goal ever override the important value of free consent? Population ethics considers the role of government, which can go from merely providing information to advocacy, providing incentives, or coercing with regard to sterilization. Some have proposed eugenic and punitive sterilization.

Proposals (e.g., The Human Betterment Foundation) and even legislation for mandatory sterilization (thirty states in the U.S. passed such laws between 1907 and 1931) appeared in the early part of this century. Since mental disease and defects that are passed on by heredity create a menace for society and the state, advocates argued the good of the whole can override the freedom of the individual. The Nazi eugenic laws and practices at this time have become notorious.[41]

In the second half of the twentieth century, only a few advocates (e.g., Joseph Fletcher) have proposed some eugenic sterilization.[42] The horrors occasioned by Nazi practice, the erroneous scientific foundation of the eugenic movement in the early part of this century, the fear of errors, the hubris of making eugenic decisions for others, the overly intrusive role of the state, and the continuing and growing emphasis on the freedom and rights of all, have contributed to the general consensus against eugenic sterilization. Some proposals have been made to cut off welfare funds to poor women who have children and refuse to undergo sterilization, but such proposals have not received much support.[43]

The fact that there is little or no discussion of punitive sterilization in the recent literature hints at a consensus against the practice today. However, Francis Hürth, a conservative Roman Catholic theologian, in the 1930s proposed limited cases in which punitive sterilization might be justified. Pope

Pius XI went out of his way not to condemn punitive sterilization in his 1931 encyclical *Casti connubii.* Proponents maintain that if the state can inflict capital punishment for certain crimes it can also inflict the lesser punishment of sterilization in limited appropriate cases. Critics reply that punitive sterilization does not achieve the purposes of punishment and does not even inhibit future sex crimes.[44] There appears to be no support for punitive sterilization today.[45]

Abortion

Abortion, or the interruption of pregnancy, also constitutes a means of fertility control. This section will very briefly explain the logical application of one's moral position on abortion to judgments about abortion as a means of fertility control.

All those who oppose abortion as a general principle also oppose abortion as a means of fertility control. Those who hold that from the first moment of conception the zygote should be treated as an individual human being, or who attribute a high value to the early conceptus, oppose forms of contraception that work as abortifacients. Here again technological developments blur the clear distinction between contraception and abortion. Doubts about how the IUD actually works led some to condemn it as abortifacient because of the theory that the IUD prevents the implantation of the early conceptus in the endometrium of the uterus.[46] Those who hold this view of the early conceptus strongly oppose the new RU486 pill, which definitely works as an abortifacient. On the other hand, those who do not attribute any value or great value to the early conceptus have no moral qualms about the RU486.

Many (e.g., Beverly Harrison)[47] who advocate the morality of abortion in general recognize significant moral differences between abortion and contraception. Some attribute more value and worth to the fetus as it develops in the maternal womb. Consequently abortion (at least after the first few weeks) should not be used as the regular and ordinary method of fertility control for a number of possible reasons—the danger of some risk to the mother, the problems caused by multiple abortions, and the value that is attributed to the fetus. However, abortion could still be used in the case of contraceptive failure.

Fertility control has always been significant for humankind, but contemporary scientific, social, philosophical, theological, and feminist developments have focused even more attention on this issue. The debate about fertility control within marriage continues to see much dissent by Catholics from the hierarchical teaching.

Notes

1. Angus McClaren, *A History of Contraception from Antiquity to the Present Day* (Oxford: Basil Blackwell, 1990).
2. John T. Noonan, Jr., "Contraception," in *Encyclopedia of Bioethics,* Warren T. Reich, ed., 4 vols., (New York: Macmillan, 1978), vol 1 204–16; Noonan, *Contraception: A History of Its Treatment by the Catholic Theologians and Canonists*, enlarged ed. (Cambridge: Belknap Press of Harvard University Press, 1986); Noonan, "The History of Contraception: Seven Choices," in *The Contraceptive Ethos: Reproductive Rights and Responsibilities*, ed. Stewart F. Spiecker, William B. Bondeson, and H. Tristram Engelhardt, Jr. (Dordrecht, Holland: D. Reidel, 1987), 3–14. See also McClaren and John M. Riddle, *Contraception and Abortion from the Ancient World to the Renaissance* (Cambridge: Harvard University Press, 1992).
3. Noonan, *Contraception: A History*, 9–30, 46–49.
4. Ibid., 30–36.
5. Ibid., 56–139.
6. Josef Fuchs, *Die Sexualethik des heilegen Thomas von Aquin* (Cologne: Bachey, 1949).
7. Noonan, *Contraception: A History*, 387–414.
8. Kurt W. Back, *Family Planning and Population Control: The Challenge of a Successful Movement* (Boston: Twayne, 1989).
9. Richard M. Fagley, *The Population Explosion and Christian Responsibility* (New York: Oxford University Press, 1960), 194–95.
10. Ibid., 195–209.
11. For an overview of the teaching of the hierarchical magisterium, see John Gallagher, "Magisterial Teaching from 1918 to the Present," in *Human Sexuality and Personhood* (St. Louis: Pope John Center, 1981), 191–210; Joseph A. Selling, "Magisterial Teaching on Marriage 1880–1968: Historical Constancy or Radical Development?" in *Historia: Memoria futuri: Mélanges Louis Vereecke,* ed. Réal Tremblay and Dennis J. Billy (Rome: Editiones Academiae Alphonsianae, 1991), 351–402.
12. John Rock, *The Time Has Come: A Catholic Doctor's Proposals to End the Battle Over Birth Control* (New York: Alfred A. Knopf, 1963).
13. Louis Janssens, "Morale conjugale et progestogenes," *Ephemerides theologicae lovanienses* 39 (1963): 787–826.

14. Louis K. Dupré, "Toward a Re-examination of the Catholic Position on Birth Control," *Cross Currents* 14 (Winter 1964): 63-85.
15. Josef Maria Reuss, "Eheliche Hingabe und Zengung," *Tübinger Theologische Quartalschrift* 143 (1963): 454–76.
16. William van der Marck, "Vruchtbaarheidsregeling," *Tijdschrift voor Theologie* 3 (1963): 386–413.
17. Robert Blair Kaiser, *The Politics of Sex and Religion: A Case History in the Development of Doctrine, 1962–1984* (Kansas City, Mo.: Sheed and Ward, 1985).
18. Pope Paul VI, *On the Regulation of Birth: Humanae vitae* (Washington: United States Catholic Conference, 1968).
19. Charles E. Curran, Robert E. Hunt, et al, *Dissent In and For the Church: Theologians and Humanae Vitae* (New York: Sheed and Ward, 1969).
20. Janet E. Smith, *Humanae vitae: A Generation Later* (Washington: Catholic University of America Press, 1991); Smith, ed., *Why Humanae vitae Was Right: A Reader* (San Francisco: Ignatius, 1993).
21. Andrew M. Greeley, William C. McCready, and Kathleen McCourt, *Catholic Schools in a Declining Church* (Kansas City, Mo.: Sheed and Ward, 1976), 153.
22. Archbishop John R. Quinn, "New Context for Contraception Teaching," *Origins* 10 (1980): 263–67.
23. Stanley Samuel Harakas, "Eastern Orthodox Bioethics," in *Bioethics Yearbook I: Theological Developments in Bioethics: 1988–1990* (Dordrecht, Holland: Kluwer, 1991), 85; Chrysostum Zaphiris, "The Morality of Contraception: An Eastern Orthodox Opinion," *Journal of Ecumenical Studies* 11 (1974): 677–90.
24. Fred Rossner, "Contraception in Jewish Law," in *Jewish Bioethics,* eds., Fred Rossner and J. David Bleich (New York: Sanhedrin, 1979).
25. Hassan Hathout, "Islamic Concepts and Bioethics," in *Bioethics Yearbook I,* 104–06.
26. Prakesh N. Desai, "Hinduism and Bioethics in India," in *Bioethics Yearbook I,* 50.
27. Christine Overall, *Ethics and Human Reproduction: A Feminist Analysis* (Boston: Allen and Unwin, 1987); Susan Sherwin, *No Longer Patient: Feminist Ethics and Healthcare* (Philadelphia: Temple University Press, 1992).
28. For my estimation of the effects of the contraception revolution, see my *Transition and Tradition in Moral Theology* (Notre Dame, Ind.: University of Notre Dame Press, 1978), 29–58.
29. Efstratios Demetriov and David W. Kaplan, "Adolescent Contraceptive Use and Parental Notification," *American Journal of Diseases of Children* 143 (October 1989): 1166–72.

30. James F. Keenan, "Prophylactics, Toleration, and Cooperation: Contemporary Problems and Traditional Principles," *International Philosophical Quarterly* 20 (June 1989): 205–20.
31. Administrative Board, United States Catholic Conference, "The Many Faces of AIDS: A Gospel Response," *Origins* 17 (1987): 481–89.
32. "Reaction to AIDS Statement," *Origins* 17 (1987): 489–93. See also Michael D. Place, "'The Many Faces of AIDS': Some Clarifications of the Recent Debate," *America* 158 (1988): 135–41.
33. National Conference of Catholic Bishops, "Call to Compassion and Responsibility: A Response to the HIV/AIDS Crisis," *Origins* 19 (1989): 421–34. See James F. Drane, "Condoms, AIDS, and Catholic Ethics," *Commonweal* 118 (1991): 188–92.
34. Committee on Adolescence of the American Academy of Pediatrics, "Contraception and Adolescents," *Pediatrics* 86, no. 1 (July 1990): 134–38.
35. John C. Ford and Gerald Kelly, *Contemporary Moral Problems II: Marriage Questions* (Westminster, Md.: Newman, 1963), pp. 315–77.
36. Kevin D. O'Rourke and Philip Boyle, eds., *Medical Ethics: Sources of Catholic Teachings* (St. Louis: Catholic Health Association, 1989), 292–97.
37. John P. Boyle, *The Sterilization Controversy: A New Crisis for the Catholic Hospital?* (New York: Paulist, 1977), 5–38.
38. Karen Lebacqz, "Sterilization: Ethical Aspects," in *Encyclopedia of Bioethics*, ed. Warren T. Reich, 609–12.
39. Ruth Macklin and Willard Gaylin, eds., *Mental Retardation and Sterilization: A Problem of Competency and Paternalism* (Hastings-on-Hudson, N.Y.: Hastings Center, 1981).
40. *Committee Opinion 63: Sterilization of Women Who Are Mentally Handicapped* (Washington: American College of Obstetrics and Gynecology, 1988).
41. Stephen Trombley, *The Right to Reproduce: A History of Coercive Sterilization* (London: Weidenfeld and Nicolson, 1988).
42. Joseph Fletcher, *Morals and Medicine* (Boston: Beacon, 1960), 168.
43. Lebacqz, *Encyclopedia of Bioethics*, 1609–12.
44. John McCarthy, *Problems in Theology II: The Commandments* (Westminster, Md.: Newman, 1960), 124–29.
45. John Kenyon Mason, *Medico-Legal Aspects of Reproduction and Parenthood* (Brookfield, Vt.: Gower, 1990), 75–77.
46. Richard A. McCormick, *Notes on Moral Theology 1965 though 1980* (Washington: University Press of America, 1981), 108–09.
47. Beverly Wildung Harrison, *Making the Connections: Essays in Feminist Social Ethics*, ed. Carol S. Robb (Boston: Beacon, 1985), 115–34.

~ 7 ~

Is There Any Good News in the Recent Documents from the Vatican about Homosexuality?

I maintain, together with many others, that official hierarchical Roman Catholic teaching should accept the moral value and goodness of committed homosexual relationships striving for permanency and including homogenital sexual relations.[1] The most recent two documents from the Congregation for the Doctrine of the Faith—the 1992 "Some Considerations Concerning the Response to Legislative Proposals on the Non-Discrimination of Homosexual Persons"[2] and the 1986 "Letter to the Bishops of the Catholic Church on the Pastoral Care of Homosexual Persons"[3] strongly reiterate the teaching that homosexual relations are always and everywhere wrong. This chapter will examine these two documents (primarily the 1986 Letter, because the 1992 Considerations deals primarily with legislation and will be discussed in the next chapter) to see if they indicate any basis for the hope that the official hierarchical magisterium will ever change its moral teaching.

What this chapter discusses from an academic perspective has become a burning existential question for many today—should they leave the Roman Catholic Church because of its present teaching and strong unwillingness to ever change this teaching? This academic and theological study alone does not pretend to solve anyone's personal question, but it might furnish some helpful information. This chapter starts with a prejudgment, but attempts to examine objectively these two documents as they stand on the basis of the texts themselves and the context. The first part will deal with the case for the negative answer to the question—the documents show no openness whatsoever to any possible change in the hierarchical teaching. The second part will attempt to indicate some bases for maintaining that a change in the hierarchical teaching is possible.

The Negative Response

Universal and all-inclusive statements remain difficult to verify and most academics rightly shy away from such pronouncements. However, I begin this section with just such a proposition. All those who share my position on the moral goodness of committed homosexual relationships have severely criticized these two documents. This section will not attempt to summarize all these criticisms, but will very briefly summarize the moral teaching of these two documents and will discuss at some length why the congregation felt it necessary to maintain that even the homosexual orientation, as distinguished from homosexual behavior, constitutes an objective disorder.

The documents make the point that the moral teaching of the hierarchical magisterium remains absolutely clear—homosexual activity is always wrong. "It is only in the marital relationship that the use of the sexual faculty can be morally good" (1986 Letter, n. 7, p.380).[4] This "clear position cannot be revised by pressure from civil legislation or the trend of the moment" (n. 9, p. 380). The 1986 Letter recognizes that increasing numbers of people today, even within the church, are bringing enormous pressure to bear on the church to change its teaching. Such a position reflects, even if not entirely consciously, a materialistic ideology which denies the transcendent nature of the human person as well as the supernatural vocation of every individual. These reasons are profoundly opposed to the teaching of the church (nn. 8–9, p. 380).

The moral reasons leading to the conclusion taken by the hierarchical magisterium come from scripture, tradition, reason, and the teaching of the church. The Letter cites scriptural passages in support of its conclusion—Gn 3, 19: 1–11, Lv 18: 22 and 20: 13; I Cor 6: 9; and Rom 1: 18-32 (n. 6, pp. 379–80). In keeping with its pastoral nature, the 1986 Letter does not go into the tradition of the church, but simply points out that the present teaching has been the constant and traditional teaching of the church (n. 8,

p. 380). The church's position is "founded on human reason, illumined by faith" (n. 2, p. 377). The Letter forcefully insists that the proper pastoral care of homosexuals clearly proposes the true teaching of the hierarchical magisterium. Bishops are warned to be especially cautious of any programs pressuring the church to change its teaching even while claiming not to. It is wrong to present the teaching of the magisterium as if it were an optional source for the formation of conscience. "All support should be withdrawn from any organizations which seek to undermine the teaching of the church, which are ambiguous about it, or which neglect it entirely" (n. 17, p. 382).

This summary of the moral teaching and pastoral recommendations of the Letter of the Congregation for the Doctrine of the Faith indicates how forcefully and decisively this teaching has been proposed. No similar document with such admonitions and concrete pastoral measures to reinforce the teaching of the hierarchical magisterium has ever been issued. Is it any wonder that all those who share the position of working for change in the teaching of the hierarchical magisterium have unhesitatingly and strongly criticized the document? Such a presentation of the teaching on homosexuality provides not even the slightest basis for a possible change in the teaching.

The congregation found it necessary not only to condemn homosexual acts, but also to describe the homosexual orientation itself (for which the individual person is ordinarily not responsible) as an objective disorder. The 1986 Letter emphasizes the objective disorder of the homosexual orientation, inclination, and condition more than any other point.

A great number of commentators have strongly disagreed with this understanding and have been quite perplexed about it.[5] The document provides no psychological or psychiatric evidence to support its position. Why did the congregation so forcefully emphasize this point?

Logically this emphasis is closely related to the position taken by the congregation on the morality of homosexual acts and legal discrimination against gays and lesbians. The Letter strongly emphasizes the disordered nature of the homosexual orientation or inclination precisely because other recent documents had neglected it or even given the impression there was nothing disordered about the orientation. The Letter itself gives a partial glimpse of this history (n. 3, p. 379).

"The Declaration on Certain Questions Concerning Sexual Ethics" issued by the Congregation for the Doctrine of the Faith on December 29, 1975, addressed the issue of homosexuality. The Declaration distinguished between "temporary homosexuals and homosexuals who are permanently such because of some innate drive or a pathological condition which is considered incurable." This condition, however, cannot justify homosexual acts. Homosexual acts are "disordered by their very nature" and "deprived of the essential ordination they ought to have."[6] Thus the Declaration distinguishes between the homosexual condition or orientation and homosexual acts, which are said to be always disordered. The 1986 Letter refers only to the Declaration, but other interesting developments occurred after the Declaration in the United States.

In November 1976 the National Conference of Catholic Bishops issued "To Live in Christ Jesus," a pastoral letter dealing with all aspects of the moral life. The very brief discussion of homosexuality in this pastoral letter begins by recognizing that some persons find themselves through no fault of their own to have a homosexual orientation. Homosexuals have the same basic human rights as everyone else and should also have an active role in the church community. "Homosexual activity, however, as distinguished from homosexual orientation, is morally wrong."[7] Since the orientation is not described as morally wrong or disordered, and since the orientation is contrasted to the morally wrong acts, one could conclude legitimately that the orientation itself is not disordered and is neutral or even good. Some American bishops on the basis of this document in their own individual statements and teachings repeated the distinction between the orientation and the morally wrong activity.[8] Pope John Paul II in his address to the American bishops in Chicago in 1979 praised them for rightly saying that homosexual activity, as distinguished from the homosexual orientation, is morally wrong.[9]

The 1986 Letter perceptively recognized that, in accord with its own moral methodology, the condemnation of homosexual acts logically involves the recognition that the homosexual orientation itself is objectively disordered.

A preliminary step requires a proper understanding of the term "disordered." According to the 1986 Letter, the homosexual orientation is not a sin but is an objective disorder (n. 3, p. 379). This same Letter later speaks of homosexual activity as being a moral disorder (n. 7, p. 380). The letter thus uses the term "disordered" to describe both the homosexual orientation and homosexual activity.

Every human moral act contains two aspects—the objective and the subjective. The objective refers to the rightness or wrongness of the act in itself, whereas the subjective refers to the culpability or the responsibility of the agent who does an objectively wrong act. "Right and wrong" are the most correct terms to use about the objective aspect of the act; "culpability or sin" refer to the subjective aspect. The Catholic moral tradition in common with many other moral traditions has recognized that various factors might affect the culpability or sinfulness of the person who does a morally wrong act. Thus the present hierarchical teaching maintains that homosexual acts are objectively wrong, but various factors might affect the subjective culpability or sinfulness involved (n. 11, p. 381). In the tradition of Catholic moral theology, an act is objectively wrong because it is disordered. Thomas Aquinas long ago referred to law as an ordering of reason. The divine law, the natural law, and human law involve an ordering of reason. A disordering constitutes an objective wrongness which thus goes against the divine, natural, or human law.[10]

But why was it necessary for the congregation to maintain that the homosexual orientation, condition, or inclination constitutes an objective disorder?

The documents under consideration help to provide an answer by mentioning significant aspects of the hierarchical magisterium's teaching about moral methodology in determining whether or not an act is objectively well-ordered or disordered. The moral ordering of acts is determined by their ends. Teleology and the principle of finality play an important role in the moral methodology employed in hierarchical Catholic sexual teaching. The 1975 Declaration maintains that respect for the finality of the sexual act guarantees the moral goodness of the act.[11]

Natural law has been described as the participation of the eternal law in the rational creature. God has made us, and human reason by examining human nature can discover how we are to act. However, natural law does not involve a heteronomous or extrinsic understanding of law. We are not to do something just because God commands it. God made us to achieve our own happiness and fulfillment. By acting in accord with our nature and God's plan or law we achieve our true happiness. Thus the 1986 Letter maintains that every morally disordered act prevents one's own fulfillment and happiness by acting contrary to the creative wisdom of God (n. 7, p. 380).

But how do we know God's creative plan and the proper finality and ordering of human acts? The theory of natural law behind hierarchical Catholic sexual teaching, as illustrated in the 1975 Declaration, discovers the plan of God by looking at the nature and purpose of the sexual faculty or power. The sexual faculty exists for the twofold purposes of procreation and love union of male and female. This twofold finality must be respected in every sexual act and grounds the norm that it is only in the marital relationship that the use of the sexual faculty can be morally good.[12] The 1975

Declaration applies these principles and norms to all the particular sexual questions. Thus, for example, artificial contraception between spouses is wrong because it goes against the procreative finality of the act. Homosexual relations are judged wrong because both finalities are missing—procreation and the love union of male and female.[13]

The 1986 Letter follows the same approach. "To choose someone of the same sex for one's sexual activity is to annul the rich symbolism and meaning, not to mention the goals, of the creator's sexual design. Homosexual activity is not a complementary union able to transmit life and so it thwarts the call to a life of that form of self-giving which the gospel says is the essence of Christian living" (n. 7, p. 380).

The teleology or finality fundamental to this natural law theory also controls with regard to the evaluation of inclinations. Note that the very word "inclination" itself has teleological overtones. One is inclined to certain ends or purposes. In fact Thomas Aquinas develops his fundamental approach to natural law on the basis of the three inclinations in human beings—what they share with all living things, what they share with animals, and what is specific to human beings as such. The order of the precepts of natural law is according to the order of the natural inclinations. Good is to be understood in terms of the end.[14] Logic demands that if the act is disordered, the inclination or orientation to that act is also disordered. The end determines the judgment about the inclination or orientation. Stealing is morally disordered, so the inclination or orientation to steal is disordered. If the inclination or orientation to a certain end is good or neutral, then the act itself is good or neutral. The logic of the moral theory demands that if the homosexual act is disordered, then the inclination or orientation to that act is also disordered. The congregation from its perspective could not continue to allow Catholic statements to imply or even maintain that the homosexual orientation is neutral or good.

Thus the 1986 Letter clearly states, "Although the particular inclination of the homosexual person is not a sin, it is a more or less strong tendency ordered toward an intrinsic moral evil and thus the inclination itself must be seen as an objective disorder" (n. 3, p. 379). If the orientation or inclination is neutral or good, then the act is neutral or good.

The objectively disordered nature of the homosexual orientation is also logically necessary to support the position taken by the congregation on the legal aspects of homosexuality. Laws have been proposed and enacted to prevent discrimination against people because of race, ethnicity, gender, age, or sexual orientation. The congregation holds that rights such as the right to work, to housing, and so forth, are not absolute. They can be legitimately limited for objectively disordered external conduct. The homosexual orientation is not the same as race, gender, age, or ethnic origin. It is an objectively disordered orientation. Homosexuals thus can and should be treated differently by the law, whereas persons of different races, ethnic origins, gender, or age should not be discriminated against and treated differently.[15] Logically the moral and legal positions taken by the Congregation for the Doctrine of the Faith require the congregation to insist that the homosexual orientation is objectively disordered, even though so many have criticized that claim.

Thus this section proves that the congregation has a strong, forceful, aggressive, and unequivocal commitment to the present position on homosexuality. In no other issue has the hierarchical magisterium in general taken such practical initiatives to ensure that this official teaching is so clearly enunciated and pastorally protected against contrary encroachments. This approach constitutes very bad news indeed for those calling for a change in the teaching. One can readily understand why such proponents have been so negative about the recent documents.

Positive Aspects

Can these documents provide any basis for the possibility of change in the teaching of the hierarchical magisterium on homosexuality? Invoking Rynne's Law constitutes one possible approach. Xavier Rynne was the pseudonymous author whose "Letters from Vatican City" first appeared in *The New Yorker* during the sessions of Vatican II and provided the English-speaking world with an inside view of the workings and machinations of Vatican officials and bureaucrats. In a 1981 book Francis X. Murphy claims to have discovered in an analysis of the ecclesiastical events described by Rynne a definite pattern of change discernible in the doctrinal, moral, disciplinary, and structural aspects of the church. When faced with a new or evolving position or issue in which many people and theologians are calling for change, the magisterium staunchly and forcefully refuses to acknowledge any possibility of change. However, change soon occurs. Rynne's Law maintains that with the publication of a papal or hierarchical document that expresses a refusal to budge on the issue, an unwitting acknowledgment has been made of the fact that the turnabout is already in process. Actual change is thus accomplished by "reverse English."[16]

What about Rynne's Law? No one can doubt that Murphy has properly interpreted Rynne. A few years ago the heretofore coy Murphy publicly acknowledged that he was/is Xavier Rynne. However, is Rynne's Law true? Those looking for a change in the hierarchical teaching on homosexuality can find great solace in Rynne's Law. All must acknowledge the very forceful and unprecedented defense of the existing teaching on homosexuality made in the most recent documents. The application of Rynne's Law thus provides great hope even in the midst of the massive evidence to the contrary.

Undoubtedly Murphy–Rynne can point to many occasions in which Rynne's Law has been verified. However, in more recent times one looks in vain for illustrations of Rynne's Law. Begin with the issue of contraception. The hierarchical magisterium has been adamant and, despite massive disagreements by Catholic spouses in practice and Catholic theologians in theory, the hierarchical magisterium has not changed its teaching. In fact the hierarchical magisterium has even devised a new defense for the teaching. The church in bearing witness to the message of Jesus must often be countercultural. Even though the majority of people espouse a particular position, the church in the tradition of the prophets must remain faithful to and continue to practice and bear witness to the truth.[17] (I do not see how such a countercultural emphasis is compatible with the traditional Catholic recognition that its moral teachings are based on natural law which is common to all human beings.) Proponents of change in other areas of sexuality, church structures, and the role of women in the church have also been disappointed. Perhaps Rynne's Law needs more time in order to become effective. But perhaps the law itself is somewhat biased and not always true.

Can proponents of change appeal to anything other than Rynne's Law in their analysis and interpretation of recent hierarchical documents on homosexuality? My response is yes. The 1986 Letter itself offers some basis for a positive answer, but this support is muted and barely visible to the naked eye. Yet its reality cannot be denied. The support exists not on the level of the specific conclusions about homosexuality, but on the level of moral methodology. Again the 1986 Letter deals primarily with pastoral approaches, but it also mentions ever so briefly some of the methodological aspects of the Roman Catholic tradition in moral theology. Five methodological aspects mentioned there provide significant bases for changing the hierarchical teaching—the role of reason; the realization that God's law and the natural law are based on what is for human good, fulfillment, and perfection; the role of the sciences; the critical interpretation of the scripture;

and the living tradition of the church with the dependent role of the hierarchical teaching office. The proponents of change in the teaching on homosexuality have appealed to these same methodological understandings to make their point. This section will now examine each of these issues.

The Role of Reason. The 1986 Letter states that "the Catholic moral viewpoint is founded on human reason illumined by faith . . ." (n. 2, p. 377). The Roman Catholic tradition has consistently insisted on the importance of both faith and reason and has asserted that faith and reason cannot contradict one another. The significant role of theology in the Catholic tradition flows from the importance of human reason. Catholic theology rests on the twofold aspect of faith seeking understanding and understanding seeking faith. The role of reason has been prominent in moral theology. Catholic moral teaching has traditionally been based on the natural law or human reason and not directly on scripture or revelation. Human reason by reflecting on human nature can arrive at true ethical wisdom and knowledge. Contemporary Catholic social teaching recently appeals, and correctly so, to all people of good will.

Of course the ultimate problem comes from determining whose reason or what reason. The 1986 Letter and contemporary hierarchical teaching on sexuality in general understand reason in terms of a manualistic concept of natural law which determines the proper ordering of acts on the basis of the faculty or the power from which they come.

Logically, reason constitutes a more general and broader term than natural law which is a particular understanding of human reason. The present theory of natural law actually did not exist prior to the individual teachings which it supports. The theory actually arose as a way to explain consistently, coherently, and systematically all the existing particular teachings. The Roman Catholic tradition has consistently recognized a mutual relationship between theory and practice. The theory changes, develops, and is modified in the light of the developing practices. Reason as the more general reality can and should critically evaluate the existing theory or method which is being employed.

The methodological approach followed in the 1975 Declaration is basically the same as that on which the later Letter is based. Many Catholic theologians have strongly criticized that methodological approach. For our purposes it suffices just to mention some of those criticisms—a failure to give enough importance to historical and cultural developments; a passive role for human reason merely discovering the values embedded in human nature; an overly deductive methodology based on eternal, universal principles founded on human nature; an overemphasis on the finality of the sexual act and faculty and not enough emphasis on the person; a physicalism which too readily identifies the moral aspects of the act with the physical aspects; a deontological ethical model based on natural law which claims too great a certitude for its conclusions and applications; and a failure to pay enough attention to the experience of people.[18]

Those who disagree with the official hierarchical teaching on homosexuality have a different understanding of the meaning of sexuality for gays and lesbians. The historical Catholic emphasis on the goodness of human reason and its ability to come to true ethical wisdom and knowledge can be the basis for criticizing the very way in which reason is understood and employed in the teaching of the hierarchical magisterium.

Morality and Human Fulfillment. The Roman Catholic insistence on faith and reason and the goodness of reason stems from the central Catholic emphasis on mediation, or sacramentality, as it is sometimes called. According to the principle of mediation the divine is mediated in and through the human. The human is not evil, but good and positively related to the divine. As a result Catholic theology has strongly acknowledged that the glory of God is the human person come alive. God's law, if you want to use that term, calls for all human beings to come to their fulfillment and happiness. Thomas Aquinas in the very beginning of his *Summa theologiae* maintains that the ultimate end of human beings is happiness.[19] In this context morality is intrinsic in the sense that what is moral and good constitutes human happiness and perfection. (Of course the Catholic tradition understands the human person in the broader context of community and not as an isolated individual.) In the best of the Catholic tradition, something is commanded because it is good and not the other way around.[20] The 1986 Letter strongly supports this classical Catholic approach, although using it for its own purposes. "As in every moral disorder, homosexual activity prevents one's own fulfillment and happiness by acting contrary to the creative wisdom of God" (n. 7, p. 380).

This very principle, however, can and has been used against the existing hierarchical teaching. Yes, the questions of what constitutes true humanity and true fulfillment generate much debate, but the question remains about what actually does serve the fulfillment and happiness of gays and lesbians.

The Role of the Sciences. A third somewhat related methodological issue concerns the role of the sciences in the moral judgment. The Catholic approach which is so open to the human and human reason must also be open to learn from the human sciences. The sciences can tell us quite a bit about the human and hence about morality. On the other hand, each individual science is limited and cannot simply be identified with the totality of the human. The human includes all the different aspects—the psychological, the sociological, the eugenic, the biological, the physical, the psychic. Human moral judgments must take all these aspects into account, but the human moral judgment comprises the ultimate and all-inclusive judgment. Nothing in this finite world is ever perfect from every possible perspective. We all know the problems and difficulties in determining the proper balance among all these aspects. Think, for example, about the contemporary debate over sacrificing environmental concerns to economic concerns or vice versa. Sociologists, for example, might be able to achieve very important data by invading other people's privacy, but we say no to such approaches in the name of the human. Thus the Catholic tradition in its contemporary understanding recognizes the importance but also the limitations of a particular science or all the empirical sciences taken together.

The 1986 Letter recognizes and accepts the epistemological place of the sciences in Catholic understanding. The congregation claims that the Catholic moral perspective finds support in the more sincere findings of the natural sciences, which have their own legitimate and proper methodology and field of inquiry (n. 2, p. 379). "The church is thus in a position to learn from scientific discovery but also to transcend the horizons of science and to be confident that her more global vision does greater justice to the rich reality of the human person in his [*sic*] spiritual and physical dimensions created by God, and heir, by grace, to eternal life" (n. 2, pp. 377-379). The last part of the quotation appears to be overly defensive, but the basic thrust is in keeping with the best of the Catholic self-understanding.

Those who disagree with the present hierarchical teaching frequently appeal to contemporary psychiatry and psychology, although the practitioners of these disciplines do not all agree about the reality of homosexuality.[21] The human moral judgment embraces more than the psychological and the psychiatric, but these aspects remain very significant.

The Use of Scripture. The Catholic approach, as distinguished from some Reformation approaches, has rejected the axiom of the scripture alone. The Catholic emphasis on tradition, the role of the church and the Holy Spirit, and the use of reason form the basis for the rejection of *sola scriptura*. In the first part of the twentieth century, Catholic hierarchical teaching firmly rejected the critical historical analysis of the scripture, but ever since Pope Pius

XII's *Divino afflante Spiritu* in 1943 Catholics in general have accepted and used critical biblical scholarship.[22] One cannot go directly from a scriptural text embedded in its own historical and cultural circumstances to the present with its very different historical and cultural circumstances.

The Catholic approach in general and in the manuals of moral theology insists that its moral teaching is based primarily on human reason. Since Vatican II moral theology has given more importance to the role of scripture, but the sexual teaching still claims to have a rational and natural law basis. Reason and the scripture cannot be opposed.

The 1986 Letter of the congregation actually spends much more time discussing the scriptural basis for its judgment than the rational and natural law basis. The Letter focuses on the causes of confusion regarding the church's teaching with special emphasis on recent scriptural interpretations. The congregation cites and explains seven different texts to prove that homosexual relations are morally wrong. The 1986 Letter rejects the new exegesis of scripture "which claims variously that scripture has nothing to say on the subject of homosexuality, or that it somehow tacitly approves of it, or that all of its moral injunctions are so culture-bound that they are no longer applicable to contemporary life. These views are gravely erroneous and call for particular attention here" (n. 4, p. 379). Thus the document explains why it pays so much attention to the scriptures.

Despite this strong condemnation of some contemporary interpretations of scripture, the congregation remains true to the Catholic approach and even explicitly recognizes historical and cultural differences between the scriptures and our times. "It is quite true that the biblical literature owes to the different epochs in which it was written a good deal of its varied patterns of thought and expression (*Dei verbum*, 12). The church today addresses the gospel to a world which differs in many ways from ancient days. But the world in which the New Testament was written was already quite diverse from the situation in which the sacred scriptures of the Hebrew people had been written or compiled, for example" (n. 5, p. 379). The Letter explicitly recognizes that its own conclusion about homosexuality does not logically follow from this above understanding of the scripture. "What should be noticed is that, in the presence of such remarkable diversity, there is nevertheless a clear consistency within the scriptures themselves on the moral issue of homosexual behavior" (n. 5, p. 379). Note the "nevertheless."

Many scholars from Derrick Sherwin Bailey in 1955 down to the present have used the understanding of the scriptural diversity and conditioning accepted by the congregation to justify homogenital behavior between constitutional homosexuals in a committed relationship.[23] Thus one can appeal to the methodological understanding of the role of scripture in determining Christian morality as proposed by the 1986 Letter to come to a very different moral judgment about homosexual behavior.

The Living Tradition and the Role of the Hierarchical Magisterium. Without doubt the most discussed and the most significant issue in contemporary Catholic morality concerns the role of the hierarchical teaching office. While forcefully and even aggressively defending the hierarchical teaching on homosexuality, the 1986 Letter briefly indicates an understanding of that hierarchical magisterium which recognizes its somewhat limited and dependent role. The hierarchical magisterium is not the only or the highest authority in determining Catholic moral teaching in general.

An earlier section pointed out that the Catholic tradition sees the morally obligatory as what is for the good, the perfection, and the fulfillment of the human person called to live in community. Thus something is commanded because it is good. Consequently, the hierarchical magisterium itself does not make something true or good but must discover this basic truth or goodness. The hierarchical magisterium does not constitute the only or the highest source of truth and goodness in the Catholic tradition.

The 1986 Letter refers to "the church's living tradition" (n. 5, p. 379). This comparatively innocuous reference is most significant. The document could have omitted the word "living" but it did not. Tradition thus is a living reality. The church grows and develops. The experience of Vatican II underscored the reality of living tradition. The church must understand, appropriate, and live the word and work of Jesus in the light of the historical and cultural situation of today. Too often in the past, tradition was understood to be something that stopped fifty years earlier. A recognition of living tradition means that the church in general or the hierarchical magisterium in particular cannot just repeat what has been said in the past.

The 1986 Letter explicitly cites *Dei verbum*, n. 10 (The Dogmatic Constitution on Divine Revelation of the Second Vatican Council) to show that the hierarchical magisterium is not the only source of knowledge and truth. "It is clear, therefore, that in the supremely wise arrangement of God, sacred tradition, sacred scripture, and the magisterium of the church are so connected and associated that one of them cannot stand without the other.

Working together, each in its own way under the action of the one Holy Spirit, they contribute effectively to the salvation of souls" (n. 5, p. 379).

The 1986 Letter thus recognizes the magisterium functions in relationship to scripture and tradition. The very paragraph cited above in the 1986 Letter from the Dogmatic Constitution on Divine Revelation spells out in greater detail what that relationship entails. "The task of authentically interpreting the word of God, whether written [scripture] or handed on [tradition] has been entrusted exclusively to the living teaching office of the church, whose authority is exercised in the name of Jesus Christ. This teaching office is not above the word of God, but serves it, teaching only what has been handed on, listening to it devoutly, guarding it scrupulously, and explaining it faithfully by divine commission and with the help of the Holy Spirit. . . ."[24] Thus the hierarchical magisterium is the servant of the scripture and tradition. The three sources are not on an equal plane.

One influential commentary on The Dogmatic Constitution on Divine Revelation stresses the significance and consequences of such a view of the magisterium:

> When seen against this background, the explicit emphasis on the ministerial function of the teaching office must be welcomed as warmly as the statement that its primary service is to listen, that it must constantly take up an attitude of openness toward the sources, which it has continually to consult and consider, in order to be able to interpret them truly and preserve them—not in the sense of "taking them into custody" (to which sometimes the activity of the teaching office in the past may have tended), but as a faithful servant who wards off attempts at foreign domination and defends the dominion of the word of God both against modernism and against traditionalism. At the same time the contrast between the "listening" and the "teaching" church is thus reduced to its true measure: in the last analysis the whole church listens and, vice versa, the whole church shares in the upholding of true teaching.[25]

The author of this commentary is Joseph Ratzinger. Ratzinger sees in this paragraph of the Constitution a theology of the word and a renewed theology of the laity as totally rejecting the understanding of *solo magisterio*.[26] Those who are calling for a change in the hierarchical teaching on homosexuality accept, endorse, and propose just such an understanding of the magisterium in their attempt to change its teaching.

One cannot deny that the recent forceful reiteration of the hierarchical teaching on homosexuality is bad news for those trying to change that teaching. However, the 1986 Letter recognizes significant methodological approaches in the Roman Catholic tradition which are the same approaches employed by those who are trying to change the teaching. In the final analysis the methodological aspects are more important and will have more of an influence than the particular teaching itself.

Practical Conclusions

I believe that the methodological approaches traditionally associated with Roman Catholicism's discussion of morality support the arguments calling for a change in the hierarchical magisterium's forceful condemnation of all homosexual behavior. However, I am not a Pollyanna. This change will still take time, patience, much frustration, and great resolve. The factors aligned against such a change constitute a powerful force and will not quickly and readily disappear. Look at the record. The Roman Catholic Church has not changed on any of the significant points that have been discussed in the last twenty-five years.

In theory, in accord with the perspective of the hierarchical magisterium, change can only occur on those matters which are of church law and not of divine or natural law. The ordination of married men serves as one such example of church law. But even here the hierarchical magisterium refuses to change its teaching, even though more and more church communities are unable to celebrate the Eucharist together. The Eucharist has always served as the heart and center of Catholic life, but Catholic bishops are now busy preparing, devising, and carrying out non-Eucharistic liturgies. Thus change has not occurred even on a matter that all admit is not by anyone's definition unchangeable.

Matters of natural law by definition are said to be unchangeable precisely because they are the law that God has set down from all eternity and by definition cannot be changed. The church did not make these laws. God made them and the church cannot change them. I believe that just such an understanding lies behind the strong rhetoric used in defense of such teachings. God is on our side, and we are defending God's law against all comers. Opponents point out that even Thomas Aquinas recognized that the secondary conclusions of the natural law are removed from the first principles and can admit of exceptions.[27] But the hierarchical magisterium has never recognized such an approach.

The support at the present time for a change in the hierarchical magisterium's teaching on homosexuality is weak if compared with those seeking a change in the teaching on artificial contraception for married couples. If the Catholic church's hierarchical magisterium will not change its position where the arguments, the pressure, and the numbers seem so strong, it is not going to change very quickly on the issue of homosexuality.

As all recognize, the hierarchical magisterium finds change difficult and above all is most reluctant to admit that its teachings have been wrong and need to change. Perhaps the most significant change of Vatican II on a specific issue concerned the teaching on religious liberty. The major issue concerned not the teaching itself but the problem of change. How could the church teach in the twentieth century what it denied in the nineteenth? The problem was solved by a theory of development which claimed that the historical circumstances had changed so that the church was right in both centuries.[28] I believe the unwillingness to admit that its teaching has been wrong constitutes the major reason why the hierarchical magisterium has not changed its teaching on artificial contraception. For all practical purposes Pope Paul VI admitted that in his encyclical *Humanae vitae.*[29]

Most of the problem areas in discussion today in the Catholic Church concern the issue of sexuality. I am sure many unconscious fears, anxieties, and power questions are involved in these issues. I do not have the competency to explore these matters. However, some very legitimate fears and questions also exist. Where should the church draw the line? The church cannot merely accept everything being done today. A one-sided individualism infects many aspects of contemporary life including sexuality. Fear of what will follow if some changes are made grounds another strong reason in favor of the status quo.

Some maintain that change on homosexuality and other issues does not occur because of a few powerful personalities holding office in the church. Undoubtedly personalities do make a difference, but the opposition to change comes from deeper sources than just a few personalities. In other words, changes in personalities are not necessarily going to open the door to change.

I do not underestimate the forces working to uphold the status quo, but I still believe that the Catholic tradition, approach, and methodology in morality give grounds to support a change in the hierarchical magisterium's teaching on homosexuality.

Notes

1. Different authors use different ways to arrive at this conclusion. For an overview see *Homosexuality in the Church: Both Sides of the Debate,* ed. Jeffrey S. Siker (Louisville, Ky.: Westminster/John Knox, 1994); *Homosexuality and*

Ethics, ed. Edward Batchelor (New York: Pilgrim, 1980); Anthony Kosnik, et al., *Human Sexuality: New Directions in American Catholic Thought* (New York: Paulist, 1977), 200–209. My position sees these relationships as morally good for the constitutional homosexual, but falling short of the normative ideal of sexuality. See Charles E. Curran, *Critical Concerns in Moral Theology* (Notre Dame, Ind.: University of Notre Dame Press, 1979), 59–80.

2. Congregation for the Doctrine of the Faith, "Some Considerations Concerning the Response to Legislative Proposals on the Non-Discrimination of Homosexual Persons," *Origins* 22 (1992): 173–77.
3. Congregation for the Doctrine of the Faith, "Letter to the Bishops of the Catholic Church on the Pastoral Care of Homosexual Persons," *Origins* 16 (1986): 377–82.
4. The reference refers to the paragraph numbers of the document and the page in *Origins*. All subsequent references are to the 1986 Letter unless explicitly indicated.
5. For a perceptive analysis and critique of the Vatican's position on homosexual orientation, see Robert Nugent, "Sexual Orientation in Vatican Thinking," in *The Vatican and Homosexuality,* ed. Jeannine Gramick and Pat Furey (New York: Crossroad, 1988), 48-58.
6. Congregation for the Doctrine of the Faith, "Declaration on Certain Questions Concerning Sexual Ethics," *The Pope Speaks* 21 (1976): 66.
7. National Conference of Catholic Bishops, "To Live in Christ Jesus," as cited in *Homosexuality and the Magisterium: Documents from the Vatican and United States Bishops,* ed. John Gallagher (Mount Ranier, Md.: New Ways Ministry, 1986), 9.
8. Archbishop John R. Roach, "Statement on Homosexuality," January 1978, in *Homosexuality and the Magisterium,* 10; Archbishop John R. Quinn, "A Pastoral Letter on Homosexuality," May 5, 1980, in *Homosexuality and the Magisterium,* 25; Archbishop James A. Hickey, "Letter on Homosexuality," April 5, 1984, in *Homosexuality and the Magisterium,* 94–95.
9. Pope John Paul II, "In Love, Faithful to the Truth: Address to the Episcopal Conference of the United States, October 5, 1979," *The Pope Speaks* 24 (1979): 352.
10. John Mahoney, *The Making of Moral Theology: A Study of the Roman Catholic Tradition* (Oxford: Clarendon, 1987), 224–58.
11. 1975 Declaration, n. 5, *The Pope Speaks* 24 (1979): 64.
12. Ibid., nn. 4–5, pp. 62–64.
13. Ibid., 64 ff.
14. Thomas Aquinas, *Summa theologiae* 4 vols. (Rome: Marietti, 1952), I II, q. 94, a. 2.

15. "Some Considerations," nn. 10-16, pp. 176–77.
16. Francis X. Murphy, *The Papacy Today* (New York: Macmillan, 1981), 2–3.
17. For a description of the hierarchical teaching on contraception as prophetic, see Pope John Paul II, *The Role of the Christian Family in the Modern World—Familiaris consortio* (Boston: Daughters of St. Paul, 1981), n. 29, p. 47.
18. Richard A. McCormick, *Notes on Moral Theology 1965 through 1980* (Washington: University Press of America, 1981), 668-682.
19. Aquinas, *Summa*, I, q. 1-5.
20. Mahoney, 235–45.
21. For appeals to psychiatry and psychology in ethical discussions of homosexuality, see many of the authors in Batchelor, *Homosexuality and Ethics.*
22. Gerald P. Fogarty, *American Catholic Biblical Scholarship* (San Francisco: Harper, 1989).
23. Derrick Sherwin Bailey, *Homosexuality in the Western Christian Tradition* (London: Longmans, Green 1955), 29–63.
24. Dogmatic Constitution on Divine Revelation, n. 10, in *The Documents of Vatican II*, ed. Walter M. Abbott (New York: Guild, 1966), 117–18.
25. Joseph Ratzinger, "Dogmatic Constitution on Divine Revelation, Chapter II," in Herbert Vorgrimler, ed., *Commentary on the Documents of Vatican II*, 5 vols. (New York: Herder and Herder, 1968), vol. 3, 197.
26. Ibid., 196.
27. Aquinas, *Summa*, I II, q. 94, a. 5.
28. John Courtney Murray, "Vers une intelligence du dévelopment de la doctrine de l'Église sur la liberté religieuse," in Jerome Hamer and Yves Congar, eds. , *Vatican II: La liberté religieuse, declaration 'Dignitatis humanae personae'* (Paris: Cerf, 1967), 111–47.
29. Pope Paul VI, *On the Regulation of Birth: Humanae vitae* (Washington: United States Catholic Conference, 1968), n. 6, p. 4.

~ 8 ~

Law, Public Policy, and Gay and Lesbian Rights

This chapter addresses the issue of sexual orientation and human rights from the perspective of Roman Catholicism. Logically this complex question has a number of different facets—the moral teaching about homosexuality, whether the teaching is proposed for all humankind and should be found convincing by those who do not share Catholic faith, the way in which religion should engage in public discourse, the relationship between morality and law, and finally the different aspects of law moving from the legality or illegality of homosexual acts, the rights of homosexual persons not to be discriminated against in our society, the provision of certain benefits to same sex couples, and the legal acceptance of gay marriages.

Focusing the Issue

From a logical perspective an important connection, although not necessarily an absolute agreement, exists between one's moral and one's legal position. If one believes that taking the life of a convicted criminal is morally wrong, one opposes capital punishment; the opposite is true as well. However, the connection is not absolute. One could be morally opposed to drinking alcoholic beverages but willing to respect the freedom of others to do so within American civil society. With regard to homosexuality, those who morally approve committed same sex relations invariably favor lesbian and gay rights ranging from no discrimination to the according of legal benefits to a committed couple in a same sex relationship. Those who view homosexual genital relations as immoral are more reluctant to support gay legal rights in their many dimensions. Thus one's position about the morality of homosexual genital behavior has a very important but not decisive influence on one's approach to legality and the civil rights of gay and lesbian persons.

As the previous chapter indicated, the Roman Catholic Church, like other religious bodies and society in general, experiences much ferment and discussion today in the area of sexuality in general and homosexuality in particular. The official hierarchical teaching of the Catholic Church condemns homosexual genital behavior since its criterion for the moral use of genital sexuality is limited to the context of a heterosexual marriage. However, many contemporary Catholic moral theologians have disagreed and called for a change in the existing hierarchical teaching. These disagreeing theologians come from two different positions. The one sees committed homosexual unions as morally good but lacking something that is found in heterosexual marriage. The second position sees the quality of the relationship as the moral criterion for both heterosexual and homosexual unions.[1]

Those who, like myself, disagree with the hierarchical teaching (I have adopted the first of the two positions mentioned above)[2] would be supportive of protecting gay and lesbian persons from discrimination in civil society and also approving same sex domestic partnerships with legal and social ramifications. I would not favor gay marriage as just another form of marriage. Thus the great importance of one's position on the morality of homosexual genital relationships and the need to give significant consideration to that question in any discussion about the civil rights of gay and lesbian people. But for three reasons this chapter is not going to develop the question of the morality of homosexuality from the Catholic perspective.

First, such a discussion would be repetitive. I and many others have written extensively on the issue and further discussion would add little or nothing to what has already been done.[3] Second, the very nature of the Roman Catholic Church with its hierarchical teaching office makes their position privileged and in the technical sense of the word "authoritative." I personally defend the rights of Catholics to dissent in theory and in practice from the hierarchical teaching on homosexuality. Many theologians do dissent from this teaching, and many committed gay couples continue to practice their Catholic faith. But the pope and bishops are the hierarchical teachers and the spokespersons for the positions of the church. Other Catholic individuals and groups are free to speak out on the issues and even propose positions contrary to the hierarchical teaching office, but they are not themselves authoritative spokespersons for the Roman Catholic Church, nor are they looked upon as such. Third, from a realistic perspective, the hierarchical magisterium is not going to change its teaching on homosexuality in the near future, having refused even to change its teaching on artificial contraception within marriage. In our American civil society, the hierarchical magisterium with its present moral teaching will continue to be the authoritative spokesperson for the Catholic Church even though there are other dissenting voices. As a result this chapter will focus on the Catholic understanding of the relationship between morality and law in general and how it bears on civil rights for gays and lesbians when one begins with the moral position of the hierarchical magisterium.

Some preliminary questions already mentioned in the introduction need to be addressed. Most, if not all, in the Catholic tradition—whatever their position on the issue of homosexuality—hold that the moral teaching is proposed for all humankind and not just for Catholics. Historically, Catholic moral teaching was based on the natural law which claimed to be common to and binding on all human beings. Appeals were not made primarily to revelation but to reason. More recently Catholic theology and teaching have incorporated more specifically theological and scriptural aspects into their approaches to morality but still claim that such teaching is applicable to all and can be convincing to all humankind.[4] Think of the modern papal encyclicals which are addressed to all people of goodwill. The United States bishops believe their position on nuclear disarmament, the economy, and abortion apply to all in society and should be convincing to those who do not share Catholic faith.[5]

Religion in general and Catholicism in particular have a right to try to influence and persuade society about what they believe to be for the public good. Roman Catholicism, more than any other Christian church, has appealed to reason and common human warrants in its approach to social morality, thus making it somewhat easier to hold a dialogue in an attempt to persuade all other citizens. Personally I do not think specifically religious language should be excluded from the public square. If you believe that the Christian Bible calls for justice for all, you have a right to argue and work for such a position in the public sphere. However, to be convincing to others, one cannot simply appeal to authority as such, be it biblical or church or whatever. However, biblical stories such as the Prodigal Son or the Good Samaritan can appeal to many people who do not share the same faith. Religious perspectives should not automatically be excluded from public discourse in the public square, but not everything that religions claim to be morally wrong should be prohibited by law or public policy. Law must have a truly political or civil purpose. What is such a truly political purpose? Most would recognize the public good or the common good as the criterion of a truly political purpose. Many differences arise about what constitutes this public good.[6] This chapter will discuss the thorny and fundamental question of the relationship between morality and law.

Two Different Theories

What is the understanding of the relationship between morality and law in the Catholic tradition? In this regard some significant development has occurred in recent Roman Catholic understanding at Vatican II.

As in other matters the Catholic tradition has given special attention to Thomas Aquinas. Aquinas, in his *Summa theologiae,* understood morality to be based on the natural law, which is the participation of the eternal law in the rational creature. Human law is derived from natural law. In fact, human law is truly a law and obliges only to the extent that it is derived from natural law. If something is not in accord with natural law, it will not be law but a corruption of law. The human law either directly promulgates the conclusions of the natural law (e.g., murder is a crime) or specifies what the natural law leaves undetermined (e.g., driving on the right side of the street).[7]

Aquinas, however, emphasizes that morality and law are not identical. He answers in the negative the question if it belongs to human law to prohibit all the vices. Human law is imposed on the multitude of human beings, the greater number of whom are not perfect in virtue. Human law should prohibit only the more grievous vices from which the greater number of people can abstain and especially those that are harmful to others and without which human society cannot be conceived, such as murder and theft.[8] Elsewhere Aquinas approves of Augustine's toleration and regulation of prostitution. His discussion of Augustine occurs in the context of his consideration of tolerating the rights of infidels. Human rule is derived from divine rule and should imitate it. The omnipotent and perfect God permits some evils to occur in this world lest greater goods would be taken away or more evils would occur. Human legislators can follow the same principle of tolerating evil lest certain goods are impeded or greater evils follow.[9] The principle of tolerating evil becomes very significant in subsequent debates.

Thomas also explicitly holds that the law should not command all the acts of all the virtues but only those that are ordered to the common good.[10]

The Thomistic approach thus recognizes two important differences between morality and law. Human law looks only to the common good and human law can and at times should tolerate evil. Both of these characteristics of human law are open to wide interpretation.

Two comments made in the pre-Vatican II Roman Catholic Church show the different approaches to toleration. William J. Kenealy in 1948 argued in favor of the Massachusetts law which forbade the sale, manufacture, exhibition, and advertising of contraceptives. He maintained that the majesty of our civil law should not sanction a perversion of God's natural law. No concern here is even given to the possibility of toleration.[11]

John Courtney Murray, writing in the 1950s about morality and law, points up the differences at times between the strictness of Catholic morality in sexual matters, which appalls libertarians, and the laxness of Catholic governments, which equally appalls puritans. Murray points out that in 1517 the number of prostitutes in the city of Rome (governed by the pope) considerably surpassed the number of married women. With a realistic shrug of the shoulders Murray laconically remarks that the figures are not edifying but they are interesting.[12] Here one gets quite a bit of toleration. Thus prudential judgments bear great weight with regard to both the principle of toleration as well as to what might be harmful to the common good. Here, too, one sees how the disposition of people, history, and so many other factors might enter into whether or not and to what degree one accepts toleration.

Vatican II proposed a different understanding of the relationship between morality and law. The council did not deal explicitly with the question of morality and law but it did discuss the role and function of government and law in a democratic society in its Declaration on Religious Freedom. The document in this case is following the approach of the American Jesuit, Murray. One should point out that the final document of the council on religious freedom does not follow Murray's viewpoint totally, but it does accept his understanding of the role and function of law in a pluralistic democratic society.[13]

Some wanted to see the issue of religious freedom treated primarily as a theological question based on the freedom of the act of faith or a moral question based on the freedom of conscience. Murray, on the other hand, frames the issue as formally a juridical or constitutional issue which has foundations in theology, ethics, and political philosophy. The understanding of constitutional government and its proper role grounds Murray's approach to religious freedom.[14]

The Declaration on Religious Freedom deals with the jurisprudential and constitutional question in its discussion of the limits of religious freedom. When can and should government intervene in the exercise of religious freedom? In so doing the council proposes what Murray himself called the basic principle of the free society and what he thinks secular experts consider the most significant sentence in the Declaration—"For the rest, the usages of society are to be the usages of freedom in their full range. These require that the freedom of man [*sic*] be respected as far as possible and curtailed only when and insofar as necessary."[15] In the use of all freedoms the moral principle of personal and social responsibility is to be observed. But society has the right to defend itself against abuses committed under the pretext of freedom. Here juridical norms in conformity with the objective moral order are to determine when the coercive force of law can intervene. Law can and should intervene to protect public order which constitutes the basic component of the common good. The public order involves an order of justice and rights, public peace, and public morality.[16]

In his own writings, Murray develops somewhat the meaning of these concepts. Murray sees an important distinction between the common good and the public order based on the distinction between society and the state. In the constitutional tradition the state plays only a limited role within society. The purposes of the state are not coextensive with the purposes of society. There are many other groups and institutions within society besides the state. The state as a part of society uses its coercive power for the benefit of society. On the basis of the distinction between society and the state, Murray makes the distinction between the common good and the public order. The pursuit of the common good devolves upon society as a whole—all its members and all its institutions in accord with the principles of subsidiarity, legal justice, and distributive justice. The public order is a narrower concept indicating where the coercive power of the state may be used. The public order involves an order of justice, of public morality, and of public peace. Murray does not develop these but only mentions, for instance, that public morality comprises certain minimal common standards accepted among the people.[17]

Murray properly recognizes significant shifts represented by this teaching. The Catholic Church has now accepted the theory and practice of a limited, free, constitutional, democratic state.[18] Yes, there is no doubt that the Catholic Church has learned much from the Enlightenment and its understanding of the political order which at one time it strongly opposed. Catholicism has traditionally seen the individual as a part or member of the broader society and political community. In the language of the contemporary debate, Roman Catholicism has strongly favored a communitarian understanding of humankind. In the words of Aquinas and Aristotle, the human being is social and political by nature. From this perspective Roman Catholicism has been very slow to recognize the legitimate freedom and rights of individuals in political societies—to say nothing about freedom and rights within the church itself. The Declaration on Religious Freedom shows that the Catholic Church has finally accepted the notion of the limited, democratic, constitutional state. However, Catholicism is not accepting an individualistic anthropology and the absoluteness of free choice. Although the church has not given enough importance to freedom in the past, still freedom cannot be absolutized and must exist together with justice, truth, and charity.[19] To make sure that the communitarian dimension remains, I emphasize that the state's promotion and protection of justice also includes social justice.

The differences between these two understandings of the relationship between morality and law are significant but not total. First, the Thomistic approach begins with the moral law and then brings in common good and toleration to show that the legal can legitimately differ from the moral at times. The second approach begins with the freedom of the person; the coercive force of law must be justified by the requirements of the public order. The first position begins with the moral law and thus seems to give a presumption to the moral law, whereas the second position begins with the freedom of the person and gives the presumption to this freedom. This difference is very significant because it shapes the way the whole issue is looked at. The first position begins with the moral law and then sees if one can tolerate an evil. The second approach sees the issue as the right of the individual to act in accord with one's own conscience provided that the public order is not disproportionately hurt.

Second, the Thomistic and older approach makes the common good the purpose of law, whereas the Vatican II approach makes the public order the criterion for a proper use of the law. The public order is less expansive and inclusive than the common good and by definition forms just a part of the common good. The Declaration on Religious Freedom calls public order the basic element of the common good.[20]

Third, the older Thomistic understanding does not explicitly mention the role of freedom in the common good and in reality downplays the role of freedom. The Vatican II position emphasizes the role of freedom as a constitutive part of the common good of society and the need of the state to promote and protect that freedom. Thus one can readily see that the second approach as found in the Vatican II would find it easier to justify and defend the basic rights of lesbian and gay persons against discrimination in work, housing, public accommodations, and other areas.

Before applying this understanding to the rights of lesbian and gay persons, a possible objection arises. Is this theory on religious liberty really applicable to the question of morality and law in general and to the particular question of lesbian and gay rights? Murray's explanation underscores the religious freedom issue as being primarily a juridical and constitutional question that has broad implications and is not limited only to the issue of religious freedom. Murray's approach begins with a complex insight—the free human person under a government of limited powers. Religious liberty is not primarily a theological or ethical issue but a legal and jurisprudential one.[21] The Declaration on Religious Freedom begins by recognizing the growing sense of the dignity of the human person and the increasing demand that human beings should act on their own responsible freedom and not be driven by coercion. This requires that constitutional limits be placed on the power of government so there be no encroachments on the rightful freedom of the person and of associations. This demand for freedom in human society especially regards the quest for values proper to the human spirit—above all the free exercise of religion in society.[22] Thus there can be no doubt that the Declaration is providing criteria for the proper role of government not only in matters of religious freedom but in all matters of the responsible use of human freedom and its legitimate limitations through the coercive power of the state.

In addition, the right to religious freedom is comparable to the human right not to be discriminated against. Both are ultimately based on the dignity of the human person. The right not to be discriminated against is a fundamental human right and not just a remote or secondary human right. All free societies accept such an understanding of the right not to be discriminated against. However, just as there are limits on the rights to religious freedom, so too there can and should be limits on the right not to be discriminated against. The same basic principles are to be followed in both cases.

The Rationale in Favor of Nondiscrimination

The argument in favor of the rights of gays and lesbians not to be discriminated against begins with the principle that the freedom from discrimination "be respected as far as possible and curtailed only when and insofar as necessary." The presumption favors such a right to nondiscrimination or freedom from discrimination. Such a right can only be limited by the demands of the public order. In terms of the rights of others being violated, one possible limitation will be mentioned here. Can religious groups opposed to homosexual acts be forced to hire and employ people who are sexually active homosexuals? One could argue that their religious freedom to practice their own religion will thus be compromised by the state. I note this limitation here but will not delve any further into the issue.

The protection of gays and lesbians against discrimination in the same way as protection based on race or gender does not seem to be opposed to justice and social justice, but rather is a demand of justice. Such nondiscrimination does not harm the rights of others. Obviously having sex with a minor should be a criminal offense for both heterosexuals and homosexuals.

The criterion of public peace does not seem to raise any question for preventing discrimination against gays and lesbians, but the criterion of public morality has at times been invoked. The criterion of public morality, at the minimum, is contrasted with private morality. The very fact that one believes a certain action is morally wrong does not justify discriminating against people who do that action. The prior question concerns making illegal what one considers immoral. I know nobody in the Catholic tradition today who is arguing that homosexual acts between consenting adults in private should be illegal. Public morality is somewhat difficult to determine and to apply in a pluralistic society. One reason frequently invoked to justify some restrictions on the rights of gays and lesbians is the deleterious influence on marriage and the family that would come from the recognition of such rights. The Catholic tradition has always given great importance to the family as one of the three natural societies (family, state, and church) and seen the need to protect and promote the institutions of marriage and the family.[23] Will laws prohibiting discrimination against gays and lesbians apparently weaken marriage and the family?

Most authorities today recognize that no one chooses her or his sexual orientation. The *Catechism of the Catholic Church* accepts this understanding.[24] Thus individuals are not going to choose to be lesbian or gay so they can avoid marriage. In a certain sense one could argue that people who choose to be single are a greater threat to marriage and the family. However, no one has proposed any discrimination against single people. But there is a much more pertinent comparison. The Catholic approach to marriage sees divorce and remarriage as morally wrong. From this perspective divorce and remarriage constitute a threat to the institution of marriage with its characteristic of indissolubility. The sanctioning of divorce by law negatively affects marriage and the family more than protecting gays and lesbians against discrimination. Catholics today are not even bothering to oppose or change the civil law on divorce, let alone calling for discrimination against divorced and remarried people.[25]

Thus the human right of gays and lesbians not to be discriminated against cannot be overturned by the demands of the public order. Such discrimination would be wrong. In the light of the methodology and conclusions proposed above, this chapter will now examine other approaches to the question.

Summary and Critique of Other Positions

Roman Catholic bishops in the United States have been divided in their positions about laws preventing discrimination against gays. Cardinals O'Connor of New York, Bernardin of Chicago, and Law of Boston (through the Massachusetts bishops) have opposed legislation outlawing discrimination against gays. However, Archbishops Quinn of San Francisco, Roach of St. Paul, Whealon of Hartford, and Weakland of Milwaukee have all supported nondiscrimination legislation,[26] and the bishops of Florida and Oregon have opposed state proposals that would prohibit laws protecting the rights of homosexuals.[27]

A very curious document came from the Congregation for the Doctrine of the Faith in 1992 concerning legislative proposals on discrimination against homosexuals. The document was originally sent privately only to the bishops in the United States, was made public by an unofficial Catholic group, and then subsequently published with a few changes by the Vatican. According to this document sexual orientation is not comparable to race, ethnic background, sex, or age with regard to nondiscrimination because it is an objective disorder and is essentially private and unknown unless the person chooses to publicly so identify oneself. Homosexuals have the same rights as all human persons, but these rights are not absolute and can be limited, for example, in the placement of children for adoption or foster care, the employment of teachers or athletic coaches, and military recruits. In releasing the document for publication the Vatican spokesperson also released an explanation of the document. These considerations were originally given to the bishops of the United States as a background resource for whatever help they might provide the bishops and were not intended as an official and public instruction of the congregation. These observations also do not pass judgment on any responses already made by bishops or state conferences in the United States. [28] Archbishop Quinn of San Francisco pointed out that the bishops of California and himself had opposed discrimination against gay and lesbian persons and their policy will continue even after the Vatican document.[29]

As might be expected, the position accepting discrimination or some limitation of the human rights of lesbian and gay persons often follows the Thomistic approach and begins with the moral teaching of the church. Cardinal Joseph Bernardin of Chicago, a well-respected, moderate prelate, opposed a proposed gay rights ordinance that came before the Chicago City Council in 1986. In defending his position, Bernardin explained that in the case of gay rights legislation he seeks to balance two values—first, no person should be discriminated against because of sexual orientation and, second, the normativeness of heterosexual marital intimacy for genital relations.[30] Bernardin insists, of course, that he is speaking about public morality—those areas where the state can legitimately legislate. "As a teacher of morality and a citizen, I want to protect the rights of all citizens but I cannot support public protection or sanctioning of sexual activity or a way of life which compromises the normativeness of heterosexual marital intimacy."[31] My purpose is not to refute in depth the Bernardin position but simply to note the underlying theory on which it is based. One begins with a moral teaching regarding the normativeness of heterosexual marital intimacy and moves from there to public policy or legislation. Here Bernardin apparently sees no reason to prevent the move from morality to legislation or any reason to tolerate the evil he sees. By invoking public morality, and in the light of other approaches, one would expect Bernardin to prove that such nondiscrimination would have a negative effect on marriage and the family. But the Chicago Cardinal moves from morality to legality without any other considerations.

One scholar, John M. Finnis, rejects the Thomistic view of the relationship between law and morality and appeals to the Vatican II understanding to support his position of some restrictions on gay and lesbian civil rights. Finnis describes the standard modern European position according to which the state is not authorized to make adult homosexual acts in private a punishable offense, but states can discourage homosexual conduct and orientation.[32] Finnis, a Catholic philosopher, uses the moral theory associated with Germain Grisez and himself to argue for the immorality of homosexual genital relations. The moral acceptance of homosexual relations is an active threat to the stability of existing and future marriages. A political community which judges that the family and family life are of paramount importance for the community can rightly judge that it has a compelling interest in denying homosexual conduct or a gay lifestyle as a humanly acceptable choice and form of life and is thereby doing what it properly can as a community to discourage such conduct.[33]

In conjunction with his basic thesis that the state cannot criminalize consensual adult homosexual acts in private but can discourage homosexual orientation and lifestyle for the good of society, Finnis develops and defends what he calls an instrumental, not a basic, intrinsic, or constitutive understanding of the common good.[34] A constitutive, basic, or intrinsic notion of the common good denies the subsidiary function of the state and authorizes the state to direct people to virtue and to deter those from vice by making even private and consensual adult acts of vice a punishable crime.

Finnis identifies such an intrinsic, basic, and constitutive notion of the common good with Aristotle and the principle laid down by Thomas Aquinas in his T*reatise on Princely Government,* according to which government should command whatever leads people toward their ultimate heavenly end, forbid whatever deflects them from that end, and coercively deter people from doing evil and induce them to morally decent conduct. In a footnote Finnis claims that in two places in the *Summa* (which we mentioned above) Aquinas qualifies but does not abandon this approach.[35]

Finnis proposes an instrumental notion of the common good as found in the Vatican II teaching on religious liberty. This teaching on religious freedom first insists that everyone has the right not to be coerced in religious matters because religious acts transcend the sphere of government. Second, the council puts limits on religious freedom and here Finnis quotes the passages about public order including the protection of the rights of all citizens, public peace, and public morality. However, the common good, in order to protect the institution of marriage, justifies restricting the rights of homosexuals.[36] Thus Finnis claims to be following what I have called the Vatican II approach to the relationship between law and morality, and he comes to a conclusion diametrically opposed to mine.

However, I do not think Finnis appreciates and follows the full approach to the role of morality and law found in the Declaration on Religious Freedom and in the work of John Courtney Murray. He never cites what Murray called the basic principle of the free society and the most significant passage of the Declaration from the perspective of secular experts—freedom is to be respected as far as possible and curtailed only when and insofar as necessary.[37]

Nowhere in his discussion of law and morality does Finnis mention freedom, let alone the presumption in its favor. He fails to point out that freedom is a very important component of the common good. Finnis' article also nowhere explicitly recognizes the reality of pluralism on the issue of homosexuality in our society. The logic of his argument seems to rest on the fact that all human beings not only accept the conclusion of his moral analysis of homosexual acts but also the moral theory on which it is based. In reality, as already pointed out, gay rights would not disproportionately harm marriage and family precisely because one's sexual orientation is not a matter of free choice. In addition, Finnis always uses the broader term "common good" rather than the narrower term "public order," although he does cite the Declaration's understanding of public order as the fundamental part of the common good. By its nature public order is less inclusive than the common good.

Finnis uses the Declaration on Religious Freedom to prove his point that the common good of society is instrumental and not basic or constitutive, but he ignores and apparently does not accept the broader jurisprudential and constitutional framework within which this teaching on religious liberty is set.

In general, most of the defenders of some possible discrimination against gay and lesbian persons not only do not use the Vatican II approach to the proper understanding of the relationship between morality and law, but also they do not accept its basic principles. In opposing a homosexual rights bill for their state, the bishops of Massachusetts maintained that the passage of legislation of this type would be seen by many as a step toward legal approval of the homosexual lifestyle. This concern is heightened by a common perception in our country that whatever is declared legal by that very fact becomes morally right. The tragic experience about abortion in this country in the last ten years shows the need for great caution in this area.[38] This understanding thus fails to recognize the distinction between morality and law found in the Declaration on Religious Freedom. As bishops their role is to propose the teaching of the church, in this case the proper role of the coercive force of government and law and the presumption in favor of freedom. Likewise, they fail to recognize that the civil law allows divorce and remarriage and does not discriminate against divorced people, but the Catholic Church still maintains its moral teaching on divorce. Catholic bishops have not made any attempt to change divorce legislation. It seems the Massachusetts bishops are looking at the question of gay and lesbian rights only through the narrow prism of their experience with abortion and they thereby fail to appreciate both the theory proposed in the Declaration on Religious Freedom and the experience gained from other issues such as divorce.

I think that the statement of the Massachusetts bishops helps to explain why those who hold the immorality of homosexual genital relations do not understand the relationship between morality and law in the light of Vatican II's teaching on the role of the state as found in its Declaration on Religious Freedom. First, in their own mind there exists a more direct relationship between morality and law than the conciliar understanding. They were probably trained in the older approach and have never really seen the issue in the light of the theory of the role of the state behind the teaching on religious liberty. It is easier to accept this theory when it safeguards the freedom of what they hold to be morally right (religious liberty) than when it might promote what they hold to be morally wrong (homosexual genital behavior).

The recent opposition of the United States Roman Catholic bishops to abortion as a matter of public policy has become the all-important analogy in their minds. These bishops have closely linked morality and law on this issue. (I have argued against changing the existing permissive law on abortion on the basis of the conciliar view of the relationship between morality and law. However, I recognize that someone else using such an understanding of law who sees the fetus as a truly individual human being could justify restrictive abortion legislation.) To separate morality and law on the gay and lesbian rights issue might open the door to some relaxation in their struggle against legal abortion. It seems that abortion has become so significant an issue in their approach that the American Catholic bishops will do nothing that will in any way tend to weaken their legal approach to abortion. As noted earlier, the legal aspects of divorce are a closer analogue to the legal aspects and rights of homosexual persons.

I think something else is also at work today in the mentality of the United States Catholic bishops. There is a moral rigorism present which too readily identifies the moral and the legal. In the language of the older approach, there is less willingness to tolerate evil now than there was in the past. Think, for example, of the opposition of the United States Catholic bishops to using condoms to prevent the spread of AIDS.[39] If there ever was a clear case of counseling the lesser of two moral evils or tolerating an evil (from their perspective) to avoid a greater one, this would be the case. I will leave it to people more expert than I to say where this rigorism comes from—Anglo–Saxon mentality, Irish and French rigoristic Jansenism, the all-controlling influence of the abortion debate. One thing is sure—there is a rigorism showing itself today in the American Catholic bishops' reaction to questions of morality and public policy.

One might expect those arguing in favor of nondiscrimination laws for lesbian and gay persons, especially when writing from a more scholarly perspective, to appeal to the Vatican II understanding of the role of the state and the relationship between morality and law. But as a matter of fact I have not found such approaches. John Touhey argues against the document of the Congregation for Doctrine of the Faith and in support of the civil rights of gay and lesbian persons on the basis of the principle of toleration—the older approach. He cites Augustine, Aquinas, and the Catholic response in England to the Wolfenden Report in justifying the invocation of toleration here. He buttresses his argument by showing that such rights will not undermine the social fabric especially with regard to marriage and the family.[40]

Robert Nugent, who has written extensively on the issues of homosexuality and who has exercised a very significant pastoral ministry to lesbians and gays, also argues against the 1992 Document of the Congregation for the Doctrine of the Faith calling for restrictions on the rights of homosexual persons. Nugent takes up the arguments of the congregation and explicitly refutes them without developing a positive rationale of his own on the relationship between morality and law. He maintains, for example, that sexual orientation is comparable to age, sex, gender, and race as a basis for nondiscrimination in the civil forum. Nugent insists that the Vatican respect its own distinction between sexual orientation and action and also shows that gay rights would not be harmful to marriage, the family, and the common good.[41]

Richard A. Peddicord also argues that the Catholic teaching should accept and promote the civil rights of gay and lesbian persons with no restrictions or discrimination. Peddicord sets up his understanding of the issue as a conflict between the justice tradition of the church, with its heavy contemporary emphasis on human rights and its sexual teaching. He thus argues for the primacy of the justice aspect especially in the light of the fact that the civil rights of gays and lesbians will not harm marriage, family, and the common good. Peddicord uses this statement of the issue precisely because many of the proposals made by bishops, for example, Cardinal Bernardin's approach, uses such an understanding and sees the issue in terms of the tension between those two.[42]

In my judgment, it is surprising that Catholic defenders of gay and lesbian civil rights do not employ the Vatican II understanding of the role of government and law. Nugent's and Peddicord's arguments would be even stronger within that context. However, both of them have chosen to respond to the issue on the same basis that others have used to argue for some limitation of civil rights.

Domestic Partnership Laws

What about domestic partnership laws? At the very minimum logic recognizes that on the basis of the Vatican II approach described above it will be much harder to justify domestic partnership laws for gays than to justify nondiscrimination laws. The right not to be discriminated against is a very basic and fundamental human right, whereas domestic partnership laws do not touch on such a fundamental human right. Perhaps even more significant in the light of the theory is the fact that rights against discrimination are basically an immunity—a freedom from unjust discrimination. The Vatican II theory proposed above recognizes that freedom must be promoted as much as possible and curtailed only when necessary. However, domestic partnership laws do not involve an immunity or a freedom from but rather an entitlement—a positive giving of some benefit. The Vatican II approach is much more open to justifying immunities than entitlements.

The factual situation also bears out the contention that given the hierarchical Catholic teaching on homosexuality and especially homosexual genital relations, it is more difficult to justify domestic partnership laws than nondiscriminating human rights laws for gays and lesbians. I have found no one holding the hierarchical moral teaching who argues in favor of domestic partnership laws. Archbishop John Quinn of San Francisco, who has been a strong supporter of nondiscrimination and the rights of gays and lesbians, has opposed across the board domestic partnership laws.[43]

Domestic partnership laws recognize and encourage homosexual unions by providing legal recognition and certain benefits for the couple involved. This is much more than just respecting the basic human rights of all, including homosexuals. Those who are morally opposed to a position can more readily grant civil rights to those they accuse of being morally wrong than positively support a same-sex union they consider to be morally wrong. By recognizing unions other than the union of marriage, society at the very minimum detracts somewhat from its protection and promotion of marriage.

However, an argument can be made for domestic partnership laws, but I admit it is not nearly as convincing as the argument for nondiscrimination against gay and lesbian persons. At the very minimum such partnership laws are not going to discourage heterosexual people from getting married. Even the *Catechism of the Catholic Church* recognizes that people do not choose their sexual orientation. Consequently, domestic partnership laws are not going to entice some people into a homosexual union who otherwise would have become married. In reality it seems that such provisions for domestic partnerships will not denigrate or harm the institutions of marriage and the family.

To justify support for such partnership laws, the Catholic tradition could appeal to the general principle of counseling the lesser of two moral evils.[44] This principle is somewhat related to the general toleration principle—one can tolerate evil to insure that greater good or lesser evil will occur. On an individual basis one could counsel a person who is determined to be homosexually active to live in a stable and faithful homosexual relationship as a lesser evil than engaging in promiscuous homosexual genital encounters. In an analogous way one can argue in favor of domestic partnership laws as a way of avoiding the greater evil of promiscuous sexual liaisons. By promoting stable relationships one avoids a greater evil.

Again, the comparison with divorce is most apropos. The civil law not only allows divorce but it also provides civil recognition and benefits to divorced and remarried people. Catholic leaders are not engaging in any activities to change the present divorce law. In both cases the civil law is protecting and promoting to some degree a union that Roman Catholic teaching opposes. But giving legal provision and benefits to divorced and remarried people is more opposed to the Catholic understanding of marriage than domestic partnership laws precisely because people freely choose to divorce and remarry, but people ordinarily do not freely choose their sexual orientation. Thus one could maintain that the provision of domestic partnership laws does less harm to marriage and the family than do the existing laws about divorced and remarried people. However, in the present rigoristic environment, I do not think American Catholic bishops would make or accept this argument for domestic partnership laws.

In conclusion, this chapter has focused on the morality and law relationship in the Roman Catholic tradition to see how the official hierarchical moral teaching on homosexuality, especially homosexual genital relations, relates to the legal issues of civil rights for gay and lesbian persons. The approach to the morality–law relationship found in Vatican II has not been explicitly employed very often in this discussion, but such an approach offers a very firm foundation for laws protecting gays and lesbians against discrimination. On the other hand, such an approach at best provides a less firm foundation for supporting domestic partnership legislation.

Notes

1. For an overview of the positions of the many United States Catholic moral theologians calling for a change in the present hierarchical teaching on homosexuality, see Robert Nugent and Jeannine Gramick, *Building Bridges: Gay and Lesbian Reality in the Catholic Church* (Mystic, Conn.: Twenty-Third Publications, 1992), 146–56.
2. See Charles E. Curran, *Catholic Moral Theology in Dialogue* (Notre Dame, Ind.: Fides, 1972), 184-219; *Transition and Tradition in Moral Theology* (Notre Dame, Ind.: University of Notre Dame Press, 1979), 59–80; *Critical Concerns in Moral Theology* (Notre Dame, Ind.: University of Notre Dame Press, 1984), 73–98.
3. Ibid.
4. Charles E. Curran and Richard A. McCormick, eds., *Readings in Moral Theology No. 7: Natural Law and Theology* (New York: Paulist, 1991).
5. J. Bryan Hehir, "The Church and the Political Order: The Role of the Catholic Bishops in the United States," in *The Church's Public Role,* ed. Dieter T. Hessel (Grand Rapids, Mich.: Wm. B. Eerdmans, 1993), 176–97.
6. For a further development of my thinking on these issues see Charles E. Curran, *The Church and Morality: An Ecumenical and Catholic Approach* (Minneapolis, Minn.: Fortress, 1993), 65–91.
7. Thomas Aquinas, *Summa theologiae* (Rome: Marietti, 1952),I II, q. 95, a. 2.
8. Ibid., I II, q. 96, a. 2.
9. Ibid., II II, q. 10, a. 11.
10. Ibid., I II, q. 96, a. 3.
11. William J. Kenealy, "Contraception: A Violation of God's Law," *Catholic Mind* 46 (1948): 552–64.
12. John Courtney Murray, *We Hold These Truths: Catholic Reflections on the American Proposition* (New York: Sheed and Ward, 1960), 163.
13. For the development of the Declaration itself and Murray's role in it, see Richard J. Regan, *Conflict and Consensus: Religious Freedom and the Second Vatican Council* (New York: Macmillan, 1967).
14. John Courtney Murray, *The Problem of Religious Freedom* (Westminster, Md.: Newman, 1965), 19–22.
15. Declaration on Religious Freedom, n. 7, in *The Documents of Vatican II,* ed. Walter M. Abbott (New York: Guild, 1966), 687. Murray's comments are found on p. 687, fn. 21. In this edition the footnotes in italics are the official footnotes of the documents, while those in regular type are unofficial footnotes added by Murray himself.

16. Ibid., n. 7, pp. 685–87.
17. Murray, *Problem of Religious Freedom*, pp. 28–31: Declaration on Religious Liberty, *Documents of Vatican II*, fn. 20, p. 686.
18. Ibid., fn. 21, p. 687.
19. For a fuller discussion, see *Catholicism and Liberalism: Contributions to American Public Philosophy*. ed. R. Bruce Douglass and David Hollenbach (Cambridge: Cambridge University Press, 1994).
20. Declaration on Religious Freedom, n. 7, in *Documents of Vatican II*, 687.
21. Murray, *Problem of Religious Freedom*, 26.
22. Declaration on Religious Freedom, n. 1, in *Documents of Vatican II*, 675.
23. Margaret A. Farley, "Family," in *The New Dictionary of Catholic Social Thought*, ed. Judith A. Dwyer (Collegeville, Minn.: Liturgical Press, 1994), 371–81.
24. *Catechism of the Catholic Church* (Vatican City: Editrice Vaticana, 1994), n. 2358, p. 566.
25. For Catholic approaches, both historical and contemporary, to divorce laws, see Philip J. Grib, *Divorce Laws and Morality: A New Catholic Jurisprudence* (Lanham, Md: University Press of America, 1985).
26. Richard A. Peddicord, *Gay and Lesbian Rights: A Question: Sexual Ethics or Social Justice?* (Kansas City, Mo: Sheed and Ward, 1996), 63–95.
27. Florida Bishops, "On Discrimination Against Homosexual Persons," *Origins* 23 (1993): 395–96; "On File," *Origins* 24 (1994): 388.
28. Congregation for the Doctrine of the Faith, "Observations Regarding Legislative Proposals Concerned With Discrimination Toward Homosexual Persons," *Origins* 22 (1992): 175–77.
29. John R. Quinn, "Civil Rights of Gay and Lesbian Persons," *Origins* 22 (1992): 204.
30. Joseph L. Bernardin, "I Too Struggle," *Commonweal* 113 (1986): 682–84.
31. Ibid., p. 684.
32. John M. Finnis, "Law, Morality, and 'Sexual Orientation'," *Notre Dame Law Review* 69, no. 5 (1994): 1049–55.
33. Ibid., 1055–70.
34. Ibid., 1070–76.
35. Ibid., 1073. In my judgment, Thomas Aquinas in the *Summa* does modify such an approach by invoking the common good as the criterion grounding the purpose of human law. However, Thomas Aquinas holds a very inclusive concept of the common good.
36. Ibid., 1072–73.

37. Declaration on Religious Freedom, n. 7, in *Documents of Vatican II*, p. 687 and fn. 21.
38. "Bishops Oppose Homosexual Rights Bill," *Origins* 14 (1984): 73–74.
39. United States Catholic Bishops, "Called to Compassion and Responsibility: A Response to the HIV/AIDS Crisis," *Origins* 19 (1989): 429.
40. John F. Touhey, "The Principle of Toleration and the Civil Rights of Gay and Lesbian Persons," *New Theology Review* 7 (August 1994): 35–46.
41. Robert Nugent, "The Civil Rights of Homosexual People: Vatican Perspectives," *New Theology Review* 7 (November 1994): 72–86.
42. Peddicord, *Gay and Lesbian Rights*.
43. John R. Quinn, "Letter to Mayor Art Agnos," *Origins* 19 (1989): 50.
44. For the classical treatment of the principle in the manuals of moral theology, see I. Aertnys and C. Damen, *Theologia moralis*, 17th ed., 2 vols. (Rome: Marietti, 1956) vol. 1, n. 379, p. 366.

~ 9 ~

The Theory and Practice of Academic Freedom in Catholic Higher Education

The history of church-sponsored higher education in the United States shows repeated tensions over the issue of academic freedom. In the nineteenth century controversy arose between sponsoring churches and the Darwinian theory of evolution proposed by many in the academy.[1] Today the American Association of University Professors (AAUP), which has set out and monitored the standards of academic freedom, still grapples with the problem of academic freedom in church-related institutions. The 1940 Statement of Principles on Academic Freedom and Tenure, drawn up by the Association of American Colleges and the AAUP and subsequently affirmed throughout American higher education, contains an exception for religious institutions: "Limitations of academic freedom because of religious or other aims of the institution should be clearly stated in writing at the time of the appointment."[2] The AAUP today is clearly uncomfortable with such a limitations clause, but has not been able to come up with an agreed-upon understanding of academic freedom in church-sponsored institutions.[3]

This chapter will treat academic freedom in Catholic higher education. Historically Catholic higher education until the 1960s was strongly opposed to academic freedom for its own institutions and also for all American colleges and universities in general. In the later 1960s and early 1970s, a total change occurred with the mainstream of Catholic higher education firmly accepting academic freedom for itself. However, a few Catholic thinkers in the United States and some minor institutions staunchly opposed academic freedom. The authorities of the Catholic Church in the Vatican have never fully accepted the American understanding of academic freedom, but until this time they have done nothing to prevent its practical operation.[4]

Although Catholic colleges and universities in general have accepted academic freedom for over twenty years, the theoretical debate and practical determinations about the future of academic freedom have become more prominent at the present time in the light of the concerns of the Vatican and many different circumstances. The contemporary debate about academic freedom for Catholic higher education in the United States contains many aspects and levels. This chapter will discuss the meaning of academic freedom, the defense of academic freedom, the institutional understanding of Catholic higher education, and the struggle over the future of academic freedom in such institutions.

The Understanding of Academic Freedom

Before 1960 Roman Catholics in the United States strongly opposed the term and the concept of academic freedom. Many who oppose the accepted American understanding of it today take a different tack. Official church documents from the Vatican recognize the importance of academic freedom but insist on limits to it.[5] Others who limit and restrict academic freedom insist that it can be understood in many different ways. William J. Byron, who proposes ecclesial limits on it, begins a major article by saying, "There are perhaps as many descriptions of academic freedom as there are academics at work in the academy."[6] Carl J. Peter's article on the subject bears the title, "The Many Faces of Academic Freedom."[7] Such an appeal to a pluralism of understandings paves the way for accepting a limited, or special, Catholic notion of academic freedom.

Does a pluralism of understandings of academic freedom exist? In one sense, yes. Many different understandings of the subject prevail in different parts of the world. Academic freedom does not mean the same thing in Europe as in the United States.[8] These discrepancies arise from the different historical circumstances under which it came to be formulated and accepted. The German tradition, for example, has traditionally insisted on the academic freedom of the learner or the student, an aspect which theoreticians in the

United States did not discuss until much later.[9] However, even within the United States, different understandings and interpretations of academic freedom exist.[10] No one can deny such pluralism and diversity.

However, in the United States there exists an agreed-upon operational understanding of academic freedom that has been proposed, especially in the 1940 Statement of the Association of American Colleges and the AAUP, endorsed by the major academic societies, incorporated into the bylaws and faculty handbooks of American higher education in general, and almost universally accepted in the academy. The AAUP continues to comment on the meaning and procedures of academic freedom and to monitor compliance with its standards. These operational norms and practices are partial in the sense that they respond only to one aspect of the subject and even then do not adequately cover that one aspect. However, the framers and promoters of these norms and procedures deserve great credit because the American higher education community has voluntarily accepted them as normative.

In keeping with the United States' historical scene, academic freedom protects the teaching, research and publication, and extramural utterances of the professor against interference by the administration or governing body of the institution, often in response to pressure from outside the institution. In all these areas the faculty member also has correlative responsibilities. Academic tenure serves as the primary means of protecting academic freedom, although nontenured faculty are said to have the same academic freedom as a tenured professor. A tenured faculty member can be terminated only for "adequate cause" (incompetence, moral turpitude, *bona fide* financial exigency) in accord with elaborate due process proceedings calling for a committee of faculty peers to judge the case in the first instance with the final decision made by the governing board of the institution on the basis of the compiled record.[11]

This operational understanding of academic freedom is far from perfect. The understanding and the correlative norms protect only one aspect of academic freedom (that of the professor); do not cover that aspect completely (for that academic freedom might also be threatened by one's colleagues); insist on the procedural judgment by peers that does not necessarily guarantee fairness and justice; and protect some (the tenured) more than others (the nontenured). In my judgment such an understanding and procedure are good but far from complete and perfect. However, the best can often be the enemy of the good.

The Defense of Academic Freedom

The precise question concerns whether or not Catholic institutions of higher learning can accept this theory and practice of academic freedom. Theodore Hesburgh, former longtime president of the University of Notre Dame, has pointed out that the question of academic freedom for Catholic institutions arises especially in the case of theology. If Catholic theologians in a Catholic college enjoy it, then all other academics there will also have it.[12] In other words, making the case for the academic freedom of Catholic theologians is hardest to do because of the very nature of Catholic theology.

As a matter of fact, the mainstream of Catholic higher education since the late 1960s has accepted academic freedom in practice, but surprisingly little attention has been paid to the reasons for accepting such freedom. A later section will show that some very practical reasons threatening the continued existence of Catholic higher education had an influence on this swift and total change, but survival and growth can never become ultimate values that overrule everything else.

In deciding whether Catholic higher education should accept academic freedom, what is the primary question to be addressed? Why did some other churches, and the Catholic Church in particular, originally sponsor and support institutions of higher learning? Why do churches support other institutions such as hospitals and social service organizations? The ultimate reason is that the church maintains such institutions are good for the church in the light of its mission and purpose. The church should not sponsor institutions of higher learning if such sponsorship is not for the good of the church. The church, consequently, should consider the case for academic freedom in higher education on the basis of whether or not such an institutional arrangement is good for the church.

Those who oppose such an approach in Catholic higher education make their argument precisely on the basis of what is good for the church. The consistent rejection of academic freedom before 1965 emphasized that the hierarchical magisterium of the church has the God-given task to safeguard, protect, and promote the truths of revelation and does not depend on academic discussions that have no such promise of divine help.[13] In the contemporary debate, William J. Byron insists on ecclesial limits on academic freedom.[14]

Such an argument about academic freedom in Catholic higher education is analogous to the questioning of it for the country as a whole in the 1940 Statement. "Institutions of higher education are conducted for the common good and not to further the interest of either the individual teacher or the institution as a whole. The common good depends upon the free search for truth and its free exposition."[15] The very nature of the case, the arguments of those opposed, and the analogy of the justification of academic freedom based on the good of society as a whole, all clearly show that defenders of academic freedom must prove that such freedom is for the good of the church in church-sponsored institutions.

These paragraphs will summarize such a rationale for academic freedom in Catholic higher education which I have developed elsewhere in greater detail.[16] The academic freedom and autonomy of the Catholic college or university cohere with the affirmation of Vatican II about the legitimate autonomy of culture and the sciences.[17] The church should accept a free Catholic college just as it has accepted a free Catholic press as being in the best interests of the church itself. Academic freedom will make sure that theological discussion is never cut off prematurely. Catholic theology has always recognized and emphasized the need to understand faith in the light of tradition and contemporary reason and experience. Academic freedom for Catholic higher education thus will ensure that the Catholic tradition will always be a living tradition. Such an acceptance also bears witness to the traditional Catholic assertion that faith and reason cannot contradict one another. Especially in the United States context, such an acceptance of academic freedom bears witness to all inside and outside the church that the Catholic faith has no fear of honest dialogue and discussion of any kind. The existence of such freedom in the long run will enhance the credibility of the hierarchical teaching office in the church.

What about the problems that academic freedom will create for the church? The primary problem comes from the fact that theologians will make mistakes and perhaps influence those they teach and others to accept positions opposed to church teaching. All must recognize the problem, but it can be contained. The hierarchical magisterium always retains the right and the duty to point out that certain teachings are outside the pale of Catholic orthodoxy. Discussion by peers tests proposals by others. Such constructive criticism rightly limits the influence of a particular theologian and also safeguards the interests of the church to some degree. In the United States context, students and others always retain some skepticism about what an individual professor might say and propose on any given issue. In our society we are accustomed to the probing and questioning role of the academy. Professors by their own responsibility have the obligation to properly present and label their positions if and when they disagree with official hierarchical church teaching.

A convincing case thus can be made for academic freedom for Catholic higher education; but proponents of this position, including myself, have to recognize a very important practical problem. This position requires greater freedom for the theologian in the academy than in the church. The last section of this chapter will deal with the practical aspects of the future of Catholic higher education in the context of a more conservative church climate in which Vatican authorities are tightening the reins on Catholic theologians in the church. Such a climate makes it very difficult to convince such church authority that Catholic theologians in the academy should enjoy academic freedom.

A further issue arises among those who support and defend academic freedom for Catholic higher education. The AAUP standard maintains that even a tenured professor can be dismissed for incompetency in accord with due process proceedings with the judgment made in the first instance by faculty peers. "Competency" has never been spelled out in official AAUP documents, but it entails properly employing the method of the discipline. Catholic theology by its very nature has its own method which recognizes the sources of scripture, tradition, church teaching, reason, and experience. Someone who does not follow the method is incompetent and can be dismissed if the incompetence can be proved to a committee of faculty peers and ultimately the governing body of the institution.

Some have explicitly denied such an understanding of competence for the Catholic theologian. The crux of the matter concerns the meaning and existence of Catholic theology as a discipline in the academy. James John Annarelli has built on the approach of Schubert Ogden, who maintains that theology does not appeal to criteria of truth and meaning different from those employed by cognate disciplines. Annarelli understands Catholic theology as involving public accessibility so that Catholic theology is a university discipline like all others. In other words, the method of Catholic theology does not have anything unique about it or different from other cognate disciplines.[18]

In my judgment Catholic theology, with its specific sources and method, is different from cognate disciplines such as philosophy. What Annarelli proposes might be true of foundational theology, but not of systematic theology. In a contemporary context academics recognize the presuppositions of all disciplines. Such presuppositions are much more evident in disciplines such as feminist studies. Catholic theology presupposes its distinctive sources of revelation and church teaching. However, the judgment about incompetency in the academy must be made by academic peers and not by church authorities.

The debate about this point continues, but the crux concerns whether or not Catholic theology, with its own distinctive method, constitutes a legitimate university discipline. The practical ramifications of the question are enormous. If Catholic theology is not a true university discipline, then a very strong argument for the existence of Catholic colleges and universities no longer exists. If Catholic theology is a legitimate and specific university discipline, then one who is incompetent in its method can be dismissed on those grounds of incompetency, as judged in the first instance by peers. At the present time the AAUP appears to be willing to live with the two different approaches, so both can claim to be within the pale of the AAUP understanding of academic freedom.

The Institutional Identity of Catholic Colleges

A deeper layer of the academic freedom question for Catholic higher education involves the structural or institutional question. How does the Catholic college or university function, how is it Catholic, and how does it relate to the Catholic church?

The Magna Charta of the quick and almost total change in Catholic higher education's acceptance of academic freedom was the Land O'Lakes Statement issued in 1967 by twenty-six leaders of Catholic higher education in the United States and Canada. The opening paragraph makes the point clearly and succinctly:

> The Catholic university today must be a university in the full modern sense of the word, with a strong commitment to and concern for academic excellence. To perform its teaching and research functions effectively the Catholic university must have a true autonomy and academic freedom in the face of authority of whatever kind, lay or clerical, external to the academic community itself. To say this is simply to assert that institutional autonomy and academic freedom are essential conditions of life and growth and indeed of survival for Catholic universities as for all universities.[19]

Catholic higher education today thus sees a very close relationship between institutional autonomy and academic freedom. The mainstream Catholic colleges and universities have independent boards of trustees with a majority of lay persons and are not controlled by any church body or person. Such autonomy safeguards academic freedom in these institutions.

Institutional autonomy and academic freedom are closely related but not identical. In theory and in practice an institution could claim institutional autonomy to violate the academic freedom of its faculty. One could also have academic freedom without institutional autonomy. The institution could be owned and governed by a church group but clearly proclaim in its bylaws and official documents that the faculty enjoys full academic freedom. However, institutional autonomy does stand as a very significant way to establish and protect such freedom in Catholic institutions of higher learning.

This emphasis on autonomy in the Land O'Lakes Statement did not come primarily from a concern for academic freedom alone but from a different and more pressing concern threatening the survival and future of Catholic higher education in the United States. State and federal funding for Catholic higher education were threatened by two very significant court cases—*Horace Mann League v. Board of Public Works* (1966) and *Tilton v. Richardson* (1971).[20]

The trial of the Horace Mann case, which began in 1964 in the Circuit Court of Maryland, challenged grants totalling 2.5 million dollars made by the General Assembly of Maryland to four denominational colleges for the construction of college facilities. The two Catholic institutions were St. Joseph's College and the College of Notre Dame. The plaintiffs appealed the March 1965 negative decision of the Circuit Court to the Maryland Court of Appeals. On June 2, 1966, the Maryland court ruled that on the basis of a number of criteria three colleges, including the two Catholic institutions, were legally sectarian and thus the state grants to them involved the establishment of religion, which is prohibited by the First Amendment of the Constitution.

In April 1966 Francis X. Gallagher, the attorney for the Catholic institutions, addressed the National Catholic Educational Association and a meeting of the twenty-eight presidents of the Jesuit colleges and universities in the United States. Gallagher offered practical recommendations to guard against court challenges to the constitutionality of government aid to Catholic higher education on the basis of his experience in the Horace Mann case and the negative decision of the Maryland court. The Mann case was appealed to the U.S. Supreme Court but *certiorari* was denied.

The Catholic higher education community knew there would be further court challenges. The legal counsel for the plaintiffs in Mann was Leo Pfeffer, a well-known expert and advocate of a high wall of separation between church and state. The NCEA encouraged and sponsored a study by John J. McGrath, a canonical and civil lawyer at Catholic University, who maintained that charitable and educational institutions chartered as corporations under American law are owned by the corporation and not by the sponsoring religious body.[21]

Meanwhile, action continued in the courts. With Leo Pfeffer as lead attorney, fifteen taxpayers in 1968 challenged the constitutionality of Title I of the Higher Education Facilities Act of 1963 under which four Catholic colleges in Connecticut received federal construction grants for academic facilities in the amount of two million dollars. In spring 1970 the District Court unanimously rejected the plaintiffs' argument, but they appealed to the Supreme Court which in June 1971 ruled in favor of the four Catholic colleges in a narrow five to four decision. One of the reasons stated by Chief Justice Berger was that these colleges accepted academic freedom. Charles Wilson, one of the attorneys for the Catholic colleges, published through the National Catholic Educational Association a monograph on the subject pointing out on the basis of the decision what Catholic colleges should do to ensure that they could continue to receive state and federal funding.[22] In the late sixties in New York State, requirements for receiving state aid for higher education added another important influence to the move of Catholic institutions to juridical autonomy from the church or sponsoring religious community.[23]

The full history of this period in Catholic higher education has not been written. Elsewhere I have developed in depth the theological factors stemming from Vatican II and other cultural factors that influenced the move toward the acceptance of institutional autonomy and academic freedom for Catholic higher education.[24] But it is safe to say that the comparatively quick and total acceptance of autonomy and academic freedom in Catholic higher education would never have occurred if it had not been for the threat to government funding for these institutions. These historical circumstances and the quickly developing changes help to explain why there was no in-depth defense of academic freedom developed at this time.

A few commentators maintain that if Catholic colleges were more Catholic and not autonomous they would not lose their government funding.[25] However, another commentator points out that recent developments in Catholic church law and practice have already changed the attitude and approaches of Catholic institutions of higher learning, so that federal money should never be spent to aid these sectarian institutions.[26] On the basis of the past court decisions one can see how Catholic educators fear that any return to an earlier institutional understanding of Catholic colleges and universities would jeopardize state and federal funding.

Some Catholic institutions of higher learning have a two-tiered corporate structure that reserves certain powers to the religious community or diocese.[27] In theory the McGrath approach to legal canonical incorporation has been challenged.[28] But Catholic higher education is more committed than ever to academic freedom and institutional autonomy.

Opponents to this move by the mainstream of Catholic higher education see now the beginnings and development of the same movement that led to the secularization of many Protestant-founded colleges and universities in this country. The former provost of the University of Notre Dame has examined in detail how Vanderbilt University went secular and sees many of the same factors present in contemporary Catholic universities.[29] Catholic higher education in general has denied the charge that they have bargained away their Catholic identity by insisting on academic freedom and institutional autonomy. But such identity is and will be quite different from the pre-1965 Catholic identity of higher education. The next chapter will propose my understanding of Catholic identity in higher education.

Anomalies exist, some challenges are still raised; but the mainstream of Catholic higher education continues to proclaim its institutional autonomy and to stand up for academic freedom. However, the future structures and development of Catholic higher education with regard to academic freedom are very much in doubt.

The Future

What will happen in the future? Catholic higher educators themselves do not constitute the only decision makers who will have a say in what happens in the future. In terms of Catholic Church structures, the United States bishops and the pope with the Vatican Curia are very much involved and constitute the ultimate decision makers. The leaders of Catholic higher education recognize this fact and have tried to convince both the United States bishops and the Vatican authorities of the soundness of their position. These educators up to now have been more successful with the bishops than with Rome, although support from the bishops has waned in the light of a more aggressive position from the Vatican. In the end, on this issue as on many others, the United States bishops might very well find themselves caught in the middle between the mainstream leadership of Catholic higher education in the United States and the pope and Vatican authorities.

The United States Bishops. The leaders of Catholic higher education have made consistent, thorough, and, for a while, very successful efforts to convince the United States bishops to accept their understanding of Catholic colleges and universities as autonomous but still Catholic. The college and university presidents established a joint committee with bishops to discuss their mutual concerns. In 1977 the bishops issued a pastoral message on Catholic education, "To Teach as Jesus Did," that included a short discussion of higher education.[30] The bishops' statement recognizes the need for "responsible academic freedom" (n. 74). "While fully maintaining the autonomy concomitant to its being a college or university, the institution will manifest fidelity to the teaching of Jesus Christ as transmitted by His church" (n. 73). The language is somewhat ambiguous, but the terms autonomy and academic freedom are used and accepted. More importantly the bishops as a group in no way condemn or express doubts about the direction taken by Catholic higher education. The leaders of Catholic higher education had to be greatly pleased despite some ambiguity in wording. After all, actions speak louder than words and actions interpret words. In practice not even one single bishop publicly opposed the changes that had taken place in higher education.

In 1980 the United States Catholic bishops issued a pastoral letter devoted exclusively to higher education—"Catholic Higher Education and the Pastoral Ministry of the Church."[31] The document echoed a 1976 position paper from the College and University Department of the National Catholic Educational Association.[32] The bishops basically accepted the aspects of catholicity on campus that had been proposed by the educators. Catholic identity requires strong theology and philosophy departments, an effective campus ministry, a worshipping community on campus, fostering dialogue between faith and the modern world, and giving institutional witness to the compatibility of faith and reason. The bishops supported institutional autonomy and academic freedom without any qualification or modification while recognizing that commitment to the gospel and the teaching heritage of the Catholic church provides the inspiration and environment that make a Catholic college fully Catholic. There should be no conflict between a Catholic university and the responsibility of the hierarchy. Thus in this crucial period of great change the Catholic bishops supported the position adopted by the leaders of Catholic higher education in the United States.

A number of factors made the bishops more open to accept the position taken by the leadership of Catholic colleges and universities. The bishops, with their very difficult job descriptions, tend to be pragmatic and realistic administrators. The action of the courts and the best legal advice indicated that Catholic higher education had to accept institutional autonomy and academic freedom if it were to survive. The bishops were already experiencing the financial problems affecting Catholic elementary and high schools. The lower Catholic school system was shrinking, and its continuing existence with great financial sacrifice was causing divisive reactions among Catholic people. The bishops obviously understood and sympathized with the plight of Catholic college and university presidents. The fact that these presidents were in dialogue with the bishops and continued to publicly assert their wanting to be Catholic made it much easier to accept their decision as inevitable in the light of the circumstances. The bishops really did not have much other choice.

In addition, bishops never really had a great role in the internal governance and direction of Catholic colleges and universities. A few Catholic colleges were institutions originally owned and operated by the diocese, but the vast majority were founded and directly governed by religious communities of men and women. At this time the Jesuits ran twenty-eight colleges in the United States. The bishops were heavily involved in running grammar schools and high schools because most of them were operated by the parishes or the diocese itself. As a result, the dramatic changes in higher education did not immediately and directly affect bishops all that much, and they could more easily go along with these developments. Whatever the reasons, the bishops did not publicly oppose and even positively affirmed what had transpired in Catholic higher education. One might expect that if the original changes were accepted and lived with for many years the issue would be settled. But it is not.

In 1985 the Vatican Congregation for Catholic Education issued "Proposed Schema for a Pontifical Document on Catholic Universities" and sent this draft throughout the world for discussion.[33] The Association of Catholic Colleges and Universities (ACCU—formerly known as the College and University Department of The National Catholic Educational Association) and prominent Catholic university presidents responded very negatively to the document, which they saw as challenging and threatening their own self-understanding and operating principles.[34] The response of the National Conference of Catholic Bishops agreed with the position of the ACCU, but seven individual bishops strongly supported the proposed norms.[35]

The most significant academic freedom case in the 1980s involved me at the Catholic University of America.[36] In August 1986, the Vatican Congregation for the Doctrine of the Faith culminated a seven-year investigation by ruling that I was neither suitable nor eligible to be a Catholic theologian. On June 2, 1988, the Board of Trustees of the Catholic University accepted the declaration of the Holy See about me as binding on the university. I could no longer teach Catholic theology at Catholic University where I had been a tenured professor. The Board of Trustees tried to protect their institutional autonomy by freely accepting the Vatican judgment about me as being in keeping with their freely chosen Catholic character. The president of the university now talked about the ecclesial limits on academic freedom. I took the case to court, but the judge decided against me, insisting that "nothing in its [the University's] contract with Professor Curran or any other faculty member promises that it will always come down on the side of academic freedom."

The AAUP censured the university for violating academic freedom.[37] The accreditation evaluation team of the Middle States Association of Colleges and Schools expressed no great disapproval of what was done.[38] No cases have been raised against Catholic University's receiving federal funds of any type. As a result it seems that Catholic University was able to restrict academic freedom without suffering fatal harm, even though the academic reputation of the institution has suffered.

For the purpose of this chapter the important fact of the Catholic University of America case concerns the involvement of the most significant figures in the United States hierarchy (e.g., the archbishops of Boston, Chicago, New York, Washington). All of these as members of the Board of Trustees, which is only half clerical, made the decision to limit academic freedom. Some commentators maintain that this action was unique to Catholic University because of its special pontifical status,[39] but any board of trustees at any other Catholic institution could in theory make the same decision on the basis of its Catholic character. In addition to the bishops corporately involved in the Catholic University case, a number of individual bishops (Daniel E. Pilarczyk of Cincinnati,[40] Oscar H. Lipscomb of Mobile,[41] and Donald W. Wuerl of Pittsburgh[42]) have published articles on the need to restrict academic freedom in Catholic higher education.

Recent data indicates a growing split between bishops and those involved in Catholic higher education. To celebrate its sesquicentennial in 1991 Fordham University conducted a study of three types of Catholic institutions—higher education, health care, and social service. The first phase involved a Delphi experience that asked questions of 721 respondents from five categories—bishops, higher education, health care, social service, and others. Three hundred-ninety or 54 percent responded to this questionnaire that asked similar questions about the present and future of these institutional ministries.[43]

All respondents shared a high degree of agreement in rejecting both sectarian and secular scenarios for all these institutions and claimed that a mixed scenario should and would prevail in the year 2015.[44] Such an understanding coheres with the Catholic theological understanding of the church interacting with and serving the world.

On the exact nature of the Catholic identity, especially with regard to the institutional autonomy of these institutions, significantly greater areas of disagreement existed between bishops and higher education representatives than between bishops and people from the health care and social service institutions.[45] Seventy-seven percent of the bishops responding agreed that the diocese or religious order should have reserve powers, which extend at least to the election of the board of Catholic institutions of higher learning; while 67 percent of those associated with higher education disagreed. Only 15 percent of the bishops, but 69 percent of those from higher education, agreed that the residential bishop should not monitor what is taught at a Catholic college or university. Fifty-one percent of the bishops, but 92 percent of educators, agreed that the residential bishop should not control who is hired to teach theology at Catholic universities or colleges. Sixty-two percent of bishops disagreed with the statement that a Catholic university or college should not clear possibly controversial speakers with the residential bishop, whereas 88 percent of educators agreed. Seventy percent of the bishops agreed that a Catholic college should deny tenure to a "pro-choice" professor, while only 9 percent of educators agreed. Forty-seven percent of bishops, but only 1 percent of educators, agreed that a Catholic institution should not grant tenure to a Catholic married outside the church.

This recent data thus suggests that support of bishops for the autonomy and academic freedom of Catholic higher education is waning. As already pointed out, Catholic health care facilities and social service agencies do not have such academic freedom and autonomy and consequently the bishops and the leaders of these two fields generally agree about institutional identity and a direct relationship to the church.

One very logical explanation of the shift on the part of some bishops comes from the stronger positions recently taken by the Vatican authorities about church control over theologians, the disciplining of Catholic theologians, and the new norms proposed for Catholic higher education throughout the world.

Vatican Authorities. The history of the discussions between Vatican authorities and the leadership of Catholic higher education has been told by many of those leaders who were involved in this dialogue.[46] From the very beginning of the dialogue, the American educators have tried to convince the Vatican officials of the legitimacy of their institutions as being both autonomous with academic freedom and Catholic. The Vatican authorities have never been comfortable in theory with this position, but the American educators have been successful in practice. The Vatican congregation has at least permitted Catholic higher education in the United States to pursue this course. Catholic canon lawyers in general have agreed with the positions taken by the educational leaders. Whenever canonical issues have arisen that seem to be opposed to institutional autonomy and academic freedom for Catholic higher education, United States canon lawyers have generally given minimalist interpretations or even claimed that the canons or laws concerned do not apply in the United States situation.[47]

However, there is another side to the story. James J. Conn, an American Jesuit civil lawyer, in his recently published doctoral dissertation in canon law at the Pontifical Gregorian University in Rome concludes, on the basis of church documents, that Catholic colleges and universities should be of two types. The first category includes canonical institutions (or, as they are called, "juridicial persons"), directly under the church and church law. The second category embraces those institutions that choose to retain their Catholic identity by having a relationship with the church's hierarchy and accepting the role of the hierarchy in vigilance of faith and morals, but are not canonical institutions. All other institutions that do not want to submit themselves to ecclesiastical authority should secularize and admit publicly that they are not Catholic. The ambiguity that has been for so many years characterizing the identity of Catholic higher education and its relationship to the church should come to an end.[48]

I disagree with the basic thesis proposed by Conn. I believe an institution can be a university, with academic freedom and autonomy, and still be Catholic. Conn bases his conclusions on official Vatican documents and directives and at least makes a strong case for what is the ideal position taken by Vatican officials about higher education in the United States. This view conflicts with that proposed by the leadership of Catholic higher education. In the light of this conflict what will be the future of Catholic education in the United States?

After all the discussions and negotiations of the last twenty-five years, Pope John Paul II in September 1990 issued the Apostolic Constitution

Ex corde Ecclesiae proposing norms for Catholic higher education throughout the world.[49] In my judgment these norms are somewhat ambiguous, but they certainly do not clearly affirm the self-understanding of American Catholic higher education leaders.

The academic freedom and autonomy of Catholic colleges and universities are mentioned, but both concepts are explicitly limited. "It possesses that institutional autonomy necessary to perform its functions effectively and guarantees its members academic freedom, so long as the rights of the individual person and of the community are preserved within the confines of the truth and the common good" (n. 12). In addition, the institutional fidelity to the church requires an adherence to the teaching authority of the church in faith and morals (n. 27). Those who teach theological disciplines in these institutions must have a mandate from the competent ecclesiastical authority (Part II, a. 4). Bishops are not external agents to the university but participate in the life of Catholic colleges and universities (n. 28).

However, those defending the present self-understanding of Catholic higher education can point to some support in other parts of the document. Catholic institutions that do not have a direct juridical tie to the church (for all practical purposes all those in the United States) "with the agreement of the local ecclesiastical authority will make their own the general norms and their local and regional applications, internalizing them into their governing documents and, as far as possible, will conform their existing statutes both to these general norms and to their applications" (Part II, a. 1, 3). The general norms set forth in these documents are to be applied "in conformity with the Code of Canon Law and complementary church legislation, taking into account the statutes of each university or institute and, as far as possible and appropriate, civil law" (Part II, a. 1, 2). The ambiguity of this document stands out. Supporters of the present self-understanding of American Catholic higher education can point to the document's recognition of the local customs, laws, and existing statutes. Opponents can point to the obvious restrictions placed on autonomy and academic freedom.

Who will decide? Norms for individual countries are to be drawn up by the bishops conference and reviewed by the Holy See before becoming applicable. At the present time the United States bishops have established a committee of bishops which in consultation with the leaders of Catholic higher education are meeting to come up with the norms. The final decision is thus not far off.

The mainstream leadership of Catholic higher education that strongly resisted earlier proposed Vatican norms has greeted these final norms with enthusiastic support.[50] They apparently believe they can convince the American bishops and the Vatican to accept in practice the existing institutional autonomy and academic freedom for Catholic higher education in the United States. Their approach can marshall strong reasons in its favor.

The bishops have been supportive of Catholic higher education's new directions and would find it difficult to change now. The present understanding and practice have been in place for over twenty years and enjoy the presumption of what has been in existence for some time. To change the present system would not only be difficult but divisive and chaotic. Many trustees and administrators of these independent corporations would strenuously object to such changes.

To change the present understanding and structure of Catholic higher education in the United States could be catastrophic. Most commentators, but not all, agree that without institutional autonomy and academic freedom Catholic higher education could lose its state and federal funding. Without such funding, few Catholic institutions could survive. The United States bishops, from their own painful experience, know how difficult if not impossible it is to keep Catholic grammar and high schools operating without government support.

The Vatican authorities have always known the need for compromise. Think of the concordats that the Vatican has made over the years with different countries. Some maintain that the Vatican's willingness to compromise has been a very healthy part of the Catholic Church as an institution, but many agree with my judgment that at times the Vatican has been willing to compromise too much to defend its institutional best interests. Compromise on this issue, however, does not have the pejorative aspects of some past compromises and could fit in well with a traditional canonical approach. Roman law in general and Catholic canon law in particular have always tended to emphasize universal norms but then grant many privileges and dispensations because of local conditions and circumstances. The supporters of academic freedom and institutional autonomy can make a good practical case to continue the present course of Catholic higher education in the United States.

But opponents of such autonomy and academic freedom can marshall strong practical reasons for their position. The United States bishops have been changing in their attitude in this regard. Why should Catholic higher education be different from Catholic health care facilities and social service organizations? These later organizations serve large publics and receive much state and federal funding, perhaps even more than that which goes to higher education, but they exist and thrive with ecclesial limits on what they do. The Catholic University of America has insisted on ecclesial limits on academic freedom and has not suffered fatal consequences. Not all agree that government funding is dependent on full academic freedom. Church institutions should have the right to exercise their religious freedom to be truly Catholic.

Rome in the last seventeen years (corresponding with the present pontificate of John Paul II) has been very worried about theologians, intervened frequently to take action against them, and introduced juridical norms for controlling the practitioners of theology. The Vatican has publicly investigated and sometimes taken action against Catholic theologians—Hans Küng, Jacques Pohier, Edward Schillebeeckx, Gustavo Gutiérrez, Leonardo Boff, André Guindon, and myself. Catholic theologians throughout the world have protested these and similar actions, to no avail.[51] Two other respected German theologians have written books describing their run-ins with Vatican authorities.[52] The 1983 Code of Canon Law (over the strong objections of the American Catholic higher education leaders) required all those who teach theological disciplines in any institute of higher studies to have a mandate from a competent ecclesiastical authority.[53] In February 1989 the Congregation for the Doctrine of the Faith published a new profession of faith and oath of fidelity to be taken, among others, by those who teach disciplines connected with faith and morals in any university.[54] This strong attempt to control theologians in the academy coheres with any obvious reading of the documents from the Vatican which propose, at the very minimal as an ideal, that all Catholic colleges and universities are somehow or other responsible to the hierarchy.

Within this context a committee of United States bishops chaired by Bishop John J. Leibrecht began the process of drawing up national ordinances for this country on the basis of *Ex corde Ecclesiae*. For all practical purposes the dispute over academic freedom and institutional autonomy boiled down to the question of the mandate from competent ecclesiastical authority for teachers of theology in Catholic colleges and universities. The requirement of such a mandate would give bishops the power over the hiring and firing of theologians in the academy and thus destroy academic freedom.

The committee of seven bishops with some college and university presidents as nonvoting members or consultors circulated draft ordinances in the spring of 1993. According to this proposal, Catholic professors of theological disciplines are to be advised by academic officials of the church's expectation that they request the mandate from the competent ecclesiastical authority.[55] Note that such a proposal tries to preserve institutional autonomy by taking the institution out of the matter. However, it remains a violation of academic freedom because it gives to church authorities the say over who is hired or dismissed from an institution of higher learning. But the committee continued its consultations and discussions.

In August 1995 the committee circulated a new draft of the ordinances. The draft does not mention the mandate. A covering background sheet maintains that canon 812, which requires the mandate, must be seen in the light of the need to safeguard the orthodoxy of what is taught in Catholic institutions of higher learning and also the long, unique history of such education in this country. These ends are best achieved by a nonjuridical application of the mandate. The proposed ordinances consequently do not mention the mandate. Disputes between bishops and theologians are to be decided in accord with the earlier document, "Doctrinal Responsibilities: Approaches to Promoting Cooperation and Resolving Misunderstandings between Bishops and Theologians." This document deals primarily with the process to be followed.[56] The implication is that the hierarchical church authorities have the right to make judgments about the work of a particular theologian, but these judgments do not have any juridical effect in the academy. This draft thus shows that the committee of bishops is willing to live with the American understanding of academic freedom for theologians in colleges and universities.

The final resolution will only come after the committee proposes a new draft, the bishops vote on it, and Rome finally approves it. Time will tell about the final outcome. The resolution of this discussion over academic freedom in Catholic higher education and theology in the United States will have significant effects for the life of the church in this country.

Notes

1. For the classical history of academic freedom in the United States, see Richard Hofstadter and Walter P. Metzger, *The Development of Academic Freedom in the United States* (New York: Columbia University Press, 1955). See 363-66 for the significance of the controversy over Darwinism.
2. "1940 Statement of Principles on Academic Freedom and Tenure," in American Association of University Professors, *Policy Documents and Reports*, 7th ed. (Washington, D.C.: American Association of University Professors, 1990), 3.

3. "Report of Committee A, 1988–89," *Academe* 75 (September–October 1989): 54.
4. For the full exposition of this history see my *Catholic Higher Education, Theology, and Academic Freedom* (Notre Dame, Ind.: University of Notre Dame Press, 1990), 26–153. This present chapter brings that book up to date and emphasizes certain issues that have emerged in the discussion.
5. Pope John Paul II, "*Ex corde Ecclesiae*: The Apostolic Constitution on Catholic Universities," *Origins* 20 (1990), n. 29, p. 271.
6. William J. Byron, "The Nature of Academic Freedom and the Teaching of Theology," in *Issues in Academic Freedom,* ed. George S. Worgul, Jr. (Pittsburgh: Duquesne University Press, 1992), 70.
7. Carl J. Peter, "The Many Faces of Academic Freedom," *Origins* 20 (1991): 520.
8. Raymond F. Collins, "Academic Freedom: American and European Contexts," in *Issues in Academic Freedom*, 24–41.
9. Walter P. Metzger, "Profession and Constitution: Two Definitions of Academic Freedom in America," *Texas Law Review* 66, no. 7 (June 1988): 1269–71.
10. See, for example, "Symposium on Academic Freedom," *Texas Law Review* 66, no. 7 (June 1988): 1247–659.
11. AAUP, *Policy Documents and Reports*, 3–10 with procedural and updating documents found from 11–72.
12. Theodore M. Hesburgh, *The Hesburgh Papers: Higher Values in Higher Education* (Kansas City, Mo.: Andrews and McNeel, 1979), 75.
13. Aldo J. Tos, "A Critical Study of the Modern American View on Academic Freedom" (Ph.D. diss., Catholic University of America, 1958).
14. Byron, in *Issues in Academic Freedom*, 72–87.
15. AAUP, *Policy Documents and Reports*, 3.
16. *Catholic Higher Education, Theology, and Academic Freedom*, 154–91.
17. Pastoral Constitution on the Church in the Modern World, nn. 53–63, in *Vatican Council II: The Conciliar and Post Conciliar Documents*, ed. Austin Flannery (Northport, NY: Costello, 1975), 958–68.
18. James John Annarelli, *Academic Freedom and Catholic Higher Education* (Westport, Conn.: Greenwood, 1987), 174–79. Non-Catholic scholars have proposed similar positions. See, for example, Lonnie D. Kliever, "Academic Freedom in Church-Affiliated Universities," *Texas Law Review* 66, no. 7 (June 1988): 1477–80. For a position in agreement with mine, see Richard P. McBrien, "Academic Freedom and the Catholic Theologian," in *Issues in Academic Freedom*, 126–42.

19. Land O'Lakes Statement, in *The Catholic University: A Modern Appraisal,* ed. Neil J. McCluskey (Notre Dame, Ind.: University of Notre Dame Press, 1970), 336–37.

20. My presentation relies substantially on Joseph Richard Preville, "Catholic Colleges, the Courts, and the Constitution: A Tale of Two Cases," *Church History* 58 (June 1989): 197–210.

21. John J. McGrath, *Catholic Institutions in the United States, Canonical and Civil Law Status* (Washington, D.C.: Catholic University of America Press, 1968).

22. Charles H. Wilson, Jr., *Tilton v. Richardson: The Search for Sectarianism in Education* (Washington, D.C.: Association of Catholic Colleges, 1971).

23. Editorial, "Blaine, Bundy, and Balderdash," *America* 122 (1970): 34–35.

24. See my *Catholic Higher Education, Theology, and Academic Freedom*, 85–106.

25. Kenneth D. Whitehead, "Religiously Affiliated Colleges and Academic Freedom," *America* 156 (1987): 96–98; Phyllis Zagano, "Sectarian Universities, Federal Funding, and the Question of Academic Freedom," *Religious Education* 85 (Winter 1990): 136–48.

26. Dena S. Davis, "The American Constitution and Catholic Canon Law," *Journal of Church and State* 31 (1989): 207–18.

27. Alice Gallin, "Catholic Higher Education Today—The Challenges of Ambiguity," *Cross Currents* 43 (Winter 1993–94): 486.

28. Adam J. Maida, *Ownership, Control, and Sponsorship of Catholic Institutions* (Harrisburg, Pa.: Pennsylvania Catholic Conference, 1979). See also James Jerome Conn, *Catholic Universities in the United States and Ecclesiastical Authority* (Rome: Pontifical Gregorian University, 1991), 201–6. For an overview and criticism of the various approaches, see Robert T. Kennedy, "McGrath, Maida, Michiels: Introduction to a Study of the Canonical and Civil Law Status of Church-Related Institutions in the United States," *Jurist* 50 (1990): 351–401.

29. James Tunstead Burtchaell, "The Decline and Fall of The Christian College," *First Things*, no. 12 (April 1991): 16–29; no. 13 (May 1991): 30–8.

30. National Conference of Catholic Bishops, *To Teach As Jesus Did* (Washington: United States Catholic Conference, 1973).

31. National Conference of Catholic Bishops, "Catholic Higher Education and the Pastoral Ministry of the Church," *Origins* 10 (1980): 378–84.

32. College and University Department, National Catholic Educational Association, "Relations of American Catholic Colleges and Universities with the Church," *Catholic Mind* 74 (October 1976): 51–64.

33. Congregation for Catholic Education, "Proposed Schema for a Pontifical Document on Catholic Universities," *Origins* 15 (1986): 706–11.
34. "Association of Catholic Colleges and Universities: Catholic College Presidents Respond to Proposed Vatican Schema," *Origins* 15 (1986): 697–704; Statement of Presidents of Leading Catholic Universities of North America on the Schema for a Proposed Document on the Catholic University, sent to William Cardinal Baum, Prefect of the Congregation for Catholic Education with a cover letter signed by Theodore M. Hesburgh on March 21, 1986.
35. Congregation for Catholic Eudcation, "Summary of Responses to Draft Schema on Catholic Universities," *Origins* 17 (1988): 247.
36. For my description and interpretation see *Catholic Higher Education, Theology, and Academic Freedom,* 210–39; *The Living Tradition of Catholic Moral Theology,* (Notre Dame, Ind.: University of Notre Dame Press, 1992), 217–39. For a slightly different interpretation, see Larry Witham, *Curran vs. Catholic University* (Riverdale, Md.: Edington-Rand, 1991).
37. "Reports: Seventy-Sixth Annual Meeting," *Academe* 76, no. 5 (September–October 1990): 28.
38. Report to the Faculty, Administration, Trustees, Students of the Catholic University of America by an Evaluation Team Representing the Commission on Higher Education of the Middle States Association of Colleges and Schools, 34.
39. Joseph A. O'Hare, "Faith and Freedom in Catholic Universities," in *Vatican Authority and American Catholic Dissent,* ed., William W. May, (New York: Crossroad, 1987), 160–67.
40. Daniel E. Pilarczyk, "Academic Freedom: Church and University," *Origins* 18 (1988): 57–59.
41. Oscar H. Lipscomb, "Faith and Academic Freedom," *America* 159 (1988): 124–25.
42. Donald W. Wuerl, "Academic Freedom and the University," *Origins* 18 (1988): 207–11.
43. Charles J. Fahey and Mary Ann Lewis, eds., *The Future of Catholic Institutional Ministries: A Continuing Conversation* (New York: Third Age Center, Fordham University, 1992), 1–3.
44. Ibid., pp. 35–37.
45. Ibid., pp. 52–58.
46. Alice Gallin, "On the Road Toward a Definition of a Catholic University," *The Jurist* 48 (1988): 536–58; Ann Ida Gannon, "Some Aspects of Catholic Higher Education Since Vatican II," *Current Issues in Catholic Higher Education*

8, no. 1 (Summer 1987): 10–24; Theodore M. Hesburgh, "The Vatican and American Higher Education," *America* 155 (1986): 247–50; Robert J. Henle, "Catholic Universities and the Vatican," *America* 137 (1977): 315–22. For the documentary history of the recent discussions between Catholic higher education in the United States and the Vatican, see *American Catholic Higher Education: Essential Documents 1967–1990* , ed., Alice Gallin, (Notre Dame, Ind.: University of Notre Dame Press, 1992). For the history of Catholic higher education in this country in the twentieth century from a perspective that is not as enthusiastic about the changes since the late 1960s as the leaders of Catholic higher education, see Philip Gleason, *Contending with Modernity: Catholic Higher Education in the Twentieth Century* (New York: Oxford University Press, 1995).

47. James A. Coriden, "The Teaching Office of the Church," in *The Code of Canon Law: A Text and Commentary,* ed. James A. Coriden et al. (New York: Paulist, 1985), 571–72.

48. Conn, *Catholic Universities in the United States and Ecclesiastical Authority,* 324–28.

49. Pope John Paul II, *Ex corde Ecclesiae, Origins* 20 (1990): 265–76. Subsequent references in the text will be to the paragraph numbers.

50. James W. Sauve, "Pope John Paul II and Catholic Colleges and Universities," *America* 163 (1990): 260 ff; also my "Point of View," *Chronicle of Higher Education,* (Jan. 30, 1990): A48.

51. For most of the cases mentioned and other developments see *The Church in Anguish,* ed. Hans Küng and Leonard Swidler (San Francisco: Harper and Row, 1987).

52. Walbert Bühlman, *"Dreaming About the Church: Acts of the Apostles of the Twentieth Century* (Kansas City, Mo.: Sheed and Ward, 1987); Bernard Häring, *My Witness for the Church* (New York: Paulist, 1992).

53. Coriden, *A Code of Canon Law: A Text and Commentary,* 575–76.

54. Congregation for the Doctrine of the Faith, "Profession of Faith and Oath of Fidelity," *Origins* 18 (1989): 661–63.

55. Memorandum from Bishop John J. Leibrecht to Archbishops and Bishops, Presidents of Catholic Colleges and Universities (May 4, 1993), privately circulated.

56. Memorandum from Bishop John J. Leibrecht to Bishops, Presidents, Learned Societies, Sponsoring Religious Communities (August 25, 1995), privately circulated.

~ 10 ~

What Is a Catholic College?

The previous chapter has traced the dramatic change in Catholic higher education concerning its acceptance of academic freedom and institutional autonomy. Before 1960 the Catholic college and university identified themselves as a part of the pastoral arm of the church. In this same period other changes have also occurred such as the reduced number of religious teaching in these Catholic institutions as well as a growing professionalism on these campuses. Such significant changes have raised the fundamental question of what is a Catholic institution of higher learning.[1] The question of the Catholic identity of these institutions is further complicated by the broader issues of the identity of higher education today and the identity of the contemporary Catholic church in the United States.

The Background

American higher education itself today cannot agree about its own identity and purpose. Postmodernism has challenged the understanding of higher education generally accepted in the earlier part of this century, when the emphasis was on the autonomy and capability of human reason, value-free objective knowledge, and human progress through the developments of science and technology. The rise of diversity and pluralism has challenged this older understanding of American higher education. Deep divisions exist within many departments in our colleges and universities (e.g., English, history) about the very nature of the discipline and the proper methodological approaches to be used. Most institutions find it harder and harder to find agreement on curriculum. Power struggles are omnipresent on our campuses.

The Catholic Church itself is also experiencing an identity problem. The divisions within the church over issues of sexuality and authority are well known. Many Catholic women today, for example, find it increasingly difficult to be committed to the Catholic Church with its present understanding of the role of women. Many other women remain committed and involved but determined to bring about change in the institution. On the other hand, some Catholics have been upset with the extent of change within their church and are unwilling to support any further developments. Thus many Catholics have come to their own *modus vivendi* with the church at the present time, but such differences make it very difficult for the total church to act in a particular way or to agree on an understanding of what is church. Experiential and anecdotal evidence supports the contention that Catholic academics and intellectuals are more turned off by the church today than other Catholics. Academics especially have difficulty with pronouncements such as the latest statement from the pope on the ordination of women. Relying not on reason or argument of any kind but solely on authority, the pope decreed that the ordination of women cannot even be discussed within the church.[2] Then the Congregation for the Doctrine of the Faith claimed such a teaching is infallible.[3] However, there are probably some Catholics on Catholic campuses who agree with the recent papal pronouncement.

Catholic colleges and universities are not the only institutions that claim the title "Catholic." Catholic institutions are heavily involved in health care and also in social services, usually under the umbrella of the Catholic Charities organization. But a significant difference exists with regard to Catholic colleges and universities. Catholic hospitals and Catholic Charities organizations are seen as a direct and immediate part of the pastoral mission of the church and act in accord with Catholic teaching. Thus, for example, Catholic hospitals resist any pressure to do abortions because such procedures are against the Catholic hospital code of ethics.[4] (Problems will arise more often in the future with mergers and the formation of larger health alliances, but still the problems are not exactly the same as those confronting the identity of Catholic higher education.)

More practical aspects also raise unique problems for the discussion of the Catholic identity of Catholic colleges today. Disaffected Catholic faculty members do not want to touch the question. In addition, our faculties contain many members who are non-Catholic. Such faculty members have often tended to see themselves as second-class citizens on Catholic campuses and especially when the talk turns to Catholic identity. Some discussions of Catholic identity conjure up sectarian images which make non-Catholic faculty not only uncomfortable but downright opposed to what they hear.

Despite all these problems connected with the Catholic identity of colleges and universities, Catholic higher education continues to exist and in some senses thrive. All higher education is experiencing problems, and finances remain a long-term worry. Catholic higher education, however, is doing as well as most of its sisters and brothers. Most Catholic institutions are heavily tuition dependent, but there is no crisis situation immediately foreshadowing the closing of most Catholic colleges and universities. Why not continue doing what we are doing? Since there are no immediate threats to the continuing existence of Catholic higher education, since there are so many problems and difficulties involved in even raising the question of Catholic identity, why not just go along as we are? But still many people want to raise the question of Catholic identity. Why?

Ethical, historical, and theological reasons stand behind the quest for coming to grips with the Catholic identity of Catholic higher education. From an ethical viewpoint Catholic colleges call themselves Catholic and appeal to Catholics to attend these institutions and to support them. These institutions therefore should be Catholic or admit publicly that they are not Catholic and therefore should not appeal to Catholics for support. Most Catholic institutions of higher learning were founded by, staffed by, and supported by religious communities (in a few cases dioceses). Now independent boards of trustees are legally responsible for these institutions. However, the present boards of trustees recognize their obligation to the founding vision and support of these institutions. A moral obligation exists to continue the work of the founders.

The leaders of Catholic higher education are conscious of the historical reality in American higher education, where many institutions which originally started out as religious institutions under Protestant auspices have become secular. The list includes some of the most prestigious institutions in the country, including Harvard, Yale, and Princeton. Many of the leaders of this movement toward secularization were themselves religious people who gradually diminished the religious aspect of their institutions until finally there was none left at all. The Protestant educational enterprise for the most part voluntarily abandoned its Christian identity.[5] Some contemporary observers see the same process at work in Catholic higher education. A few Catholic institutions in the

United States in the 1960s, such as Webster College and Manhattanville, explicitly made the decision to become secular institutions, but the vast majority of colleges and universities still claim to be Catholic.[6] Thus the challenges from critics of contemporary Catholic higher education as well as the demands of truthfulness and honesty for those involved in Catholic higher education have challenged such colleges to clearly indicate how and why they are Catholic.

Theological and theoretical grounds also stand behind the search for a Catholic identity. Catholic Christians have traditionally believed that institutions of higher education are good for the church. Here the church not only can provide knowledge for its members but it can also provide for a public dialogue between theology and the world of science and knowledge that also contributes to the good of Catholic theology. However, in addition the Catholic tradition has insisted that it has something to say not only to the church community but also to the world at large and the broader society. Thus through institutions of higher learning the Catholic church can contribute to its own good and also to the good of society as a whole.

In reading some of the contemporary descriptions of Catholic higher education in the 1940s and 1950s, one suspects that a romantic nostalgia occasionally comes to the fore. Was the Catholicism of the Catholic college of that era as cohesive and all-embracing as one often hears? The literature on the subject occasionally speaks of "The Catholic Renewal" and "The Catholic Renaissance" that characterized the life of these Catholic colleges with scholastic philosophy as "the unifying and integrating element in the curriculum."[7] Such descriptions appear too romantic and a bit naive as accurate descriptions of what was happening in Catholic higher education in those days. However, no matter what the proper description of Catholic higher education in the '40s and '50s, we have to admit that we can never return to what was present then. Catholic identity in general has changed greatly and so has the reality and identity of Catholic higher education.

Catholic institutions of higher education have a twofold identity: they claim to be both American and Catholic. The move to academic freedom and institutional autonomy has underscored the commitment to be colleges and universities in the accepted sense in the United States. Can such institutions still be Catholic? How can they be Catholic?

The Meaning of Catholic

The most obvious understanding of Catholic is what is unique about the Roman Catholic Church, thus differentiating it from all other religions and

Christian churches. Catholicism differs from all other Christian religions by its emphasis on a visible church served by a hierarchy with roles of holy orders, jurisdiction, and teaching. Thus in the intellectual area the pope and bishops are authoritative teachers of the Catholic faith. No one else in the church can claim that title or role. One might try to go on and spell out other aspects of what is unique to the identity of Roman Catholicism, but one has to agree on the uniqueness and perhaps even the fundamental uniqueness based on this understanding of the visible human church with hierarchical offices of pope and bishops.

To describe any reality only in terms of what is unique to it does not tend to be an adequate and accurate description. To describe Roman Catholicism only by its unique aspects not only is unfair and wrong, but it tends to distort the very meaning of being Catholic. Every reality has aspects that are unique and aspects that are distinctive. The distinctive aspects greatly contribute to the total identity of the reality and help make it what it is, but they may be shared by many others.

Three distinctive Catholic aspects of the Catholic tradition stand out in the context of striving to understand the Catholic identity of Catholic colleges—the Catholic tradition embraces all reality and is inclusive; the Catholic tradition accepts the goodness of creation and the goodness of the human; God and the divine are mediated to us in and through creation and the human. These three characteristics deserve further explanation.

First, catholicity *touches all and includes all.* This characteristic in the classical distinction of Ernst Troeltsch distinguishes Catholicism from sects.[8] Sects do not pretend to be universal. They generally see the world as evil and remove themselves from this evil, as exemplified today by the Amish. Sectarians in this sense are very committed people, but they do not believe in a big church which is open to all and in a faith that touches and in some way respects all reality. This general characteristic of touching all reality grounds the Catholic insistence on inclusivity rather than exclusivity. The Catholic church is universal and inclusive—open to all races, all people, all parts of the world. The other two aspects of catholicity build on this fundamental theme of universality and inclusivity.

Second, the Catholic tradition accepts *the basic goodness of creation in general and of the human in particular.* Whatever has been made by God is good and is included within the Catholic understanding and embrace. Creation grounds this basic acceptance of and openness to all reality, but redemption too touches the human and all reality as illustrated in the insistence on speaking of redemption in terms of the new heaven and the new earth.

The Catholic tradition has built on the famous saying that nothing human is foreign from the Christian. The glory of God is the human person come alive. The ultimate end of creation is the glory of God and the happiness of the human being. Another traditional Catholic axiom insists that grace does not destroy nature, but grace builds on nature. In the Catholic tradition of Thomas Aquinas, the ultimate end of human beings is happiness. Happiness occurs when the human being comes to perfection and fulfillment. What constitutes happiness? According to Aquinas, human happiness involves the fulfillment of the basic and most significant of human drives—the desire to know the true and to love the good. If the intellect knows perfect truth and the will loves the perfect good, we are happy.[9] Thus the Catholic tradition accepts the basic goodness of creation and of the human.

To illustrate and develop the characteristic Catholic acceptance of the goodness of creation and the human, reflect for a moment on the traditional Catholic understanding and use of natural law in its approach to morality.[10] We all know how controversial the natural law is. Personally I have disagreed with some of its uses in Catholic moral theology, but my disagreements center on how one understands human reason and human nature. I totally agree with what might be called the theological aspect of natural law—even for people of faith, human reason reflecting on humanity and the world created by God can arrive at true moral wisdom and knowledge. Some Christians emphasize the sinfulness and fragility of the human and even claim that a sinful human reason reflecting on a broken creation and humanity cannot arrive at true moral wisdom and knowledge. The acceptance of natural law in the Catholic tradition recognizes the basic goodness and power of human reason. Notice here too the inclusiveness in the famous Catholic axiom stressing faith and reason. Karl Barth, the greatest Reformed theologian of the twentieth century, once remarked that his greatest problem with Roman Catholicism was its "and."[11] I agree with Barth that the "and" is distinctive of Catholicism, but I glory in the Catholic "and"—faith *and* reason, grace *and* nature, faith *and* works. The Catholic "and" fundamentally acknowledges the goodness of the human and of human reason. Human reason is a gift given to us by God and we are called to use it and develop it as best we can. Thomas Aquinas rests his anthropology on seeing the human being as an image of God. But how does the human being image God? The human being is an image of God precisely because like God the human being has intellect, free will, and the power of self-determination. We are like God, and we participate in God by using our intellect, free will, and power of self-determination.[12]

The acceptance of natural law also illustrates the all-inclusiveness of Catholicism. Catholics are not called to act differently in the world from all other people in their daily life and in the political, social, and economic orders. All human beings are called to act in the same way and have the power of human reason to discover how they should act. Much discussion has occurred lately about these aspects of natural law, but I am simply pointing out the significance of this quintessentially Catholic approach for our understanding of catholicity in general and the catholicity of higher education.

The third distinctive characteristic of catholicity—*the divine mediated through the human*—builds on and is intimately connected with the all-inclusiveness and the goodness of all creation aspects. Earlier chapters pointed out the importance of mediation in the Catholic tradition. Again the natural law well illustrates this mediation. How do we discern and know what God wants us to do? Do we go immediately to God to find out? No. Human reason reflecting on human nature tells us what God asks of us or what has been called the eternal law. The eternal law is the plan for all creation in the mind of God. The natural law is the participation of the eternal law in the rational creature.

Fifty years ago in every Catholic college in the United States philosophy professors following Thomas Aquinas taught that on the basis of human reason we could prove the existence of God. The image of God, so to speak, is found in her handiwork of creation. One can go from creation to the Creator—from the work of God to knowing the very existence of God.[13] At the very least the Catholic tradition recognizes that human reason raises questions of ultimate meaning, significance, and value even if some contemporary Catholics are not as convinced that reason can prove the existence of God.

Mediation plays a most distinctive role in Catholic life and thought on the explicitly religious level as such. In Catholic understanding the church is a visible human community with human leaders and members. God does not come immediately and invisibly to the individual person. Rather the saving gift of God is present and mediated in and through the visible human community with its human-divine structure called the church. The whole Catholic sacramental system rests on the concept of mediation. The human reality signifies and makes present the divine. The eucharist is a celebratory meal. Human beings often celebrate their love and friendship in a meal. Think of our holiday meals. The meal unites family and friends in love; food and drink are shared; stories are told; memories invoked; bonds strengthened. God's love is thus shared and celebrated in the very way in which human love is shared and celebrated. So for the whole sacramental system the human becomes the sign and symbol mediating the divine. This specifically religious and church aspect of mediation does not directly affect our understanding of Catholic colleges and universities, but it does underscore the primary significance of mediation in the Catholic understanding.

This understanding of catholicity with its three characteristics has been manifest throughout the history of the Roman Catholic Church. The church has been concerned about all aspects of existence and not just the explicitly religious. For our purposes, think of the interest in and concern for intellectual and artistic realities in the Catholic tradition. The Catholic Church sponsored and supported the beginning of universities in the Western world in medieval times. Notice that they were true universities in the sense of striving to be universal in scope and not just concerned with theology. For example, in the early thirteenth century the University of Paris included four faculties—Arts, Medicine, Canon Law, and Theology, with the faculty of Arts being the largest and the necessary steppingstone to the other faculties.[14] Human reason is basically good, and the church supports the quest of human reason to know the truth.

The Vatican Museum and Library well illustrate this distinctive catholicity of Catholicism. The Catholic Church has preserved many of the cultural treasures of the ancient world in its museum. Notice too that these are not necessarily Christian items but rather pertain to the culture of the world as such. Likewise the Vatican Library not only contains works with regard to theology and canon law but to all aspects of the human. With its understanding of mediation the Catholic tradition has often used the human for its own purposes as illustrated in its use of art, architecture, and music for its liturgy. However, all these realities as part of the human have a meaning and value in themselves, and the Catholic Church has also appreciated and supported the reality of knowledge and art for its own sake.

Catholicity and the Catholic College

The concept of catholicity developed here has influenced the Catholic approach to all realities. How does such an approach affect the understanding and institutional nature of the Catholic college today?

1) Too often the identity of the Catholic college is sought only on the basis of what is uniquely Catholic. Such an approach of concentrating only on the uniquely Catholic has some apparent advantages. Ninety-five percent of the college can continue doing its own thing and not worry about the Catholic nature of the institution. Non-Catholic faculty, trustees, students, and others are not concerned about the Catholic identity, and Catholic identity in no way affects them or their work in the Catholic institution. Such an approach seems to solve many problems and creates fewer obstacles than some other possibilities. Many people are rightly threatened and uneasy over a sectarian understanding of catholicity that would affect the entire institution. If the uniquely Catholic aspect were to affect the whole institution, the college would definitely be sectarian in the narrow sense and not truly an American college or university.

But in reality catholicity includes not just the uniquely Catholic but also the distinctively Catholic. The entire institution is Catholic, not just a particular part of it. Part of the distinctive Catholic identity involves the Catholic "and"—which in this case asserts that the same reality can be both an American college or university serving a broad public and Catholic interest. The Catholic tradition accepts the importance of human knowledge and human disciplines for their own sake and does not impose upon them a particular Catholic slant. These human realities have their own autonomy and their own meaning and significance. Nothing human is foreign from the Catholic college. All these other realities have a meaning and a place of their own and do not depend only on their need to be in dialogue with faith or religion. Such an understanding of a Catholic college is not sectarian. At the same time it is not merely a pragmatic acceptance of the status quo in order to preserve something in existence.

2) The Catholic college is open to all the disciplines and arts whether they involve the liberal arts, the fine arts, or professional training. One should note here the basic similarity in the meaning of Catholic and university. The word *catholic* comes from the Greek whereas the word *university* comes from the Latin, but both have the same basic root of being all-encompassing. Recall that the thirteenth-century University of Paris included the professional faculty of medicine as well as the liberal arts.

3) The Catholic tradition understands the intellect as having an intrinsic dynamic thrust that seeks the truth and will never be satisfied until it comes to the fullness of truth. The whole purpose of education is to draw the person out of her narrowness and to continually expand the intellectual horizons.

Thus the Catholic college must expose the student to the different cultures and traditions in our own country and throughout the world. The Catholic tradition thus supports the emphasis today on global education.

4) The Catholic understanding of human reason and the intellect should have some influence on how the curriculum is structured. While recognizing the universality of the objects of inquiry for the human intellect, the Catholic approach also sees the intellect as searching for more ultimate meaning and values. These questions of transcendence, meaning, significance, and value therefore should be addressed in the curriculum of a Catholic college. By the very definition of the Catholic college this means that there should be a free dialogue going on with all different approaches to meaning, significance, and values, but one important component of this search for meaning and value is the Catholic theological tradition itself.

5) The Catholic tradition values the role of the intellect and the perfection of the intellect itself as something good. The development of the intellect redounds to the good of the person. Knowledge in this approach is good not only because of the object but also in terms of the subject. For example, the Catholic tradition sees contemplation as a good in itself and not just because it is ordered to something else. In the light of this understanding the Catholic college should give an important place to the liberal arts which by definition are not justified by a more practical end. They strive to develop the intellect as such and make someone a better person without any immediate vocational payoff. No matter what the major of the individual student, the liberal arts must be a part of her curriculum in a Catholic college.

6) The Catholic tradition has always had a special concern for the poor and the needy. This distinctive but by no means unique concern should also have some curricular repercussions on the Catholic campus. The concerns of the poor and the marginalized should be heard on the Catholic campus. In addition, it might be possible to structure innovative courses by which students combine service to the poor and others with their own academic coursework. These six characteristics mentioned above refer to the primary reality of a college or university as an intellectual institution. The Catholic identity both affirms and shapes the intellectual life pursued in Catholic colleges and universities.

Too often discussions of Catholic identity emphasize more the milieu or the environment in which the intellectual endeavor of the college takes place. This emphasis on the milieu is very important and is influenced by the Catholic self-understanding, but it can never become the primary way of understanding how an institution is Catholic. The Catholic tradition upholds the dignity of the person so that respect for the individual, be she student, president, maintenance worker, or staff, should characterize the life and dealings on campus. While insisting on the dignity of the person, Catholic self-understanding has put great stress on the need for persons to exist within communities. The human person is by nature social and not just an isolated monad. The very word *college* comes from the Latin *collegium*, meaning a partnership or corporate reality. American higher education frequently speaks of the college or university as a community. The Catholic tradition recognizes the need to establish colleges as true intellectual communities in which all are working together with mutual respect in the pursuit of knowledge. However, the community from a Catholic perspective must be all-embracing thus illustrating the diversity and pluralism of our world today. Spokespersons for higher education frequently stress the need for diversity on our campuses especially in terms of the mix of students and faculty, and by definition the Catholic tradition supports such diversity.

Thus far this chapter has pointed out the implications for a Catholic college of those aspects which are distinctive of Catholic self-understanding but are also shared in common by many other people. These aspects must affect the entire institution. However, there are also uniquely Catholic aspects that affect Catholic higher education.

The uniquely Catholic identity affects many extracurricular aspects of the Catholic college. One would rightly expect the Catholic college to have a strong, well-financed, and vibrant Catholic campus ministry program. This program should include a worshipping community and an effective social justice outreach component. Note that the Catholic college itself is not a worshipping community but an intellectual community. However, the Catholic college should provide a worshipping community for those Catholics associated with the institution. Also, today the social mission of the church has taken on great importance, and a commitment to the oppressed should be a part of the Catholic ministry on campus. However, at the same time the Catholic college should encourage other religious groups to have their own campus ministries.

The uniquely Catholic identity affects the curriculum through the role of Catholic theology. The Catholic college should have a strong and very competent theology faculty. However, there is also room for other Christian theologies and for what has come to be known as religious studies. I personally think it is appropriate on such campuses to require that students take courses in theology. Likewise attempts should be made to make sure that theology is in dialogue with many other aspects of the human as represented on the campus. One advantage of a Catholic college or university is that theology and religion should not be privatized but should be an integral and essential part of the ongoing discussion among and between disciplines. The danger in so much of contemporary society is that religion becomes privatized and does not enter into the public domain. The uniquely Catholic aspect might also be developed in terms of a program or concentration in Catholic studies. This concentration could very well parallel similar developments that have taken place in other aspects of the academy such as women's studies, black studies, and so forth. Some institutions are already trying to develop such a program.

This chapter has developed the understanding of a Catholic college on the basis of Catholic identity with its twofold aspects—the unique and the distinctive. The distinctive aspects can and should be held by many other people who are not Catholic and supported by reasons that are not necessarily Catholic, Christian, or religious in orientation. Catholic by its definition tends toward universality and inclusiveness so that it will naturally share many aspects with others. A Catholic vision and understanding in its broadest sense has grounded such an understanding of the Catholic college but others can readily accept the ethos, environment, and curricular proposals that have been made in the name of the Catholic institution.

Within the American higher academy today different types of institutions exist. Some universities are heavily research-oriented whereas smaller colleges tend to emphasize teaching. Liberal arts colleges differ from more vocational or professionally dominated institutions. Land grant institutions have their own distinctive ethos, programs, and curricula.

Non-Catholics can and should be encouraged to participate in the life of the Catholic college as students, staff, faculty, and trustees. They can readily associate themselves with the understanding of the university developed here without in any way having to accept the Catholic faith. The Catholic college is not interested in converting its non-Catholic colleagues. The college does not proselytize. In fact, the presence of non-Catholics allows for the dialogue with other religions that became so important at the Vatican II.

Some understandings of catholicity in higher education talk about the need for faculty members who accept the Catholic faith and propose preferential hiring for faculty who are Catholic. However, in the understanding of catholicity proposed here, the religious faith of the individual person is not the most important reality. The most important reality concerns the willingness to accept the intellectual milieu described here. One can readily do that without being a Roman Catholic. However, I think it would be an anomaly if there were only a few faculty members who belonged to the Roman Catholic Church. At the very minimum at the present time it seems to me that one should not place that much emphasis upon the religious faith of the individual faculty member but rather one's willingness to accept the intellectual orientation and goals of the institution. Much the same applies also to trustees of such Catholic institutions.

The Catholic college or university as described here can rightly and properly appeal to the local pluralistic community for support. The Catholic college serves the intellectual needs of the community and appeals both to Catholics and non-Catholics. The service rendered by the Catholic college is primarily in the intellectual order and not in the religious order.

One might object that the catholicity of the institution as described here is somewhat vague and tenuous. To a certain extent there is some truth in that contention. However, the basic reason for such a reality emerges from the understanding of catholicity as such. Catholicism in its understanding of the world and the intellectual life does not pretend to see its position in opposition to others but rather recognizes a great deal of communality based on its acceptance of the goodness and the autonomy of the intellectual order. A somewhat similar debate is being carried out today in the discipline of Christian ethics. The question is raised whether Christians or Catholics are called to act in a different way in human society and life from other people. Many have concluded that there is nothing unique about the content of what Christians are called to do in their social interrelations in this world. There is only one basic moral order for both Christians and non-Christians. The unique aspects of Christianity do not affect the content of how people should act in the political, social, and economic orders. Let me be very clear. I am not asserting that Christian faith has nothing to do with how we live or act in this world. But I am claiming that concern for the poor, care for those in need, and struggling for justice are not uniquely Christian but can and are proposed by many who reject the Catholic or Christian faith.[15]

Precisely because the Catholic identity does not make that many unique contributions to the intellectual milieu of the Catholic college, the danger of secularization must always be faced and responded to. Secularization is the primary temptation for the Catholic, not sectarianism. For this reason it is all the more important that the institution itself continue to talk about its vision and mission and tell the story of its own existence.

But there is an even more important reason for Catholic colleges to think about, discuss, and articulate their nature and identity. Our vocations in higher education require such thought, discussion, and articulation. No vision or understanding of an institution can or should be imposed from the top down. I believe that the faculty itself must wrestle with this question of the identity of a Catholic college and strive to come up with an approach which is appropriate. The same is true for the trustees in consultation with the faculty. This Catholic vision of the college must be explicitly thought about and developed by the academic community itself, shared with the new people who join the academic community, and used as a criterion contributing to the curriculum and to the directions in which the institution should develop. The climate on most Catholic campuses today does not encourage such conversations and actions, but without them the Catholic identity of such institutions in the future will be nominal at best.

Notes

1. Recent books discussing the issue of Catholic identity of colleges and universities include: Theodore Hesburgh, ed., *The Challenge and Promise of a Catholic University* (Notre Dame, Ind.: University of Notre Dame Press, 1994); John P. Langan, ed., *Catholic Universities in Church and Society: A Dialogue on Ex corde Ecclesiae* (Washington: Georgetown University Press, 1993); David J. O'Brien, *From the Heart of the American Church: Catholic Higher Education and American Culture* (Maryknoll, N.Y.: Orbis, 1994).
2. John Paul II, "*Ordinatio sacerdotalis*: Apostolic Letter on Ordination and Women," *Origins* 24 (1994): 49–52.
3. Congregation for the Doctrine of the Faith, "Response to '*Dubium*,'" *Origins* 25 (1995): 401–3.
4. John E. Curley, Jr., "Catholic Healthcare: Identity and Integrity," in *The Future of Catholic Institutional Ministries: A Continuing Conversation,* ed. Charles J. Fahey and Mary Ann Lewis (New York: Third Age Center, Fordham University, 1992), 99–109.
5. George M. Marsden, *The Soul of the American University: From Protestant Establishments to Established Nonbelief* (New York: Oxford University Press, 1994).
6. For a summary of these discussions, see O'Brien, *From the Heart of the American Church*, 51–68.
7. For a somewhat sympathetic description of this era, see Philip Gleason,

Keeping the Faith: American Catholicism Past and Present (Notre Dame, Ind.: University of Notre Dame Press, 1989), 82–96.

8. Ernst Troeltsch, *The Social Teaching of the Christian Churches*, 2 vols. (New York: Harper, 1960), vol. 1, 331 ff.
9. Thomas Aquinas, *Summa theologiae*, 4 vols. (Rome: Marietti, 1952), I II, q. 1–5.
10. See *Readings in Moral Theology No. 7: Natural Law and Theology*, ed. Charles E. Curran and Richard A. McCormick (New York: Paulist, 1991).
11. For a Catholic perspective on the Barthian denial of "both–and," see Hans Urs von Balthasar, *The Theology of Karl Barth* (New York: Holt, Rinehart, and Winston, 1971), 40–41.
12. Aquinas, *Summa*, I II, Prologue.
13. For Aquinas' five ways of proving the existence of God, see *Summa*, I, q. 2, a. 3.
14. Thomas J. Bouquillon, "The University of Paris I," *Catholic University Bulletin* 1 (1895): 349–64.
15. For the different approaches to this debate within moral theology, see *Readings in Moral Theology No. 2: The Distinctiveness of Christian Ethics*, ed. Charles E. Curran and Richard A. McCormick (New York: Paulist, 1980).

~ 11 ~

Veritatis splendor: A Revisionist Perspective

Pope John Paul II's encyclical, *Veritatis splendor*, officially signed on August 6, 1993, has the "central theme" of the "reaffirmation of the universality and immutability of the moral commandments, particularly those which prohibit always and without exception intrinsically evil acts" (n. 115).[1]

The pope directs his remarks primarily to the state of Catholic moral theology today, but since the Catholic approach always saw its moral teaching affecting society as a whole, the encyclical makes important remarks about life in the world today. The pope had publicly mentioned his intention of writing such an encyclical on August 1, 1987, the second centenary of the death of Alphonsus Liguori, the patron saint of moral theologians and confessors (n. 5). Rumors about the preparation, the primary authors, the central themes, and even the possible scrapping of the whole idea surfaced in the intervening years. The pope himself refers to the encyclical as "long awaited" and proposes as one reason for the delay that the *Catechism of the Catholic Church* be published first (n. 5).

Overview of the Encyclical

The encyclical is addressed to "the venerable brothers in the episcopate who share with me the responsibility of safeguarding 'sound teaching'. . ." (n. 5).

The occasion for the new encyclical is the "new situation" within the Catholic Church itself. "It is no longer a matter of limited and occasional dissent, but of an overall and systematic calling into question of traditional moral doctrines on the basis of certain anthropological and ethical presuppositions (n. 4). These dissenting positions are heard even in seminaries and theological faculties with regard to questions of the greatest importance for the life of the church and souls (n.4). This reality constitutes "a genuine crisis" for the church (n.5).

At the root of these unacceptable presuppositions causing the present crisis are currents of thought which end by detaching human freedom from its essential and constitutive relationship to truth (n. 4). This explains the whole thrust of the encyclical with its title of the "Splendor of Truth" and with the very first paragraph of the introduction citing 1 Peter 1:22 about the need for "obedience to the truth." The whole structure of the document with its three chapters follows logically and coherently from the understanding of the occasion for it and the root causes of the problem.

The first chapter involves an extended reflection on the story in Mt 19:16 ff. of the rich young man who came to Jesus with the question, "What good must I do to have eternal life?" Jesus' response is that he should obey the commandments and give up all his possessions and come follow him. This comparatively long biblical reflection involves a somewhat new approach in papal teachings on moral matters. Catholic moral theology is traditionally based on human reason and natural law. However, similar but shorter reflections on biblical passages can be found in other encyclicals of the pope.[2] The pope uses this scriptural passage to point out that God's revelation includes moral commandments and that the moral life is intimately connected with faith. However, in no way does the pope abandon the Catholic emphasis on natural law, as the second chapter makes abundantly clear.

The real import of the first chapter comes from its relationship to the purpose of the entire document. "Jesus' conversation with the rich young man continues in a sense in every period of history including our own" (n. 25). The church ("the pillar and bulwark of the truth"—2 Tm 3:15) continues the teaching role of Jesus with the "task of authentically interpreting the word of God . . . entrusted only [*sic*] to those charged with the church's living magisterium, whose authority is exercised in the name of Jesus Christ" (n. 27).[3] These quotations come from the end of the first chapter and make the point that the pope today continues the work of Jesus in teaching the commandments to guide the moral life of all the followers of Jesus.

The way in which scripture is used depends on the purpose of the one using it. Here the pope's purpose has shaped and limited the use of the scripture. The moral life is understood primarily in terms of commandments (to the exclusion and underplaying of other elements such as the change of heart, virtues, vision, attitudes, moral imagination, goals, and so forth), and the role of Jesus and consequently of the church is reduced to teaching commandments. Jesus as exemplar or paradigm is left out. The risen Jesus through the Spirit as the enabler and empowerer of the Christian life is not mentioned. The moral life itself is understood in light of a legal model, with the pope following the role of Jesus proposing the commandments "with the reaffirmation of the universality and immutability of the moral commandments, particularly those prohibiting always and without exception intrinsically evil acts" (n. 115).

The second chapter has an entirely different feel and approach. The pope, carrying on the moral teaching function of Jesus, points out and condemns certain interpretations of Christian morality which are not consistent with sound teaching. The pope explicitly denies any intention "to impose upon the faithful any particular theological system, still less a philosophical one" (n. 29). However, in reality John Paul II strongly reasserts the nineteenth- and twentieth-century neoscholasticism of the manuals of moral theology within his more personalistic framework.

The general error pointed out in this section fails to recognize the importance of truth in moral theology and absolutizes freedom or conscience, cutting off their basic relationship to truth. The pope specifically mentions and condemns the most important aspects of the so-called revisionist school of Catholic moral theology (he does not use that term) that has been evolving since Vatican II—an autonomous ethic, the charge of physicalism made against the accepted Catholic teaching in sexual and medical ethics, the theory of fundamental option, and the ethical theory of proportionalism. All these in their own way have called into question the existence of some intrinsically evil acts. *Veritatis splendor* in this chapter also strongly criticizes in the broader context the absolutization of freedom, false autonomy, subjectivism, individualism, and relativism.

Chapter three develops a number of related points. The first stresses the bond between freedom and truth. Commitment to the truth above all shows forth in the willingness of people to give their lives for the truth of the gospel of Jesus. Although martyrdom represents the high point of witness to moral truth, and one to which few people are called, all Christians must daily be ready to make a consistent witness at the cost of suffering and sacrifice (n. 93). Second, universal and unchangeable norms are at the service of persons and of the society, thus showing the necessary connection between freedom and truth. Only a morality which acknowledges certain norms and rights as valid always, everywhere, and without exception can guarantee an ethical foundation of social coexistence on both the national and international levels (nn. 95–101). Third, the chapter recalls that God's grace transforms and strengthens weak and sinful human beings to be able to obey God's law (nn. 102–105). A final section on morality and evangelization contains an important section dealing with the roles of the magisterium and of moral theologians who are called to be an example of loyal assent, both internal and external, to the magisterium's teaching (nn. 106–117).

Early reaction to the encyclical has followed a somewhat predictable course.[4] Proponents of what has been called revisionism in Catholic moral theology have tended to be quite negative,[5] whereas more conservative moral theologians have been quite positive although some want the pope to go even further to a definitive and infallible magisterial judgment on the received teaching on intrinsically evil acts and to the same kind of judgment on certain understandings of faith and revelation which are even more fundamental.[6] Some more evangelically rooted scholars have lauded the pope's great emphasis on scripture and the gospel, but perhaps they do not give enough importance to how strongly the second chapter of the document holds on to neoscholastic philosophy.[7] Feminists readily find fault with the methodology involved.[8] A good number have been appreciative of the pope's dealing with the broader societal issues.[9] All of us interpret and react to the document in the light of our own understandings and interests, but we all must be careful to try to understand precisely what the pope is saying before entering into dialogue with him. In this spirit I recognize that I am coming from a revisionist position and have disagreed over the years with the papal teaching on intrinsically evil acts and dissent in the church. One commentator has pointed out that the encyclical is directed at my work.[10] However, I also find myself in agreement with many points made in the encyclical.

Positive Evaluation

I find myself in agreement with many of the pope's problems with some contemporary ethical thinking, with the positive points he makes against them, and with the applications especially in the area of social ethics. Moral truth is most important. Freedom and conscience can never be absolutized. There are many things one should not do (nn. 35–53). The Catholic tradition in the past often failed to give enough importance to freedom as exemplified in its long-standing opposition to religious freedom and the continuing problems with academic freedom. However, as the twentieth-century developed, the Catholic Church, in reaction to the danger of totalitarianism, began to give a greater role to human freedom. A very significant development occurred in Pope John XXIII's writings within two years. In *Mater et magistra* in 1961 he claimed that the ideal social order was founded on the values of truth, justice, and love.[11] In *Pacem in terris* in 1963 he added freedom to this triad.[12] Freedom is very significant, but it must be seen in its relationship to other values. The pope in *Veritatis splendor* is concentrating on freedom's relationship to truth, but it is fair to say he is not denying the other important relationships of freedom with justice and charity. One is not free to deny fundamental human rights.

Just as freedom cannot be absolutized so too conscience cannot be absolutized. Conscience cannot make something right or wrong (nn. 54-64). Adolph Eichmann claimed that he only followed his conscience, but he was rightly convicted of crimes against humanity. Conscience is called to recognize and respond to moral truth. Intimately connected with the absolutization of freedom or conscience is the false autonomy of the individual. The individual is not autonomous in the sense that the individual makes something right or wrong on her own. Here too, however, the Catholic tradition has not given enough importance to the role of creativity and the initiative of the individual. But one cannot go to the other extreme and proclaim the absolute autonomy of the individual. Any theistic morality sees the individual in relationship to and dependent on God.

The challenge is to avoid both a one-sided autonomy or a one-sided heteronomy. *Veritatis splendor* deals well with this aspect of autonomy in the first part of the second chapter (nn. 38-42). To its credit the Catholic tradition with its emphasis on participation has been able to provide a very satisfactory approach to this question. Too often the issue is proposed in terms of a competition between the divine and the human. If you have one hundred points to assign to both, then you might assign eighty to God and twenty to the human. But maybe human beings should have more and God less. The traditional Catholic emphasis on participation and mediation as mentioned in the encyclical avoids such an either or approach. The glory of God is the human person come alive. God wants us to attain our happiness and our perfection. The basic insight of Thomas Aquinas well illustrates this approach. In the Second Part of the *Summa,* Aquinas speaks of the human being as an image of God because like God she is endowed with intellect, free will, and the power of self-determination.[13] The human person imitates God by using her intellect, free will, and the power of self-determination.

Traditional Catholic moral theology following the teaching of Thomas Aquinas sees the natural law as the participation of the eternal law in the rational creature. Human reason reflecting on God's created human nature can arrive at the plan of God for us which involves our own fulfillment.[14] All theists and even some nontheists would join the Catholic tradition in denying the absolute autonomy of the human being. But the Catholic tradition does not want to embrace a heteronomy which downplays the place of self-direction and human fulfillment.

Likewise the pope properly points out the related danger of individualism in our society (n.33). The absolutization of freedom, conscience, and autonomy logically lead to individualism. The individual becomes the center of all reality and not enough importance is given to the community in general, the various communities to which we all belong, and the relationships that tie us to other human beings. In the past, the Catholic tradition has not given enough importance to the individual and sometimes in the name of community restricted the role and rights of the individual. Think of the acceptance of torture in some cases and the failure to recognize the right of the defendant not to incriminate herself. Until this century it was universally held that the state could and should use capital punishment to protect itself, but now many Catholics, recognizing more the dignity of the person, strongly oppose capital punishment. A greater emphasis is being given to the rights of the individual vis-à-vis the state, but contemporary Catholic thought in keeping with the best of its own tradition rightly rejects individualism. In the United States society today many are criticizing American individualism in the name of a more communitarian understanding of human anthropology.[15] The Catholic tradition strongly supports such a communitarian critique of individualism.

Subjectivism logically follows from all the above-mentioned approaches. The pope correctly condemns the subjectivism that makes the subject the center of right and wrong and does not give enough significance to objective reality (n. 32). Here again the Catholic tradition in the past has not given enough importance to the subject, and many recent developments in Catholic theology and philosophy have embraced the turn to the subject but this does not entail a radical moral subjectivism.

This radical subjectivism often appears in our society but without much philosophical grounding. The morality accepted by many people today proclaims that you do your thing and I'll do my thing. Just don't interfere with each other. Such subjective individualism destroys any possibility of a community of shared truths and values. To have a community one needs such shared moral values. The pope rightly points out there are rights that are always and everywhere to be acknowledged and protected. There are actions such as torture, arbitrary imprisonment, and treating workers as mere instruments of profit that should never be done (nn. 95–97). The dangers of individualism and subjectivism are present in our contemporary American society.

Finally, John Paul II points out the danger of relativism for human social living (nn. 96–101). The Catholic tradition by definition stands opposed to relativism. Catholic means universal and the pope insists on the existence of universal principles and norms. The danger in the Catholic tradition has been not to give enough importance to diversity in all its different forms. Think, for example, of the insistence on the universal language for liturgical prayer before Vatican II so that almost no Catholic understood the language of the Eucharist. The Catholic emphasis on universality too easily claimed universality for what was a historically or culturally conditioned reality. Feminism reminds us how easy it was for those in power to impose patriarchy in the name of universality.

One of the most significant debates in contemporary ethics focuses on the possibility of universality in ethics, with many either theoretically or practically denying the possibility of such universality.[16] However, the Catholic tradition with its emphasis on the one God who is Creator, Redeemer, and Sanctifier of all can never accept a relativism. We are brothers and sisters of all other human beings and called to live together with them in peace and harmony. In the midst of the pluralism and diversity of our world, universalism is more chastened than in the past and more difficult to ground and explain. I think that the pope tends to gloss over too easily some of the objections to universalism, too readily grounds it in Thomistic natural law, and at times claims too much for it. However, the Catholic tradition has correctly insisted on universality.

The signs of the times also demand some universality. We experience the lack of unity in many countries in the world including our own. Religious, ethnic, and tribal differences are the cause of war and disintegration in many nations. In the society of our own United States the divisions based on color and economic class are evident in every one of our cities. In our world, with its growing interrelatedness, we badly need to be able to communicate with one another despite religious, linguistic, ethnic, and cultural differences. In many ways the challenge to our society today is how to achieve unity in the midst of the great diversity that exists on all levels.

Negative Evaluation

My strong disagreements with the papal letter center on his understanding of and approach to contemporary Catholic moral theology and what might be described as the churchly aspect of moral theology as distinguished from Catholic social ethics. As I have already identified myself as a revisionist Catholic moral theologian, one would expect such differences to be there. Naturally, I disagree with the position that condemns the revisionist developments in moral theology, but I am even more disturbed by other aspects of the papal document.

The Role and Understanding of Law. The first objection comes from the moral model which the pope proposes in *Veritatis splendor*. Here John Paul II understands morality primarily on the basis of a legal model. Such an approach, which characterized the manuals of moral theology as illustrated in chapter three, sees morality primarily in terms of obedience to the law or the commandments of God. No one can doubt that *Veritatis splendor* employs such a model. The very first paragraph emphasizes the need for obedience to the truth, but recognizes that such obedience is not always easy. The pericope of the rich young man stresses Jesus as the teacher proposing the commandments that are to be obeyed. The first and longest of the four parts of chapter two deals with freedom and the law (nn. 35–53). Chapter two especially emphasizes the role of the natural law. Positive precepts of the natural law are "universally binding" and "unchanging." The negative precepts of the natural law oblige always and in every circumstance—*semper et pro semper* (n. 52). The third chapter continues this approach with its emphasis on laws and commands and the church's firmness in defending the universal and unchanging moral norms (n. 96).

In the judgment of many, the legal model is not the best and most adequate model for moral theology or any ethics. At the very minimum the legal model cannot adequately cover all the moral decisions that a person makes. In fact, the vast majority of moral decisions are not made on the basis of existing laws. Law directly enters into comparatively few of the moral decisions by which we live our lives. In addition, the legal model tends to restrict moral considerations only to acts and forgets about the more important realities of change of heart, vision, attitudes, and dispositions. Thomas Aquinas did not follow a legal model, but rather a teleological model based on what is the ultimate end of human beings. For Aquinas the ultimate end of human beings is happiness, and actions are good if they bring one to that end and evil if they prevent one's arriving at that end. Reality of course is quite complex, so there exists not only the ultimate end but also other ends which are not ultimate and interrelated with one another. In addition, Thomas Aquinas developed the moral life primarily in terms of human powers and habits and only brings in law at the end of his discussion of what we call fundamental moral theology.[17] The manuals of moral theology, the textbooks in the field before Vatican II, did adopt a legal model. Much has been said about the legal model, but for our present purposes it suffices to point out the inadequacy of the model and the fact that Thomas Aquinas himself adopted a different approach.

One might defend the legal model in *Veritatis splendor* precisely because the pope is dealing primarily with the existence of universal and immutable moral commandments, especially those which prohibit always and without exception intrinsically evil acts. However, at the very minimum the encyclical should have pointed out that the legal model is not the most adequate model for moral theology, and this document is dealing only with one aspect of moral theology. Neither explicitly nor implicitly does the pope make such an admission. *Veritatis splendor* thus gives the impression that it is describing the model for moral theology in general.

Ironically, someone in the Catholic tradition using the legal model tends to weaken the basic assertion of the entire encyclical that there is no opposition between freedom and law. Historically the manuals of moral theology with their legal model, ever since the seventeenth century and later debates over probabilism tended to posit an opposition between law and freedom. This assertion needs further explanation.

The Catholic tradition as illustrated in Thomas Aquinas has always insisted on an intrinsic morality. Something is commanded because it is good. For Aquinas the ultimate end of human beings is happiness. Morality involves what is good for me as a person and ultimately makes me flourish. There is no opposition between freedom and moral obligation because the moral obligation is based on what is good for the individual. This is the central point to which the pope so frequently returns in his document. However, in the manuals of moral theology ever since the probabilism controversy, a greater opposition rather than harmonious agreement exists between freedom and law. Probabilism maintains that one may follow a truly probable opinion, going against the existence of a law, even if the opinion favoring the existence of the law is more probable. The so-called reflex principle used to defend this position holds that a doubtful law does not oblige—an adage more attuned to human law than anything else. The individual starts out with one's freedom, and this freedom can only be taken away by a certain law.[18] Ironically the law model as it was employed in the manuals of Catholic moral theology in the light of the probabilism controversy emphasizes the tension and apparent opposition between freedom and law rather than the harmony which the pope wants to emphasize.

Laws Which Always and Everywhere Oblige. The major thrust of the encyclical insists on universal, immutable moral commandments which prohibit always and without exception intrinsically evil acts. In this context, note that the pope never cites the fifth commandment, "Thou shalt not kill." Everyone recognizes that killing is not always and everywhere wrong. We have justified killing in cases of self-defense and war. In fact, after much discussion and nuancing, the manuals of moral theology came to the conclusion that the intrinsically evil act which is always forbidden is the following: direct killing of the innocent on one's own authority. Thus we allowed indirect killing, killing in self-defense or in war, and capital punishment.[19]

Notice the difference between the two. Killing is a physical act which in some circumstances can be permitted. The second rule tries to account for all the possible justifying circumstances and thus states the norm that admits of no exceptions. But one has to circumscribe quite severely the generic "no killing." The pope himself in this document does not cite this very specific absolute norm that was developed in Catholic moral theology.

What, then, is the papal example of the universal, immutable condemnation of an act that is always and everywhere wrong? The answer: murder. Thus in the passage about the rich young man in Matthew, Jesus begins the commandments with, "You shall not murder" (n. 13). All would agree that murder is always wrong, because by definition murder is unjustified killing. Thus we have here three different types of norms dealing with killing. The pope cites only the very formal norm of no murder.

But there is a problem in *Veritatis splendor* from the pope's own perspective, because of a fourth formulation that is proposed. The pope wants to illustrate the point that there are intrinsically evil acts which are always and per se such on account of their very object and quite apart from the intention of the agent and circumstances. He quotes the Pastoral Constitution on the Church in the Modern World, paragraph 27, to illustrate this thesis (n. 80). The quote begins: "Whatever is hostile to life itself such as any kind of homicide. . . ." However, homicide is not an intrinsically evil act. Homicide is the physical act of killing a human being. Our language recognizes that homicide can be justifiable in certain circumstances.

But the problem might not come primarily from the pope. The official Latin version of the encyclical in its citation from the Pastoral Constitution on the Church in the Modern World uses the word *homicidium.*[20] *Homicidium* in the Latin can refer either to murder or homicide. As mentioned above, in this case the pope is citing a text from the Pastoral Constitution on the Church in the Modern World of Vatican II. Two unofficial English translations of the documents translate *homicidium* as murder.[21] However, the official translation of the papal encyclical that came from the Vatican uses the word "homicide." The error might rest with the translator and the approval of that translation by the Vatican. However, at the very minimum this goes to show how intricate and difficult it is to speak about norms that are always and everywhere obliging without any exception.

In fact, the list of actions found originally in the Pastoral Constitution on the Church in the Modern World and quoted in *Veritatis splendor* contains some actions which are not always and everywhere wrong. Both documents include abortion under the category of "what is hostile to life itself." However, the Catholic tradition has always recognized the existence of some conflict situations and concluded that direct abortion is always wrong. Indirect abortion can be justified for a proportionate reason so that abortion is not always and everywhere wrong. One would have to be stretching the point beyond belief to claim that the original clause of "whatever is hostile to life itself" means that homicide is murder and abortion is direct abortion. The reality is that any homicide or abortion is hostile to life itself, but in some circumstances might be justified.

The second category of those actions in both documents which are now claimed by the pope to be always and everywhere wrong concerns "whatever violates the integrity of the human person such as mutilation. . . ." However, Catholic moral theology has consistently recognized justified mutilation. In fact, as chapter two pointed out, the principle of totality in medical ethics justifies a mutilation of a part of the body for the sake of the whole.[22] Here again one cannot appeal to the opening clause "whatever violates the integrity of the human person" to show that the mutilation in such a context excluded medical mutilation for the good of the whole person. If the heading were the dignity or total good of the human person then one could make such a claim. By definition all mutilation goes against the physical integrity of the person, but the Catholic tradition does not say that all mutilation is wrong. The pope's efforts to uphold laws that are intrinsically or always and without exception wrong by reason of the object is fraught with difficulties.

There are such actions when the act is described in merely formal terms such as murder. One could also make the case that there are such acts when the significant circumstances are included. In reality, *Veritatis splendor* itself does not succeed in making a consistent case to prove its own position about acts that are always and intrinsically evil by reason of the object alone.

Evaluation of Contemporary Moral Theology. *Veritatis splendor* strongly disagrees with and condemns many of the developments in Catholic moral theology since Vatican II and stands opposed to the revisionist moral theology in general.

However, *Veritatis splendor* distorts and does not accurately describe the various positions attributed to so-called revisionist moral theologians. The first part of the second chapter disagrees with a school of autonomous ethics which first arose in Germany (nn. 36–37). I have disagreed with the name "autonomous" but accept the reality proposed in the sense that the moral content for life in this world is the same for Christians as for non-Christians. In my judgment, this position is in keeping with the traditional assertion that the Christian brings the human to its perfection and fulfillment. Like *Veritatis splendor* I have also disagreed with the contention that the scripture provides only *parenesis* or exhortation as some hold.[23] However, the supporters of autonomous ethics in the Catholic tradition would strongly disagree with the following description of their position. "Such norms. . . would be the expression of a law which man [*sic*] in an autonomous manner lays down for himself and which has its source exclusively in human reason. In no way could God be considered the author of this law except in the sense that human reason exercises its autonomy in setting down laws by virtue of a primordial and total mandate given to man by God" (n. 36).

Veritatis splendor in the same first part of chapter two, points out that some Catholic moral theologians have disagreed with the teachings of the hierarchical magisterium in the area of sexual morality because of their "physicalism" and "naturalistic" argumentation (n. 47). Such a statement is correct. In my opinion physicalism is the a priori identification of the human or the moral aspect with the physical, natural, or biological process. So far, so good. But the pope goes on to explain this theory in this way. "A freedom which claims to be absolute ends up treating the human body as a raw datum devoid of any meaning and moral values until freedom has shaped it in accordance with its design. Consequently, human nature and the body appear as presuppositions or preambles, materially necessary for freedom to make its choice, yet extrinsic to the person, the subject, and the human act. . . . The finalities of these inclinations would be merely 'physical' goods, called by some *premoral*. To refer to them, in order to find in them rational indications with regard to the order of morality, would be to expose oneself to the accusation of physicalism or biologism. In this way of thinking, the tension between freedom and a nature conceived of in a reductive way is resolved by a division within man [*sic*] himself" (n. 48).

Those who charge the hierarchical magisterium's teaching on sexuality with physicalism do not "treat the human body as a raw datum devoid of any meaning." The physical is one aspect of the moral or the fully human. The moral or the fully human must embrace all the aspects of the human—the physical and the spiritual, the sociological and the psychological, the eugenic and the hygienic. In keeping with the Catholic tradition, one should never be guilty of a reductionism that reduces the fully human to just one aspect of the human no matter what that aspect is. Yes, there are times when the physical is the same as the moral and the truly human, but this needs further justification to make the point.[24] In this very citation, the pope contradicts his own assertion. *Veritatis splendor* refers to this physical aspect as physical or premoral goods. Note the word "goods." They are not just "raw datum" or "extrinsic to the person." Those making the charge of physicalism take seriously the position of Pius XII that the physical and the bodily exist to serve the higher spiritual good of the person.[25] That one in theory can interfere with the physical or biological process, because of the good of the total person as a whole, seems to be very much in accord with any kind of personalism. But at the very least *Veritatis splendor* distorts the position of those who characterize hierarchical Catholic sexual teaching as guilty of physicalism. We do not absolutize freedom and we do not deny any value or meaning to the physical. In our judgment the hierarchical magisterium in this matter has absolutized the physical and the biological at the expense of the truly and the fully human.

The second part of chapter two deals with the relationship between conscience and truth. However, John Paul II also dealt with that question earlier in the encyclical. The pope claims that those who invoke the criterion of conscience as "being at peace with oneself" (he puts the words in quotation marks) are guilty of absolutizing freedom, forgetting the claim of truth, and subjectivism (n. 32).

I have proposed a theory of conscience which "attempts to explain in a more systematic and reflective way the traditionally accepted notion that joy and peace mark the good conscience which is the adequate criterion of good moral judgment and decision."[26] I explicitly point out that my approach disagrees with the position of the manuals that the judgment of conscience is based on conformity with the truth "out there." I developed this theory in dialogue with the transcendental approaches of Karl Rahner and Bernard Lonergan. However, I insist that one's judgment has to attain the true and the real value. I do put great emphasis on the subject but insist that "thus we have established the radical identity between genuine objectivity and authentic subjectivity."[27] Such an approach is proposed as a theory and others might readily disagree with it, but it does not "exalt freedom to such an extent that it becomes an absolute" nor "adopt a radically subjectivistic conception of moral judgment" (n. 32).

In the second part of chapter two on conscience, it seems that the pope's insistence on the relationship between conscience and truth has influenced him to take a position which at the very least is in opposition to the generally accepted position in Catholic moral theology. *Veritatis splendor* states: "It is possible that the evil done as the result of invincible ignorance or a non-culpable error of judgment may not be imputable to the agent; but even in this case it does not cease to be an evil. . . ." (n. 63). Thomas Aquinas maintained that invincible ignorance renders the act involuntary and excuses from sin. In other words, the evil act done in invincible ignorance is never imputable to the agent. The encyclical does not go as far as Aquinas and simply says that it "may not be imputable to the agent." However, St. Alphonsus Ligouri, the patron saint of moral theologians and confessors, goes even further than Aquinas. Alphonsus maintains that an act done out of invincible ignorance is not only not imputable but it is actually meritorious. This opinion of Alphonsus became the more common position among Catholic theologians.[28] Louis Vereecke, now an emeritus professor of the history of moral theology at the Accademia Alfonsiana in Rome and a consultor to the Holy Office, concludes his article on conscience in Alphonsus Liguori by claiming that Alphonsus' moral doctrine on conscience embraces three values—the importance of truth, the importance of reason and conscience, and the importance of freedom.[29] By so emphasizing and perhaps even absolutizing the relationship of conscience to truth, *Veritatis splendor* not only does not accept the position of Alphonsus but does not even accept the position of Thomas Aquinas, which does not go as far as Alphonsus.

The third part of chapter three addresses the theory of the fundamental option. Here also the theory is distorted. For example, the encyclical speaks of the theory as separating "the fundamental option from concrete kinds of behavior" (n. 67, see also n. 70). The theory of fundamental option distinguishes the different levels of human freedom and of transcendental and categorical acts, but it does not separate them. As Joseph Fuchs, who has written much on the fundamental option points out, the encyclical distorts the meaning of the theory by failing to recognize that the fundamental option and categorical acts happen on different levels and thus the fundamental option does not occur in the area of reflex consciousness.[30]

The fourth part of chapter three deals with the moral act, insists on acts that are intrinsically evil by reason of their object, and condemns teleological and proportionalist theories which hold "that it is impossible to qualify as morally evil according to its species—its 'object'—the deliberate choice of certain kinds of behavior or specific acts apart from a consideration of the intention for which the choice is made or the totality of the foreseeable consequences of that act for all persons concerned" (n. 79). On a number of occasions the pope points out that a good intention is not sufficient to determine the morality of an act (n. 67, n. 78). But no Catholic moral theologian I know has ever claimed that the intention alone suffices to determine the morality of an act.[31] Above I pointed out that as a revisionist I accept some acts as always and everywhere wrong if the significant circumstances (not the totality of the forseeable consequences) are included.

I have no doubt that the pope disagrees with all these recently developed theories in Catholic moral theology, but the encyclical tends to distort them and thus does not reflect their true meaning. In a certain sense they are made into straw people which then are much easier to reject. However, this is not the worst distortion in the encyclical about the present state of Catholic moral theology.

The pope claims that the "root of these presuppositions [of the dissenting Catholic moral theologians] is the more or less obvious influence of currents of thought which end by detaching human freedom from its essential and constitutive relationship to truth" (n. 4). This sentence is found in the opening introduction to the entire document. The introduction to chapter two points out "these tendencies are at one in lessening or even denying the dependence of freedom on truth" (n. 34). Note some qualification in these statements, but the fundamental problem the pope has with revisionist Catholic moral theologians is their tendency to detach or lessen human freedom's relationship to truth. Such an assertion itself is not accurate. I know no Catholic moral theologian who absolutizes freedom or detaches conscience from truth. The real question remains the proverbial one—what is truth?

As a result of this misreading of the present state of Catholic moral theology, the pope apparently sees no difference between Catholic revisionist moral theologians and the proponents of absolute freedom, conscience separated from truth, individualism, subjectivism, and relativism. Non-Catholic colleagues or any fair-minded interpreter of the present state of Catholic moral theology would readily recognize that revisionist Catholic moral theologians are not absolutizing freedom or conscience and are not supporting individualism, subjectivism, and relativism. Catholic revisionist moral theologians strongly agree with the pope in opposing these positions. That is why I made it a point earlier in this chapter to stress my strong agreement with the pope on these points.

Everyone recognizes that the pope strongly disagrees with and condemns revisionist Catholic moral positions, but the problem here is the understanding of revisionist moral theologians. Their theories are caricatured, but even worse the pope falsely accuses them of absolutizing freedom and separating it from truth and wrongly identifies them with subjectivists, individualists, and relativists.

What is going on here? I do not know. Some have blamed the pope's advisers.[32] Such an approach is a familiar Catholic tactic. When Catholics disagree with the pope it is always easier to blame it on the advisers than on the pope. On the other hand, I have never heard anyone who agreed with a papal statement say that they agreed with the pope's advisers! Popes obviously have advisers, but the final document is the pope's and not theirs. More worrisome is the fact that the pope's area of expertise is ethics. Does he really think that Catholic moral theologians who dissent on some church teachings, especially in the area of sexuality, are subjectivists, individualists, and relativists?

A realistic assessment of the contemporary state of Catholic moral theology differs considerably from the picture painted in *Veritatis splendor*. The differences between the pope and revisionist moral theologians are by no means as great as *Veritatis splendor* states. Yes, different methodologies are often at work, but revisionist moral theologians have generally agreed with the papal teaching in the area of social ethics. Likewise, revisionist moral theologians are willing to accept some intrinsically evil acts when the object of the act is described in formal terms (murder is always wrong, stealing is always wrong) or when the act is described in terms of its significant circumstances (not telling the truth when the neighbor has a right to the truth).

The primary area of disagreement concerns the understanding of the moral object: the encyclical claims that morality is determined by the three sources of morality—the object, the end, and the circumstances—and that some actions are intrinsically evil by reason of their object (nn. 71–83). The question is, how does one describe the object? As mentioned above, revisionist theologians would be willing to admit intrinsically evil acts by reason of the object if the object were described in a broad or formal way or with some significant circumstances. The earlier discussion about always obliging laws pointed out a very significant problem in the encyclical itself in describing the moral object.

Revisionists in general object to those cases in which the moral act is assumed to be identical with the physical structure of the act. These areas occur especially in the area of sexuality. As pointed out, not every killing, mutilation, taking something that belongs to another, and false speech are always wrong. Contraception, however, describes a physical act. The physical act described as depositing male semen in the vagina of the female can never be interfered with. Some people have mistakenly thought that the hierarchical teaching against contraception was based on a pronatalist position. Such is not the case. The hierarchical teaching also condemns artificial insemination with the husband's seed even for the good end of having a child. The reason why both contraception and AIH are judged wrong is because the physical act must always be there and one can never interfere with it no matter what the purpose.[33]

The charge of physicalism is intimately connected with the theory of proportionalism. Rather than describe the physical act or object as morally wrong this theory speaks of premoral, ontic, or physical evil that can be justified for a proportionate reason. This challenges the hierarchical teaching on contraception but also explains the existing hierarchical teaching on killing, mutilation, and taking property. There is no doubt that Catholic moral theologians are calling for a change in hierarchical teaching especially in the area of sexuality, but they are precisely challenging these areas in which the moral aspect has been a priori identified with the physical aspect of the act. Thus the differences between these revisionist moral theologians and the pope are much less than the encyclical recognizes. The problem is not that dissenting moral theologians absolutize freedom and/or conscience or separate them from truth. The question remains, what is moral truth?

Hierarchical Magisterium and Theologians. The confrontation and differences within Catholic moral theology in the last few decades have centered not only on the moral issues themselves but on the ecclesiological questions of the role and functioning both of the hierarchical magisterium and of theologians. *Veritatis splendor* explicitly addresses these issues in the third chapter (nn. 106–17), although the role of the hierarchical magisterium is mentioned throughout the document.

The encyclical itself deals primarily with moral truth. The ultimate question for both the hierarchical magisterium and for moral theology is what is moral truth and how do we arrive at moral truth? *Veritatis splendor* condemns many approaches in moral theology and in the broader ethical world but it never really explicitly addresses the question about how the hierarchical magisterium itself arrives at moral truth. In fact, the encyclical gives the impression that the hierarchical magisterium simply has the truth. However, the hierarchical magisterium like everyone else has to learn the moral truth. How is this done? The most frequently used phrase in this regard in the encyclical is the "assistance of the Holy Spirit." Mention is also made of the revelational aspect of morality and the hierarchical magisterium's role as the protector, guarantor, and interpreter of revelation.

The entire second chapter with its discussion of very complex theories and positions shows that the hierarchical magisterium also uses human reason in its attempt to know and explain moral truth. The Catholic insistence on mediation means that God works in and through the human and does not provide short circuits around the human. The assistance of the Holy Spirit does not exempt the hierarchical magisterium from using all the human reason necessary to arrive at moral truth. The tradition of Catholic natural law once again affirmed and developed in this encyclical maintains that its moral theology is based on human reason and accessible to all human beings. Yes, the encyclical reminds us (correctly) that human sin affects all our reasoning processes, but sin does not take away human reason's ability to arrive at moral truth (nn. 86–87). In learning moral truth the hierarchical magisterium must use human reason like everyone else.

In the last few decades, many theologians have also pointed out the experience of Christian people as a source of moral knowledge. Once again, sin affects human experience and a proper discernment is required. One cannot just work on the basis of a majority vote. However, the hierarchical magisterium itself in its Declaration on Religious Freedom of Vatican II recognized the experience of Christian people as a source of moral wisdom. The fathers of the council took careful note of these desires for religious freedom in the minds of human beings and proposed to declare them to be greatly in accord with truth and justice.[34] However, *Veritatis splendor* never mentions even implicitly that the hierarchical magisterium can and should learn from the experience of Christian people. The pope explicitly says the fact that some believers do not follow the hiercharchical magisterium or consider as morally correct behavior that their pastors have condemned cannot be a valid argument for rejecting the moral norms taught by the hierarchical magisterium (n. 112).

The Thomistic moral tradition which the hierarchical magisterium claims to follow has insisted on an intrinsic morality—something is commanded because it is good and not the other way around. The hierarchical magisterium does not make something right or wrong, but the hierarchical magisterium must conform itself to the moral truth. Thus the hierarchical magisterium must use all the means available to arrive at that truth.

In addition, the Thomistic tradition recognizes that one cannot have the same degree of certitude about practical truths as about speculative truths.[35] The hierarchical magisterium has a role in guaranteeing and protecting revelation under the inspiration of the Holy Spirit but must also use all the human means available to arrive at moral truth and live with the reality that practical truths do not have the same degree of certitude as speculative truths. One cannot expect an encyclical to say everything on the subject, but a document dealing with the splendor of truth might have been expected to say something about the nature of moral truth and how the hierarchical magisterium itself learns and knows this moral truth.

History points out that the teaching of the hierarchical magisterium in moral matters has been wrong in the past and has developed or changed. John Noonan has recently documented this change in the areas of usury, marriage, slavery, and religious freedom.[36] The fact that past teachings of the hierarchical magisterium in morality have been wrong must have some influence on how one understands the pronouncements of the hierarchical magisterium today.

The Catholic tradition itself has rightly recognized a hierarchy of truths,[37] and even the pre-Vatican II theology developed a system of theological notes to determine how core and central teachings are in Catholic faith.[38] All interpreters would admit that most of the papal teaching (I would say all, as would many others) on specific moral issues involves the noninfallible teaching office of the pope. The fact that something is *noninfallible* does not mean that it is necessarily wrong or that Catholics can disagree with it, but by definition it means that it is *fallible*. Catholic moral theologians as well as the hierarchical magisterium today must do more work to develop and talk about these different categories in the light of the general insistence on the hierarchy of truths and the older theological notes. At the very minimum the hierarchical magisterium itself must also be willing to recognize the more tentative and peripheral nature of some of its pronouncements. In addition, the hierarchical magisterium has never come to grips with the fact that some of its teachings in the past have been wrong and subsequently changed.

Veritatis splendor understands the role of the moral theologian in the light of its understanding of the hierarchical magisterium. The assumption is that the hierarchical magisterium with the assistance of the Holy Spirit has the moral truth and proclaims it. Therefore moral theologians are to give an example of loyal assent, both internal and external, to the hierarchical magisterium's teaching (n. 110).

Veritatis splendor in an adversative clause acknowledges "the possible limitations of the human arguments employed by the magisterium," but calls moral theologians to develop a deeper understanding of the reasons underlying the hierarchical magisterium's teaching and to expound the validity and obligatory nature of the precepts it proposes (n. 110). Thus there might be limitations in the arguments proposed by the hierarchical magisterium, but these in no way affect the validity of the precepts it proposes.

In condemning dissent, the present document follows the approach of *Donum veritatis*, the 1990 document of the Congregation for the Doctrine of the Faith on the role of theologians.[39] Dissent, in the form of carefully orchestrated protests and polemics carried on in the media is opposed to ecclesial communion and to a proper understanding of the hierarchical constitution of the people of God. Opposition to the teaching of the church's pastors cannot be seen as a legitimate expression either of Christian freedom or of the diversity of the Spirit's gifts (n. 113). I know no Catholic moral theologian who dissents from church teaching who would propose what she or he has done in those terms. One might argue that such a definition of dissent leaves the door open for a different type of dissent. However, the encyclical itself calls for moral theologians to give an example of loyal assent, both internal and external, to the magisterium's teaching (n. 110).

The consideration here of the hierarchical magisterium does not intend to be a thorough discussion of the role of the hierarchical magisterium or of the moral theologian. This discussion is sufficient to point out the differences that exist. Revisionist Catholic moral theologians recognize the role of the hierarchical magisterium, but insist that its teachings cannot claim an absolute certitude on specific moral issues, have been wrong in the past, and might in some circumstances be wrong today. In this light dissent is at times a legitimate and loyal function of the Catholic moral theologian. However, *Veritatis splendor* at the very minimum does not admit any kind of tentativeness or lack of absolute certitude about the teachings of the hierarchical magisterium, and in no way explicitly recognizes a positive role for dissent.

Ever since the pope announced his intention in August 1987 of writing an encyclical dealing more fully with the issues regarding the foundations of moral theology in the light of certain present day tendencies, any student of moral theology had a pretty good idea of what the encyclical would do. The pope was certainly not going to change any of the teachings that have recently been reinforced nor was he going to abandon the reasoning process behind those teachings. As a result then no one should be surprised by those aspects found in *Veritatis splendor*.

What is surprising is the fact that the pope caricatures the positions of Catholic revisionist moral theologians and refuses to recognize the great areas of agreement between them and himself. One can only wonder why *Veritatis splendor* proposes such an "either–or" or "all-or-nothing" understanding of the positions taken by Catholic revisionist moral theologians. The fundamental question remains: What is moral truth?

Notes

1. Pope John Paul II, *Veritatis splendor, Origins* 23 (1993): 297–334. References will be given in the text to the paragraph numbers in the encyclical.
2. E.g., the parable of the Prodigal Son in *Dives in misericordia*, nn. 6–7. See Pope John Paul II, *Dives in misericordia*, in *Proclaiming Justice and Peace: Papal Documents from Rerum novarum through Centesimus annus*, ed. Michael Walsh and Brian Davies (Mystic, Conn.: Twenty-Third Publications, 1991), 344–47.
3. This passage is a citation from *Dei verbum*, the Constitution on Divine Revelation of the Second Vatican Council, n. 10.
4. Symposia on *Veritatis splendor* have appeared in *Commonweal* 120 (October 22, 1993): 11–18; *First Things*, no. 39 (January 1994): 14–29. *The Tablet* (London) devoted a series of eleven articles to the encyclical beginning with the October 16, 1993 issue, pp. 1329 ff.
5. E.g., Bernard Häring, "A Distress that Wounds," *The Tablet* 247 (October 23, 1993): 1378–79; Richard A. McCormick, "Killing A Patient," *The Tablet* 247 (October 30, 1993): 1410–11; Daniel C. Maguire, "The Splendor of Control," *Conscience* 14, no. 4 (Winter 1993/1994): 26–29.

6. John Finnis, "Beyond the Encyclical," *The Tablet* 248 (January 8, 1994): 9–10; Robert P. George, "The Splendor of Truth: A Symposium," *First Things* no. 39 (January 1994): 24–25; Germain Grisez, "Revelation vs. Dissent," *The Tablet* 247 (October 16, 1993): 1329–31.
7. Stanley Hauerwas, "*Veritatis splendor,*" *Commonweal* 120 (October 22, 1993): 16–17; L. Gregory Jones, "The Splendor of Truth: A Symposium," *First Things* no. 39 (January 1994): 19–20; Oliver O'Donovan, "A Summons to Reality," *The Tablet* 247 (November 27, 1993): 1550–52.
8. Lisa Sowle Cahill, "Accent on the Masculine,"*The Tablet* 247 (December 11, 1993): 1618–19.
9. E.g., Mary Tuck, "A Message in Season," *The Tablet* 247 (December 4, 1993): 1583–85.
10. Maguire, *Conscience* 14, no. 4 (Winter 1993/94): 28.
11. Pope John XXIII, *Mater et magistra*, n. 212, in *Catholic Social Thought: The Documentary Heritage*, ed. David J. O'Brien and Thomas A. Shannon (Maryknoll, NY: Orbis, 1992), 118.
12. Pope John XXIII, *Pacem in terris*, n. 35, in *Catholic Social Thought*, ed. O'Brien and Shannon, 136.
13. Thomas Aquinas, *Summa theologiae* (Rome: Marietti, 1952), I II, Prologue.
14. Ibid., q. 91, a. 2. John Paul II cites this passage in *Veritatis splendor*, n. 43.
15. E.g., Robert Bellah et al, *The Good Society* (New York: Alfred A. Knopf, 1991); Amitai Etzioni, *The Spirit of Community* (New York: Crown, 1993).
16. For my response to this debate, see *The Church and Morality: An Ecumenical and Catholic Approach* (Minneapolis, Minn.: Fortress, 1993), 96–109.
17. Aquinas, *Summa*, I II.
18. See, for example, John Mahoney, *The Making of Moral Theology* (Oxford: Clarendon, 1987), 224–45.
19. Marcellinus Zalba, *Theologiae moralis summa II: Tractatus de mandatis Dei et ecclesiae* (Madrid: Biblioteca de autores cristianos, 1953), nn. 243–66, pp. 255–86.
20. *Acta apostolicae sedis* 85, no. 12 (December 9, 1993): 1197.
21. *The Documents of Vatican II*, ed. Walter M. Abbott (New York: Guild, 1966), 226; *Vatican Council II: The Conciliar and Post Conciliar Documents*, ed. Austin Flannery (Northport, NY: Costello, 1975), 928.
22. Zalba, *Theologiae moralis summa II*, nn. 251–52; pp. 263–68.
23. Charles E. Curran, *Toward an American Catholic Moral Theology* (Notre Dame, Ind.: University of Notre Dame Press, 1987), 57–59.

24. Charles E. Curran, *Directions in Fundamental Moral Theology* (Notre Dame, Ind.: University of Notre Dame Press, 1985), 127–37, 156–61.
25. Pope Pius XII, "The Prolongation of Life," (November 24, 1957), in *Medical Ethics: Sources of Catholic Teachings*, ed. Kevin D. O'Rourke and Philip Boyle (St. Louis, Mo: Catholic Health Association, 1989), 207.
26. *Directions in Fundamental Moral Theology*, 244.
27. Ibid., 242.
28. Louis Vereecke, *De Guillaume d'Ockham à Saint Alphonse de Liguori* (Rome: Collegium S. Alfonsi de Urbe, 1986), 555–60; James Keenan, "Can a Wrong Action Be Good? The Development of Theological Opinion on Erroneous Conscience," *Église et théologie* 24 (1993): 205–19. However, Aquinas, Alphonsus, and Pope John Paul II all recognize that the external act remains an objective disorder and is wrong.
29. Vereecke, *De Guillaume d'Ockham*, 566.
30. Joseph Fuchs, "Good Acts and Good Persons," *The Tablet* 247 (November 6, 1993): 1445.
31. Richard A. McCormick, "Killing A Patient," *The Tablet* 247 (October 30, 1993): 1410–11.
32. Fuchs, *The Tablet* 247 (November 6, 1993): 1445; McCormick, *The Tablet* 247 (October 30, 1993): 1411.
33. See "Artificial Insemination," and "Contraception," in O'Rourke and Boyle, *Medical Ethics*, 62; 92–95.
34. Declaration on Religious Freedom, n. 1, in *Documents of Vatican II*, 676.
35. Aquinas, *Summa*, I II, q. 94, a. 4.
36. John T. Noonan, "Development in Moral Doctrine," *Theological Studies* 54 (1993): 662–77.
37. Decree on Ecumenism, n. 11, *Documents of Vatican II*, 354.
38. Sixtus Cartechini, *De Valore notarum theologicarum* (Rome: Gregorian University Press, 1951).
39. Vatican Congregation for the Doctrine of the Faith, "Instruction on the Ecclesial Vocation of the Theologian," *Origins* 20 (1990): 117–26.

~ 12 ~
Evangelium vitae and Its Broader Context

On March 25, 1995, Pope John Paul II issued the eleventh encyclical of his pontificate, *Evangelium vitae.*[1] The encyclical's issuance constituted no surprise. The college of cardinals in 1991 requested such a document reaffirming life which is now seen as a more practical follow-up to the earlier (1993) and more theoretical encyclical, *Veritatis splendor.*[2]

The basic positions taken in *Evangelium vitae* are well known—the condemnations of murder, direct abortion, euthanasia, and the death penalty (its justification is practically nonexistent). The method is similar to the approaches John Paul II's encyclicals have employed in the past—the assumption of the traditional natural law teaching of the Catholic tradition on particular points, an explicit scripturally based understanding of fundamental themes and principles with a concentration in this case on the Cain and Abel story, and a commentary on contemporary cultural trends. There is little that is new in the encyclical. On the major points of murder, abortion, and euthanasia the pope expressly claims to confirm the existing teaching. The position on the death penalty is stronger and more negative than found in past papal documents but consistent with recent emphases of John Paul II.

What effect will this document have on Catholics in the United States? In my judgment, not much. As mentioned, much of the encyclical is not new. Probably the majority of Catholics and of theologians are in fundamental agreement with the thrust of the teaching on abortion and euthanasia from the moral perspective, although I have some modifications and see more grey areas and nuances and less certainties than the pope. Those who have disagreed with the teaching on these points will probably continue to do so. The opposition to the death penalty will be somewhat upsetting to some Catholics. The encyclical constitutes a practical follow-up dealing with these particular questions in the light of the more theoretical points made in *Veritatis splendor*, the 1993 encyclical. Some of the same points are developed here, but *Veritatis splendor* often caricatured the positions taken by revisionist Catholic theologians, which generally speaking does not occur in this document.

The first part of this chapter will comment on the document itself and develop three points—the positive aspects of the encyclical, two problematic aspects, and the teaching on law and public policy.

Commentary

Positive Aspects. John Paul II's basic thesis about a failure to respect the sacredness and dignity of human life in our contemporary society is shared by many people today. Our age has experienced much violence, killing, and disrespect for human life. Life is a gift of God and, although not absolute, a very fundamental and sacred value. Every human and political community rests on this fundamental right to life (nn. 1–3). *Evangelium vitae* points out many of the same problems mentioned in *Veritatis splendor*—a notion of freedom which exalts the isolated individual in an absolute way and gives no play to "solidarity"; the self "understood in terms of absolute autonomy"; "the shifting sands of complete relativism" (nn. 19–20).

The encyclical perceptively recognizes other problems in our contemporary society. Materialism and the possession of things often become all-important. Having is more significant than being. Life in this understanding can easily be reduced to just another thing or possession (nn. 22–23). An overemphasis on efficiency and technology constitutes a danger for us. The pope points out the penchant for trying to have complete control over our lives. However, we are finite creatures and will never have such full control. There are many things that happen to us in this life that we do not want and cannot control. As human beings we cannot avoid some suffering in our lives. The technological can never be totally identified with the fully human. Technology can be helpful to truly human advancement, but at times we must say no to technology and its possibilities in the name of protecting the human and our environment (n. 15).

The pope speaks up for the poor, the weak, the defenseless, the marginalized, the oppressed, and the aged and calls upon human society to help and empower these people. Too often today in our society such people are forgotten about or not respected, but human dignity does not depend on what one does, makes, or accomplishes (n. 18). Likewise the encyclical points out the danger to the ecological and environmental aspects of the earth that can come from an absolute freedom, individualism, and relativism (n. 10).

The encyclical compassionately addresses women who have had an abortion and recognizes the many factors and influences often mitigating such a decision. Although what has happened remains terribly wrong, the mercy and forgiveness of God exist in the sacrament of reconciliation (n. 99). (One phrase in this section would have caused great consternation only a few years ago—the pope considers that the aborted child is now living with the Lord. Whatever happened to limbo?).

The striving for consistency in the life issues across the board constitutes a positive aspect of the document, although the pope does not explicitly refer to the consistent ethic of life championed by Cardinal Joseph Bernardin.[3] War would be too big a topic to include, but in a passing reference the pope notes the growing tendency not to resort to war if at all possible (n. 27).

One striking aspect of the present document comes from the pope's insistence on the collegial nature of this teaching. He refers explicitly to the 1991 Consistory of Cardinals in Rome and the personal letter he sent to all bishops asking for their input (n. 5). In his solemn proclamation of the teaching on murder, abortion, and euthanasia, the pope insists on his communion with other bishops in confirming and declaring these traditional teachings (nn. 57, 62, 65). However, this collegial aspect of the document is only a very small beginning and much more needs to be done. Papal documents must have much more regular and structured input from the bishops of the world and from the people of the church.

Problematic Aspects. The primary problem comes from the document's oppositions and certainties that combine to deny the gray areas and nuances that have been a part of the Catholic moral theology tradition. The pope frames the issues in terms of the struggle between the culture of life and the culture of death. John Paul II compares this dramatic conflict between the culture of death and the culture of life with the conflict of the cross and the massive conflict between good and evil (nn. 28, 50, and throughout the encyclical). However, such a thoroughgoing opposition between the church and the world or the gospel and culture has not been the typical Catholic approach. Some Protestant approaches have seen the world primarily in terms of the opposition between grace and sin, but the Catholic tradition did not see sin as destroying the human and its basic goodness, but only infecting it.[4]

As mentioned often in this book, the Catholic position has traditionally seen the divine as mediated in and through the human. The glory of God is the human person come alive.[5] The human person is an image of God precisely because like God she has intellect, free will, and the power of self-determination. The Catholic tradition has insisted on the basic goodness of the human and of human reason. The church in its history has supported and encouraged human truth, beauty, and goodness. If anything, the danger of the Roman Catholic tradition has been its failure at times to criticize the surrounding culture.

History shows that at times the church has learned from the world—for example, the condemnations of slavery and torture and the support of political rights and the role of women. At other times the church has rightly condemned the pride, materialism, greed, and individualism too often found in the world. The pope himself recognizes the limits of his own oppositional approach by briefly pointing out some signs in our cultures that point to the victory over death even though these cultures are strongly marked by the culture of death (nn. 26–27).

The oppositional approach allows one to put one's own position under the good or the positive aspect of life while assigning those who disagree to the negative camp of the culture of death. But this is not fair. First, it tends to create a triumphalism of the church as identified with the forces of good and life and fails to recognize the church's own failures in promoting life. Second, many proponents of some abortions would not see themselves as part of the culture of death. Their position is that the early embryo or fetus is not yet a truly individual human being or person. The differences in the debate about abortion cannot be conceived so simply as a struggle between the culture of life and the culture of death.

The oppositional approach identifies one's total position with the good and does not explicitly recognize the nuances and the different levels of certitude with regard to parts of one's own position. The pope explicitly deals with exceptions to killing in the Catholic tradition as illustrated by the legitimacy of killing an unjust aggressor as a last resort in self-defense. Human life is not an absolute value and in some conflict situations human life can be taken. The official hierarchical position as phrased by the pope is, "The direct and voluntary killing of an innocent human being is always gravely immoral" (n. 57).

The Catholic tradition has solved conflict situations on the basis of the principle of double effect with its condemnation of direct killing.

However, as mentioned earlier the ethical theory of direct killing depends on an epistemological understanding of the human act which is far removed from the core gospel values. Today many Catholic theologians disagree with it and would admit more conflict situations than the concept of direct killing allows.[6] The present Catholic hierarchical teaching on direct abortion has only been in place for one hundred years. Prominent theologians in the nineteenth century admitted more justifications for abortion than the present teaching allows.[7] Recall that the ultramontanist Aloysius Sabetti approved the removal of an ectopic pregnancy, a position later condemned by the Holy Office.

The life–death, good–evil oppositional approach covers over the lack of certitude that the Catholic tradition has always recognized with regard to the theoretical understanding of when individual human life begins. For the greater part of its existence, the Catholic Church held for delayed animation according to which the human soul was infused sometime (e.g., forty to ninety days) after conception. However, even before animation, abortion was not accepted.[8] John Paul II alludes to this tradition without explicitly recalling it (n. 60). The Catholic position has maintained that in practice one must act as if the human person is present from the moment of conception. However, this is a prudential judgment that cannot claim an absolute certitude. Some in good faith and with some reason on their side could disagree with that judgment.

Even with regard to euthanasia, there are more nuances and less certitude than the life–death oppositional approach recognizes. The pope proposes the traditional Catholic understanding that one does not have to use means to keep a person alive that are disproportionate to any expected results or means that impose an excessive burden on the patient and the family (n. 65). But one cannot positively interfere to bring about death. Again, the issues involve a philosophical discussion about the difference between withdrawing a means and positively interfering to bring about death.[9] In all these cases (meaning of direct, beginning of human life, difference between withdrawing a means and positively interfering), the hierarchical magisterium's teaching rests on philosophical understandings that are removed from the core of faith. Many theologians and Catholics agree with these approaches, but others disagree without thereby becoming part of the culture of death.

A second problem concerns the continued insistence on the teaching condemning artificial contraception, even though this is not a major topic in the encyclical (nn. 13–66), and the well known papal positions on the role of women. Many of us believe that these teachings have seriously harmed the credibility of the hierarchical magisterium as a moral leader and teacher. Granted that the positions on abortion and euthanasia are based on different reasons, but such a context makes it hard for many to pay attention to what the pope says on these life issues.

Law and Public Policy. Perhaps in the United States the section on law and public policy (especially nn. 68–74) will receive the most sustained public attention. John Paul II maintains that civil law must respect and promote the basic right to life. The will of the majority or public opinion cannot override basic human rights. The present situation of permissive abortion laws in many countries shows the presence of ethical relativism, individualism, and the separation of freedom from truth. Although the pope frequently calls attention to the distressing situation of such permissive laws as a sign of the culture of death, he does not propose his teaching on civil law in the same authoritative way as he does on the moral issues themselves.

The document briefly refutes a number of reasons that have been proposed to justify permissive abortion laws. The pope claims it is never licit to vote for or obey an intrinsically unjust law such as a law permitting abortion or euthanasia (n. 73). However, the encyclical recognizes the prudential aspect in lawmaking and the difficulty in changing permissive laws. Christians must take account of what is realistically attainable. One thus can support legislation that will lessen the harm done even if some abortions are still permitted. Where permissive laws exist, the pope calls for conscientious objection for those who disagree with the law; however, recourse to violence is excluded (n. 74).

Chapter eight pointed out two different Catholic approaches today to the understanding of the proper relationship between law and morality—what was called the Thomistic approach and the John Courtney Murray–Vatican II approach. In this encyclical the pope explicitly follows the Thomistic approach. "The doctrine on the necessary conformity of civil law with the moral law is in continuity with the whole tradition of the church. . . . (and) is the clear teaching of St. Thomas Aquinas" (n. 72). Democracy cannot be reduced just to the will of the majority "but depends on conformity to the moral law, to which it, like every other form of human behavior, must be subject" (n. 70).

The earlier chapter contrasted this Thomistic approach with the Murray—Vatican II approach. The latter approach begins not with the moral law but with the freedom of the person, which, however, is limited not by the common good but by the narrower concept of the public order. Likewise the Vatican II approach recognizes freedom as a very important part of the common good. "For the rest the usages of society are to be the usages of freedom in their full range. These require that the freedom of man [*sic*] be respected as far as possible and curtailed only when and insofar as necessary."[10]

John Paul II has obviously chosen not to employ the Murray–Vatican II approach. He always begins with moral law and not freedom. He insists often on the common good as being the criterion for law and never mentions the public order (nn. 70–72). The encyclical does not develop the role of freedom in the broader common good. However, the encyclical does cite the crucial paragraph seven of the Declaration on Religious Freedom of Vatican II, which proposes the different approach to law and morality. The pope cites this paragraph to show that the purpose of civil law is "that of ensuring the common good of people through the recognition and defense of their fundamental rights and the promotion of peace and of public morality" (n. 71). In the original these three elements comprise the public order which is narrower and less than the common good. Without doubt the Thomistic approach makes it easier for the pope to show that civil law should prohibit abortion and euthanasia. This might explain why he chose such an understanding.

The Vatican II approach definitely gives a greater role to freedom and a somewhat lesser role to law in public society. However, one could employ the Vatican II theory and maintain that civil law should not allow abortion and euthanasia. The three elements of public order include the protection of the rights of all. One could argue that freedom in these cases must be restricted to protest the fundamental right to life. On the other hand, I have maintained that one could employ the Vatican II approach to come to a different conclusion about abortion laws. In the light of the differences within a pluralistic society the presumption in favor of freedom and not the moral law can argue for a more permissive law. The practical difficulties of overturning a permissive law and of enforcing a restrictive abortion law buttress the argument not to work to change the existing abortion laws in the United States. Thus I maintain that Catholics who hold the hierarchical moral teaching on abortion do not have an obligation to work to change the permissive abortion laws now existing in the United States.

One final point on this issue. Those who disagree with the encyclical on the legal issue of abortion should not accuse the pope and other church leaders of violating the separation of church and state by working for civil laws prohibiting abortion and euthanasia. In the United States, if you believe for whatever reason that basic human rights are violated, you can legitimately work for a law to protect them—but of course you must convince others. Those making such an accusation would reduce all religion to the personal and private sphere with no ability to affect public and common life. According to these principles Martin Luther King could not have worked for civil rights on the basis of his biblical understandings.

A Broader Context

The second section of this chapter will discuss the two encyclicals *Veritatis splendor* and *Evangelium vitae* in the light of the totality of papal moral teaching. I have maintained that papal social teaching has employed a different methodology from papal teaching on personal and sexual issues.[11] The two encyclicals just studied deal primarily with personal morality. A comparison with Pope John Paul II's 1995 address to the United Nations shows four very significant differences in approach.

1) The two encyclicals tend to downplay historical development and even see it as threatening the existing teaching. The emphasis is on what has been true always and everywhere. According to *Veritatis splendor,* these new approaches to Catholic moral theology reject the traditional doctrine regarding the natural law and the universality and permanent validity of its precepts (n. 4). *Evangelium vitae* proclaims and reaffirms the older Catholic teaching about life in all its dimensions because of the extraordinary increase and growth of threats to life in the modern world. This disturbing state of affairs is expanding with a new cultural climate which gives crimes against life a new and even more sinister character (nn. 3–4).

How different is the address to the United Nations.[12] John Paul II wants to reflect on "the extraordinary changes of the last few years" (n. 1) with the "global acceleration of that quest for freedom which is one of the great dynamics of human history" (n. 2). Many people at the end of this millennium are fearful for themselves and of the human future. We must learn to conquer fear through a new flourishing of the human spirit based on an authentic culture of freedom and a rediscovery of the spirit of truth (n. 16).

2) *Evangelium vitae,* as mentioned, develops its theme by contrasting the culture of life with the culture of death existing in the world today, adopting

an "either–or" or "we versus them" approach. At the United Nations, the pope took a very different tack. The answer to the present fear about the future is "neither coercion nor repression, nor the imposition of one social 'model' on the entire world. The answer to the fear which darkens human existence at the end of the twentieth century is the common effort to build the civilization of love, founded on the universal values of peace, solidarity, justice, and liberty" (n. 18). There is no "we versus them" approach here.

3) *Veritatis splendor* insists on the universal and the uniform. What is presented here is the same for all persons in all places and at all times. The "central theme" of *Veritatis splendor* is "the reaffirmation of the universality and immutability of the moral commandments, particularly those which prohibit always and without exception intrinsically evil acts" (n. 115).

At the United Nations, John Paul II was much more open to particularity, differences, and diversity. "The human condition thus finds itself between these two poles—universality and particularity—with a vital tension between them; an inevitable tension, but singularly fruitful if they are lived in a calm and balanced way" (n. 7). "To cut oneself off from the reality of difference—or, worse, to attempt to stamp out that difference—is to cut oneself off from the possibility of sounding the depths of the mystery of human life" (n. 10). Consider what would happen if the above sentence were applied to homosexuality.

4) *Veritatis splendor* and *Evangelium vitae* both presume that moral truth is easy to find and that the hierarchical magisterium has this truth and proclaims it authoritatively to all others. The entire thrust of *Veritatis splendor* rests on the splendor of truth and that people are "made holy by the 'obedience to the truth' (1 Pt 1:22)" (n. 1). At the root of the present crisis in the church lie "currents of thought which end by detaching human freedom from its essential and constitutive relationship to truth" (n. 4). The first chapter tells the story of the rich young man asking Jesus what good he must do to have eternal life. "Jesus' conversation with the rich young man continues in a sense in every period of history, including our own. . . . The task of interpreting these prescriptions was entrusted by Jesus to the apostles and to their successors, with the special assistance of the Spirit of truth: 'He who hears you hears me' (Lk 10:16)" (n.25). The church, "the pillar and bulwark of the truth," continues the teaching role of Jesus with "the task of authentically interpreting the word of God . . . entrusted only to those charged with the church's living magisterium whose authority is exercised in the name of Jesus Christ" (n. 27).

How different is the understanding of truth and the search for it in the address to the United Nations. "The truth about man [*sic*] is the unchangeable standard by which all cultures are judged; but every culture has something to teach us about one or other dimension of that complex truth. Thus the 'difference' which some find so threatening can, through respectful dialogue, become the source of a deeper understanding of the mystery of human existence" (n. 10).

There can be no doubt that significant differences in approach exist between *Veritatis splendor* as well as *Evangelium vitae* and the 1995 papal address to the United Nations. Significant continuities also exist, but the thrust of this chapter is to recognize the differences.

What explains these significant differences in the two approaches? One possible explanation concerns a basic difference between personal and social ethics. For example, Catholic social thought has always been willing to tolerate evil, which is not true in personal morality. Society rightly needs a statute of limitations, but such a statute does not exist in the moral order. The end or purpose of society is somewhat different from the end of the human person and this accounts for the differences between personal and social morality.[13] However, this difference does not seem to account for the more significant differences between the two approaches in papal moral teaching especially because the Catholic tradition, while recognizing some differences between the two areas, has tended to emphasize the continuities between them.

Perhaps the very nature of the documents under consideration explains the differences. Both *Veritatis splendor* and *Evangelium vitae* by definition are apologetic documents, defending the present teaching against those who disagree with it. On the other hand, the address to the United Nations speaks to the whole world about the need for human cooperation in working for a better humankind. Without doubt the two different genres involved here have had some influence on the different methodologies invoked in the documents themselves. However, I do not think this constitutes the total or the most basic explanation for the differences between them.

In my judgment the primary difference between the two approaches comes from the fact that in general the social documents employ a more historically conscious approach whereas the sexual and personal papal teachings employ a more classicist approach. The classicist approach tends to stress the eternal, immutable, and unchanging and adopts a more deductive methodology; whereas the historically conscious approach gives more importance to change, development, and historical differences, while employing a more inductive approach. The four differences mentioned above can be explained in a great measure by these two different methodological approaches.

All recognize the change that has occurred in the last one hundred years in hierarchical and papal social teaching.[14] The nineteenth-century papal teaching strongly condemned individualistic liberalism, the Enlightenment, and democracy. However, in the light of the growth of totalitarianism of the right, and especially of the left, in the twentieth century, papal teaching began to defend the dignity, freedom, and rights of the person. However, this does not mean that such papal and hierarchical teaching no longer had some problems with individualism or the Enlightenment. Only in the 1940s did Pius XII recognize democracy as the best form of government. Only in 1963 did John XXIII for the first time develop in a systematic way a Catholic understanding of human rights. Only in 1965 did Vatican II accept religious freedom. Significant change has occurred in hierarchical social teaching in the twentieth century.

Corresponding to the recognition of historical development and change, the hierarchical documents adopted a more historically conscious approach that begins with the concrete historical realities and not with abstract definitions or essences that are always and everywhere true. The Pastoral Constitution on the Church in the Modern World of Vatican II begins its discussion of five different areas of social morality with a consideration of the signs of the times.[15] Paul VI's *Octogesima adveniens* adopts a very historically conscious approach. "In the face of such widely varying situations it is difficult for us to utter a unified message and to put forward a solution which has universal validity. Such is not our ambition, nor is it our mission."[16] His predecessors before Vatican II would not recognize themselves in this description. In addition, Vatican II employed a historically conscious hermeneutic to justify the change in church teaching. In many ways the primary issue in the religious liberty debate at the council was the change that had obviously occurred in church teaching. The problem was solved by invoking a historically conscious hermeneutic. The historical circumstances changed and so the teaching on religious freedom has changed.[17]

There has been less change and development in personal and sexual ethics over history, but significant developments have occurred especially in sexual morality. At one time the intention of procreation was necessary to avoid mortal sin in marital sexual relations, but with the acceptance of rhythm and natural family planning one could intend not to procreate and still have marital sexual relations. However, in the last fifty years no change has occurred in the concrete norms governing personal and sexual morality. Since the issue of contraception for spouses was taken out of Vatican II, the council did not have to confront the question of change and development in this area. Hence an historically conscious methodology was not required nor was an historically conscious hermeneutic needed to justify change. Thus the recent history explains the different approaches and methodologies existing in papal teaching on social morality and on personal or sexual morality.

One final point. The invocation of an historically conscious hermeneutic to explain the change in the church's teaching on religious freedom is not adequate. There was some error involved at least at some time in the official teaching. Unfortunately, even Vatican II was unwilling to explicitly admit error in church teaching. If the council had recognized such error in past church teaching, Catholicism might have developed quite differently in the last thirty years. Consider the case of artificial contraception. Paul VI took this issue out of the council (where it might have been solved in a different way) and finally reaffirmed the ban on artificial contraception in *Humanae vitae* primarily because he could not accept the fact that the past teaching was in any way erroneous.[18]

The point of this chapter has been to show that different methodological approaches exist in papal teaching on social and personal morality and to explain why this has occurred. To explore the implications of these differences would require not only another chapter but at least a volume or two. I have tried to deal with these implications in earlier chapters and in many of my own writings in moral theology. Here I can only summarize my approach.

The different approaches in methodologies definitely raise problems of consistency and coherence for papal moral teaching. A more historically conscious approach with all that entails should also be employed in personal and sexual morality. However, such an approach by no means excludes the existence of some absolute moral norms (e.g., unjustified killing of human beings, adultery) and very significant continuities in the teachings. But it does call for some changes and the recognition that certitude and truth are much harder to come by on specific moral issues.

Notes

1. Pope John Paul II, *Evangelium vitae*, in *Origins* 24 (1995): 689–727. Subsequent references in the text will be to the paragraph numbers of the document.
2. "Communique: College of Cardinals Meeting," *Origins* 20 (1991): 747.

3. For a discussion of Cardinal Bernardin's theory see Joseph Cardinal Bernardin, *Consistent Ethic of Life*, ed. Thomas G. Fuechtmann (Kansas City, Mo.: Sheed and Ward, 1988).
4. For a classical discussion of the different models of relationships between Christ and culture, see H. Richard Niebuhr, *Christ and Culture* (New York: Harper, 1956).
5. *Evangelium vitae* actually quotes the famous saying of St. Irenaeus of Lyon, "*Gloria Dei vivens homo*" (n. 34). But the pope fails to develop the important understanding that the divine is mediated in and through the human.
6. See for example *Readings in Moral Theology No. 1: Moral Norms and Catholic Tradition,* ed. Charles E. Curran and Richard A McCormick (New York: Paulist, 1979).
7. John R. Connery, *Abortion: The Development of the Roman Catholic Perspective* (Chicago: Loyola University Press, 1977), 213–69.
8. Ibid., 88–123.
9. Alastair Norcross and Bonnie Steinbock, eds., *Killing and Letting Die*, 2d ed. (New York: Fordham University Press, 1994).
10. Declaration on Religious Freedom, n. 7, in *The Documents of Vatican II*, ed. Walter M. Abbott (New York: Guild, 1966), 687.
11. Charles E. Curran, *Tensions in Moral Theology* (Notre Dame, Ind.: University of Notre Dame Press, 1988), 87–109.
12. Pope John Paul II, "U.N. Address: The Fabric of Relations Among People," *Origins* 25 (1995): 293–99. Subsequent references in the text will be to the paragraph numbers.
13. John Courtney Murray, *We Hold These Truths: Catholic Reflections on the American Proposition* (Kansas City, Mo.: Sheed and Ward, 1960), 286.
14. For my development of this point, see my *Directions in Catholic Social Ethics* (Notre Dame, Ind.: University of Notre Dame Press, 1985), 5–69.
15. Pastoral Constitution on the Church in the Modern World, nn. 47, 54–56, 63, 73, 77, in *Documents of Vatican II*, 249–50, 260–62, 271–72, 282–83, 289–90.
16. Pope Paul VI, *Octogesima adveniens*, n. 4, in *Catholic Social Thought: A Documentary Heritage*, ed. David J. O'Brien and Thomas A. Shannon (Maryknoll, N.Y.: Orbis, 1992), 266.
17. Richard J. Regan, *Conflict and Consensus: Religious Freedom and the Second Vatican Council* (New York: Macmillan, 1976).
18. Robert Blair Kaiser, *The Politics of Sex and Religion: A Case History in the Development of Doctrine 1962–1984* (Kansas City, Mo.: Sheed and Ward, 1985).

~ *Epilogue* ~

The Future of Moral Theology

The previous pages have dealt with the historical development of moral theology and some of the current issues in the discipline. What will be or should be the future of moral theology? The manuals or *Institutiones theologiae moralis* served as the basic textbooks in the discipline from the 1600s to Vatican II. The narrow purpose and focus of these textbooks cannot survive in the future. The understanding of sin and the theory and practice of the sacrament of penance have changed dramatically since Vatican II. Before 1965 Catholic schoolchildren in the United States were drilled in the importance of what was then called "confession" and the need for frequent, even weekly, confession. Long lines of people waiting to go to confession could often be seen in Catholic churches on Saturday afternoons and evenings. Parish missions once a year made confession a central part of their message. At a minimum, church law required all Catholics to confess their sins once a year. The law explicitly referred to mortal sin but in practice this aspect was often forgotten.[1] Seminarians and religious were required to go to confession at least once a week.[2]

The importance and frequency of confession in Catholic life fit into a broader picture. Preachers and teachers often appealed to the fear of hell as a motive for living the Christian life. Mortal sin became a very threatening reality because it merited eternal damnation. To miss mass on a Sunday or holy day of obligation was a mortal sin. The temptation for pastors and teachers was to use the threat of mortal sin as a club to ensure obedience to a moral or legal provision. The Catholic emphasis on confession stressed the difference between Protestants and Catholics. In a pre-ecumenical environment the emphasis on such differences constituted a very significant aspect of Catholic life.[3]

However, great changes in both practice and theory have developed since Vatican II. Catholic people go to confession (or in the better and more correct terminology "celebrate the sacrament of reconciliation") much less frequently than a generation or two ago. Many practicing Catholics have not been to confession in years. The pre-Vatican II teaching stressed that one could not receive communion in the state of mortal sin (e.g., after having missed Sunday mass). Today in Catholic churches practically the whole congregation receives communion every Sunday. This practice shows that the view of sin is not what it once was.[4]

The understanding or theory of sin has also developed in contemporary Catholic approaches. The manuals as illustrated in the approach of Aloysius Sabetti, understood sin as a free transgression of any law obliging in conscience. Such an approach insisted almost exclusively on the matter of the act itself so that act X is a sin, act Y is a venial sin, and act Z is a mortal sin. Such an approach fit in perfectly with and followed from the Tridentine requirement that sins had to be confessed according to number and species. The specific distinction of sins depends on the different formal objects of the act. The same material act could constitute a number of formally different sins. A male religious with a vow of chastity having sexual relations with a married relative commits four different sins against chastity, religion, familial relations, and justice. The numerical distinction of sins depended on the different sinful acts that are done. If a bad act is morally interrupted and then begun again, there are two sins.[5]

Without doubt the manuals proposed an objective and legalistic view of sin. However, at least in theory and in a matter of a comparatively few lines they recognized that mortal sin was more complex than just a serious violation of God's law. Three conditions were required for mortal sin—grave matter, full advertence, and full consent. Advertence and consent are acts of the intellect and will and show the subjective aspects that must be present for mortal sin to occur. However, the presumption is that such advertence and consent are present and only *per accidens* can grave matter not be a mortal sin because of these subjective factors. Throughout the entire textbook, the assumption always remains that grave matter involves grave or mortal sin.[6]

Contemporary approaches to sin have moved away from the one-sided objective and legalistic approach of the manuals. The importance of the subject in philosophy, the increasing recognition of the psychological aspects of human acts, and the growing emphasis on the person in Catholic moral theology after Vatican II strongly argue against an overly objective view of mortal sin. The material object alone cannot be determinative of such sin.[7]

In my judgment the legal model for understanding morality and sin should give way to a relationality–responsibility model. The moral life is seen in terms of the person's multiple relationships with God, neighbor, world, and self. Mortal sin involves a breaking of these relationships. The external act must be viewed and judged in the light of these basic relationships. By definition mortal sin is not just an external act but rather the breaking of the relationship with God and others. Even the older approach based on the manuals had to admit that the confessor cannot know for certain the true interior disposition and reality of the person who is confessing sins.[8]

The earlier discussion about the fundamental option made the same basic point about sin. Mortal sin involves a fundamental orientation in the depths of one's core freedom and cannot be reduced only to the external act. Here again it is important to recognize the basic distinction between mortal sin and the external act itself as morally right or morally wrong. A particular act can and should be judged to be right or wrong (e.g., telling a lie is wrong), but on the basis of that act alone one cannot know if the relationship with God and neighbor has been broken or if a fundamental option has been changed. The conclusion is obvious and far-reaching. One cannot judge the existence of mortal sin solely on the basis of the external act. In fact, no external judgment can ever know if mortal sin is truly present or not. This approach has significant ramifications for our understanding and practice of the sacrament of penance.

The newer approach to sin has dramatically changed our whole understanding of penance. The present terminology about penance—"sacrament of reconciliation" instead of "confession"—shows the change: Confession comes from the central reality of the penitent confessing sins according to number and species; reconciliation sees the sacrament precisely in relational terms and follows from the relational understanding of sin proposed above. Penance involves a reconciliation with God, neighbor, world, and self. The church is the sacrament of Jesus, and we become reconciled to Jesus in and through our reconciliation with the church. The primary judgment is not the judgment made by the confessor about the dispositions of the penitent but the proclamation by the church of the saving judgment of God in mercy and forgiveness. The sacrament is the celebration of the saving judgment of God through Jesus in the Holy Spirit made present in the church.[9]

At the present time Catholic discipline recognizes in unusual or emergency situations the possibility of celebrating the sacrament of penance in a communal way without the specific confession of sins. I believe there should be a multiplicity of rites for celebrating the sacrament of penance. The mystery of God's forgiveness in and through the church is so multidimensional that no one ritual can symbolize all the aspects of this mystery. Individual and specific confession of sins can be a very deep religious experience of God's forgiveness and should always be an option for the celebration of penance. However, the communal absolution without individual and specific confession of sins emphasizes very important aspects of the mystery of forgiveness especially in terms of reconciliation and the community aspect of the sacrament. Our present discipline with regard to the sacrament of reconciliation is much too restrictive.

One final point. The sacrament of penance is becoming a marginalized reality for many contemporary Catholic Christians. As a result people are losing a sense of sin. The older approach overemphasized and distorted somewhat the reality of sin, but sin remains a very important reality in human existence and in the Christian understanding. We cannot afford to lose the proper sense of sin and the proper meaning of continual conversion and reconciliation in the moral life. This need only underscores more urgently the call for different ways to celebrate the sacrament of reconciliation.

The newer understanding of sin and of the sacrament of reconciliation challenges the very structure and focus of the manuals of moral theology. There is no future for the manuals as they have existed in the past.

The Present Crisis

What about the present crisis in moral theology? What will happen in the future? To begin with, one must understand the root causes of what the pope has called "the crisis in moral theology," brought about by the widespread disagreement and dissent from hierarchical teachings. Moral theology is the theological discipline today which experiences the most tension between the hierarchical teaching authority and theologians. Both practical and theoretical reasons help to explain why moral theology is at the center of the storm today. From the practical perspective, the test case for authority is whether or not it is acknowledged and followed in practice. More speculative areas are not all that neuralgic precisely because people as a whole are not that interested in them. The average person in the pew does not enter into debates about the Trinity, the nature and salvific role of Jesus, and the issues of methodology and anthropology. Authority comes into play when it affects the practical life of people. As a result the major issues of contention in the Roman Catholic Church in the United States and in the world today tend to emphasize practical ecclesiology and morality.

Moral theology serves as the bridge between the speculative and the practical. By its very nature, it deals with the bottom line of what people should do in practice. In explaining the role of theologians the hierarchical magisterium wants to keep apart the speculative and the practical aspects. Speculation belongs to theologians, practical pastoral teaching belongs to the pope and the bishops. Such an approach has the merits of clearly defining the difference between the hierarchical role and the theological role but it is much too simple.[10] Moral theology tries to tie together the speculative and the practical. As mentioned often in these pages, moral theology is the critical, systematic, and thematic reflection, in a scientific way, on Christian life and action. Since moral theology deals with the practical, some tensions will always exist between moral theology and the hierarchical teaching office of the church.

In addition, the very nature of Catholic moral theology contributes to the tension between church authority and theologians. Earlier chapters have pointed out that Catholic moral theology based its teachings on natural law and human reason. This emphasis on reason grounds an intrinsic morality that insists something is commanded because it is good and never the other way around. By contrast dogmatic theology recognizes the primacy of faith and revelation while still according a significant role to reason, seeking an understanding of faith. The hierarchical teaching authority has insisted that its moral teaching is not simply based on the will of authority but is grounded in God's natural law. However, at the same time the magisterium claims to teach the natural law with a special authority. Here lies the basic source of the tension. What if one experiences a conflict between authority and reason on a particular issue? How will the crisis be resolved in the future? Only time will tell, but I believe that in the end the Catholic tradition calls for the hierarchical magisterium itself to be subordinate to reason and moral truth.

What about dissent in the church from noninfallible teachings? I cannot accept John Paul II's one-sided understanding and condemnation of dissent. It is appropriate here to summarize briefly the three fundamental reasons—theological, ecclesiological, and philosophical—justifying dissent from what has been officially called noninfallible teaching. The theological reason recognizes what Vatican II in its decree on ecumenism has called the hierarchy of truths.[11] Not all Catholic teachings are of the same importance or centrality. The pre-Vatican II neoscholastic theologies also recognized this point by assigning different "theological notes" to teachings to determine just how central they are to Catholic Christian faith. These different notes went all the way from a matter of defined faith to probable opinions.[12] One must distinguish what is core to faith from what is more remote and peripheral. Specific moral teachings on complex issues which the hierarchical magisterium admits are based on reason and not faith cannot be that core and central to faith. Earlier chapters pointed out how the church over time has spelled out the teaching on killing to account for possible conflict situations. The precise statement of the teaching today maintains that direct killing of an innocent person on one's own authority is always wrong. Notice that such a teaching depends on a philosophical distinction between direct and indirect killing. On such philosophical questions there can and do exist differing positions in the church today, precisely because such distinctions are quite complex and open to different interpretations. Such specific teachings cannot be a matter of the core of Catholic faith. The distinction between what is core and what is remote refutes the charge often made against progressives in the Catholic Church of indulging in cafeteria Catholicism—that is, picking and choosing what one wants to believe. On matters core to the faith there has to be agreement, but disagreements can exist on those aspects that are remote and somewhat peripheral.

The ecclesiological grounds for the possibility of dissent from noninfallible magisterial teaching are found in the recognition that the hierarchical teaching office does not exhaust the teaching office in the church. The primary teacher is the Holy Spirit. Through baptism all Christians share in the teaching office of Jesus just, as they share in the priesthood of Jesus. Vatican II pointed out the prophetic aspect in the church which is different from the hierarchical office. The whole body of the faithful cannot err in matters of belief.[13] The Declaration on Religious Freedom recognized the truth about religious freedom already existing in the experience of human beings before the hierarchical magisterium official taught it.[14]

The philosophical basis for dissent comes from the logical reality that as a general principle is applied to more specific and concrete circumstances it is harder to claim that the principle is always true. Thomas Aquinas recognized that in moral issues circumstances can enter in that change the nature of the reality. According to Aquinas, the secondary precepts of the natural law oblige usually and in most cases, but not always. Ordinarily one has an obligation to give back to the owner what is being held as a deposit. However, if the owner of a sword now comes back, threatening to kill someone, and wants the sword, the person who is keeping it has no obligation to give it to him.[15] Thus in the application of general moral principles to very specific moral issues, the hierarchical teaching office cannot claim to have a certitude that excludes the possibility of error.

In discussions about dissent, I have often invoked the late-nineteenth- and twentieth-century distinction between infallible and noninfallible teaching. I appreciate the contemporary debate about infallibility, but the distinction shows that the Catholic Church has recognized the point I am trying to make about dissent. These "noninfallible" teachings (there has never been an infallible teaching on a specific moral issue) are fallible.

In practice it will be difficult for the hierarchical magisterium to accept the position that its application of general moral principles to specific moral issues might be wrong. The present overemphasis on authority and authoritarianism only seems to be making any change more difficult. History proves, however, that church teaching on specific moral issues such as slavery, the role of women in the world, human rights, the justification of the marriage act, usury, religious freedom, the rights of the accused, and many other issues has changed over the years.[16] The present impasse will not be overcome unless the hierarchical teaching office recognizes that it has been wrong in the past. Such a recognition will not be easy but it is necessary.

Without doubt the role and use of authority in the Catholic Church constitutes the biggest issue in the life of the church today. Authority has a very important role of promoting and protecting the unity of the church. To preserve and foster unity in the church today is not easy. How to reconcile both unity and legitimate diversity lies at the heart of many problems facing all societies and communities in our world today. Think of the former Yugoslavia, Rwanda, Ireland, and our own country, especially its metropolitan areas. In theory, for the church the situation lies in that distinction between what is core and central to faith and what is more peripheral and remote. In the past, church authority has too readily seen unity in terms of uniformity across the board. Much more room for diversity exists within the Catholic church than the hierarchical magisterium has been willing to admit.

However, those of us who are calling for changes and greater diversity in the Catholic church must follow the same principle in order to protect and promote the unity of the church which is always going to be fragile and in danger. Perhaps we can learn something from the struggles in contemporary

American Protestantism. Many Catholics today naively think that American Protestant churches have no problems because they do not have the same authority problem that exists in Roman Catholicism. However, mainstream churches such as Episcopalians, Presbyterians, and United Methodists have lost about 30 percent of their membership since 1970. Robert Wuthnow points out that a very significant problem for contemporary mainstream Protestants in the United States has been the danger of single-issue politics. People are more committed to single issues than to the community of the church and hence often leave the church community because of the particular issues they favor or disagree with.[17] I have urged progressive Roman Catholics to stay in the church and strive to change the church. In a theological sense almost all the divisive issues today are not central or core even though, existentially, they may be very significant for individual persons. I can appreciate that some people feel they can no longer live in the church because of these issues that so personally touch them, but I have always urged people to stay and work for change within the church. The church is not a voluntary society where like-minded people gather together primarily for the individual's own good. The church is God's community to which we are called and we all have a role to make that community more faithful to the word and work of Jesus. The church will always know the tension between freedom and authority and between unity and diversity, but I hope we can live with these tensions in a more mature Christian way in the future.

The present crisis in moral theology, apart from one's interpretation of it and reaction to it, has had one very important negative effect on the discipline itself. The crisis has tended to limit and distort the focus of moral theology. As many previous chapters in this book indicate, the crisis has been about particular actions—what has often been called quandary ethics. As a result the primary emphases in the post-Vatican II moral theology have been the same as the focus and emphasis of the manuals—specific actions viewed from the minimalist perspective of being right or wrong. Other aspects of moral theology have not received that much emphasis.

Future Developments

How should or will moral theology develop in the future? Moral theology's development will depend heavily on its different publics—the church, the academy, and the broader world. Each of these will contribute to the agenda of moral theology and no one can really predict what will be happening in these areas. However, both the nature of Catholic moral theology, and the understanding of its history give some direction to the discipline. The characteristics of catholicity and mediation provide perspectives for the future development of Catholic moral theology.

Catholicity with its all-inclusiveness recognizes the many different dimensions of morality. Morality and ethics involves much more than just an analysis of human acts to determine whether they are right or wrong. Quandary ethics will always have a place in moral theology, but it cannot be the only or even the primary consideration. There exist different levels or aspects of morality which must be considered in any systematic understanding of morality. A fundamental distinction involves the subject pole and the object pole of morality. The more general aspect of the subject concerns the basic orientation, fundamental option, or—in biblical terms—the conversion of the person, involving a radical change of heart. Discipleship constitutes another way of describing this reality. In addition to these basic orientations, more specific virtues, attitudes, and dispositions also characterize the person. In a sense these aspects of the subject are the most important realities in the moral life because they influence and affect all human actions. As the biblical adage reminds us, the good tree brings forth good fruit. Intentionality and motivation also constitute important aspects of the moral life and deserve attention in the development of moral theology. All these aspects of the subject call attention to the need for growth and development in the Christian moral life. On the objective level, values, principles, and norms are important considerations and move from the more general to the more specific. Life constitutes a very basic value. Respect for life is a principle that should influence our actions. The prohibition of targeting noncombatants in a just war constitutes a moral norm. Concrete decision making or conscience in one sense brings the subjective and objective poles together. The different levels or realities involved in understanding the moral life can be explained in different ways, but the discipline must take all these different dimensions or aspects into account.

Contemporary discussions often speak of three different approaches to ethics—a virtue approach, a principled approach, or a casuistic approach.[18] The inclusivity and catholicity of moral theology call for all three approaches, although particular studies can legitimately concentrate on one or the other. The Catholic "and" tends to avoid either–or approaches and insists on inclusivity.

The catholicity of moral theology and the tradition has meant that moral theology is concerned about all of God's creation and all of God's people within that creation. The doctrine of creation grounds this catholicity and universality. Historically the danger in the Catholic tradition of moral theology has been to so stress the universality of ethics that it has not given enough importance to historicity, diversity, and particularity, and has failed to recognize how power and privilege could corrupt a seemingly neutral, universalist perspective. Liberation theology and feminist ethics have insisted on beginning with the experience of the oppressed. A tension will always exist between the universal and the particular; between a neutral, objective, universal starting point and a committed, particular starting point for moral theology. However, the Catholic "and" insists on holding on to both aspects. Catholic feminist ethics, with its particular starting point, has been and I trust will continue to be open to dialogue with all others in terms of working for a more just world.[19]

The Catholic, inclusive, and mediational aspects of moral theology recognize the multiple dialogue partners for the discipline. As a theological discipline moral theology must incorporate the appropriate aspects of systematic theology—God, Trinity, Christology, the Holy Spirit, eschatology, ecclesiology. A very important dimension of moral theology which has not received the attention it deserves in the past concerns the relationship to sacraments and liturgy. The church is primarily church as it gathers to celebrate the Eucharist and the sacraments. The spiritual and moral life must be seen in relationship to sacramental and liturgical life. In addition to all the pertinent aspects of systematic or dogmatic theology, moral theology also is related to the scripture. This requires moral theology to be acquainted with the many different approaches to scripture today but also to examine the different ways in which the scriptures are used in moral theology. In my perspective, scripture will have more to say on the more general aspects such as fundamental orientation or virtues and less immediate relevance for specific actions, such as capital punishment, which are more embedded in particular historical and cultural circumstances.

Since moral theology sees the divine mediated in and through the human, human reason and the human sciences are most important for moral theology. In the recent past, Catholic moral theology before Vatican II was wedded to a somewhat Thomistic philosophy. Now there exist many different philosophical dialogue partners for moral theology. In addition, moral theology must also be in dialogue with all the appropriate human sciences. These sciences come into play especially in dealing with special questions in moral theology such as the economic, political, and legal aspects.

The first part of this book has emphasized the importance of the history of the discipline of moral theology. This history has a meaning and validity in itself, but it can also shed light on the nature of the discipline and how it might better develop now and in the future. The discipline of moral theology needs more historical studies.

The catholicity of moral theology calls for a very inclusive discipline that must be in dialogue with many other disciplines and perspectives. By its very nature moral theology constitutes a complex reality. The temptation to simplistically ignore this complexity is ever present. To deal with all the aspects of moral theology is a complex and somewhat daunting task, but it is necessary to be true to the nature of the discipline.

In the future there will probably continue to be many studies of particular issues, methodological aspects, and historical dimensions. In the light of the great inclusiveness and complexity of the discipline, one wonders if there will be many attempts at a synthetic and systematic development of moral theology. Two reasons argue somewhat in favor of attempting to do systematic approaches to moral theology despite the great complexity. First, courses will continue to be taught in moral theology on college, seminary, and university levels. Some of these courses will aim to present a systematic overview of the discipline.

Second, the Catholic tradition has always tried to develop systematic theologies. At times these attempts might too easily have forgotten the pluralism and diversity that exist, but the Catholic theological approach based on faith seeking understanding has traditionally emphasized the importance of striving for such systematic syntheses. The *summae* of the past stand as strong testimony to this tradition. However, the problems and difficulties in formulating new *summae* are very strong.

The very nature of Catholic moral theology should continue to influence the future development of the discipline. But it is difficult to predict exactly how this development will take place since moral theology relates to its three different publics—the church, the academy, and the wider world. Events and developments in these areas will definitely influence the future development of moral theology.

Notes

1. *Codex iuris canonici* (Westminster, Md.: Newman, 1961), canon 901.
2. Ibid., canons 595 and 1367.

3. For the origin of the important role of sin and confession in Catholicism in the United States in the nineteenth century, see Jay P. Dolan, *The American Catholic Experience: A History from Colonial Times to the Present* (Notre Dame, Ind.: University of Notre Dame Press, 1992), 225–30.
4. See *The Fate of Confession*, ed. Mary Collins and David Power, Concilium, n. 190 (Edinburgh: T. and T. Clark, 1987).
5. Aloysius Sabetti, *Compendium theologiae moralis*, 7th ed. (Ratisbon and New York: Fr. Pustet, 1892), nn. 124–34, pp. 85–97.
6. Ibid., n. 128, p. 88. Sabetti in practice follows the presumption of mortal sin when the matter is grave but does not explicitly formulate that approach. For an explicit formulation, see Marcellino Zalba, *Theologia moralis summa I: Theologia moralis fundamentalis* (Madrid: Biblioteca de Autores Cristianos, 1952), n. 630, p. 623.
7. Timothy E. O'Connell, *Principles for a Catholic Morality*, rev. ed. (San Francisco: Harper and Row, 1990), 77–102.
8. Charles E. Curran, *Directions in Fundamental Moral Theology* ((Notre Dame, Ind.: University of Notre Dame Press, 1985), 99–118.
9. James Dallen, *The Reconciling Community: The Rite of Penance* (New York: Pueblo, 1986).
10. Congregation for the Doctrine of the Faith, "Instruction on the Ecclesial Vocation of the Theologian," *Origins* 20 (1990): 117–26.
11. Decree on Ecumenism, n. 11, in *Documents of Vatican II*, ed. Walter M. Abbott (New York: Guild, 1966), 354.
12. Sixtus Cartechini, *De Valore notarum theologicarum* (Rome: Gregorian University Press, 1951).
13. Dogmatic Constitution on the Church, n. 12, in *Documents of Vatican II*, 363–64.
14. Declaration on Religious Freedom, n. 1, in ibid., 676.
15. Thomas Aquinas, *Summa theologiae*, 4 vols. (Rome: Marietti, 1952), I II, q. 94, a. 4.
16. John T. Noonan, Jr., "Development in Moral Doctrine," *Theological Studies* 54 (1993): 662–77.
17. Robert Wuthnow, *The Restructuring of American Religion: Society and Faith Since World War II* (Princeton, N.J.: Princeton University Press, 1988).
18. James F. Keenan and Thomas A. Shannon, "The Contexts of Casuistry: Historical and Contemporary," in *The Context of Casuistry*, ed. James F. Keenan and Thomas A Shannon (Washington: Georgetown University Press, 1995), 221–31.
19. Charles E. Curran, Margaret A. Farley, and Richard A. McCormick, eds., *Feminist Ethics and The Catholic Moral Tradition: Readings in Moral Theology No. 9* (New York: Paulist, 1996).

Index

Catholic health care and service institutions, identity of, 190–91; and Catholic Charities, 202; and Catholic hospitals, 44, 202